Culture and the Arts
in Education

Culture and the Arts in Education

CRITICAL ESSAYS ON SHAPING HUMAN EXPERIENCE

Ralph A. Smith

FOREWORD BY **George Geahigan**

Teachers College, Columbia University
New York and London

National Art Education
Association

KH

Published by Teachers College Press, 1234 Amsterdam Avenue, New York, NY 10027 and the National Art Education Association, 1916 Association Drive, Reston, VA 20191.

For reprint permission, grateful acknowledgment is made to the following publishers. Trustees of Boston University: "Arts Education as Liberal Education," *Journal of Education* 175:3 (1993):1–14. Polish Scientific Publications PWN: "Philosophy and Theory of Aesthetic Education," *Dialectics and Humanism* 15:1–2 (1988):31–45. National Art Education Association, Reston, VA: "Problems for a Philosophy of Art Education," *Studies in Art Education* 33:4(Summer 1992):253–266. National Society for the Study of Education: "Toward Percipience: A Humanities Curriculum for Arts Education," in Bennett Reimer and Ralph A. Smith, eds., *The Arts, Education, and Aesthetic Knowing*, Part II, pp. 51–60, 1992. *Review of Research in Visual Arts Education*: "Concepts, Concept Learning, and Art Education," *Review of Research in Visual Arts Education* (renamed *Visual Arts Research*) 11 (Winter 1979): 715. Board of Trustees of the University of Illinois: "Fig. 1: A Percipience Curriculum (K–12)" in Albert William Levi and Ralph A. Smith, *Art Education: A Critical Necessity* (Urbana: University of Illinois Press, 1991), p. 206; and from *The Journal of Aesthetic Education* "The Artworld and Aesthetic Skills: A Context for Research and Development" 12:2 (April 1977):117–132; "Art, the Human Career, and Aesthetic Education" 15:3 (July 1981):9–25; "Teaching Aesthetic Criticism in the Schools" 7:1 (January 1973):38–49; "Re-moralization and Aesthetic Education" 17:1 (Spring 1983):5–13; "An Excellence Curriculum for Art Education" 21:4 (Winter 1987):52–61; "Teaching Music as One of the Humanities" 25:3 (Fall 1991):115–28; "The Uses of Cultural Diversity" 12:2 (April 1978):5–10. Art Department, National Changhua University of Education (Taiwan): "Aesthetic Education: A Critical Necessity," in *Culture, Society, and Art Education*, INSEA Congress Proceedings (1995), pp. 268–282.

Library of Congress Cataloging-in-Publication Data

Smith, Ralph Alexander.
    Culture and the arts in education : critical essays on shaping human experience / Ralph A. Smith ; foreword by George Geahigan.
      p. cm.
    Contains previously published work.
    Includes bibliographical references and index.
    ISBN 0-8077-4655-X (cloth : alk. paper)—ISBN 0-8077-4654-1 (pbk. : alk. paper)
    1. Arts—Study and teaching—United States 2. Aesthetics—Study and teaching—United States. I. Title.

NX303.A1S65 2005
700'.71—dc22   2005050614

ISBN-13:
978-0-8077-4654-7 (paper)
978-0-8077-4655-4 (cloth)

ISBN-10:
0-8077-4654-1 (paper)
0-8077-4655-X (cloth)

Printed on acid-free paper
Manufactured in the United States of America

13 12 11 10 09 08 07 06   8 7 6 5 4 3 2 1

7/12/06

To the University of Illinois at Urbana–Champaign for support of aesthetic education for over half a century

Contents

vii

Foreword

F EW PEOPLE are considered statesmen within their chosen profession, but this, indeed, is an apt characterization of Ralph Smith within the field of art education. During the course of a distinguished career, he has come to be recognized as one of the preeminent theorists of art education and a major figure in the reconceptualization of arts education during the postwar period. As founder and editor of the influential *Journal of Aesthetic Education*, he has been in a unique position to raise issues, promote dialogue, and shape educational policy in the arts. And in his many books and articles, he has drawn upon a wide-ranging scholarship to articulate a comprehensive philosophy of education in the schools, one that enjoys the agreement of many thoughtful professionals, not only in the visual arts, but in other arts disciplines as well.

This compilation of major articles, book chapters, and addresses provides an opportunity to study the development of his thinking over the past three decades. The essays in this volume record his efforts to construct a defensible rationale for the arts in general education and a workable curriculum for art education in the public schools. They also reveal an ongoing concern about misguided policy proposals that continue to be advanced for using the arts and the aesthetic in educational settings.

For Smith, the problem of justifying art education within the school curriculum rests, ultimately, on the distinctive value of the arts in human life. To inquire into the nature of aesthetic value, however, confronts the educator with one of the most intractable problems in aesthetics. The ubiquitous presence of the arts testifies to their importance, but philosophers have yet to reach a consensus about why they are valuable. Smith is one of only a handful of theorists to systematically negotiate this difficult terrain, and in these essays we see him returning repeatedly to this question as aestheticians and philosophers continue to ponder this problem and as his own philosophy matures. His ultimate conclusions about the importance of the arts rests upon an instrumental conception of aesthetic value: works of art are valuable instrumentally insofar as they lead to worthwhile experiences. Experiences with works of art, in turn, are valuable not only because they are intrinsically enjoyable and gratifying, but also because they have the power to shape a viewer's character and provide humanistic insights into the world and the self. Although the benefits that art provides are principally personal rather than social, he argues that society and culture as a whole benefit from being made up of fulfilled, culturally literate human beings.

In his later essays, Smith draws upon the work of Ernst Cassirer, Nelson Goodman, Albert William Levi, and others, in emphasizing the cognitive nature of aesthetic experiences. Because the arts make unique contributions to the character and intellectual development of students (their constitutive and revelatory powers), they must be considered distinctive school subjects in their own right. But this implies a curriculum grounded in the humanities. If the value of the arts resides in their potential to provide worthwhile experiences, the principal mission of art education should be to equip students with those capacities and dispositions that would enable them to understand and appreciate works of art and, thus, to access this value. In contrast to educators who would subscribe to a curriculum based upon studio practice, then, he argues for a curriculum devoted principally to the humanistic study of works of art. The curriculum Smith envisions would focus principally on the secondary grades. It would be general in the sense that it would be devoted to education of the nonspecialist rather than the professional practitioner. And it would be common in that students would learn similar concepts and skills, and take similar units of work, albeit with some provision being made for individual interests. The locus of study would be exemplary works of art, both traditional and contemporary. Most of these would be selected from the Western heritage, but students would have opportunities to study works from other cultural traditions as well.

Although his overall conception of a "percipience," an "excellence," or a "humanities" curriculum in the arts remains essentially unchanged, later essays in this volume offer elaborations and refinements. In his most recent essays, Smith argues for a range of instructional methods and he provides descriptions of a sequential curriculum that extends into the elementary school. Such a curriculum would begin in grades K–3 with an informal introduction to works of art and a gradual familiarization with aesthetic concepts and qualities. Much of this learning would occur through the creative activities that now dominate art education in the early grades. Gradually these activities would merge in grades 4–6 into a more formal type of perceptual training through the introduction of systematic exercises in responding to works of art. Grades 7–9 would be devoted to developing a sense of art history: of an ability to "think of art in terms of time, tradition, and style," principally through a chronological survey of Western art. In grades 10 and 11, students would study selected master-

pieces of art in depth, both works of Western art and works from other cultural traditions. Finally, in grade 12 students would have the opportunity to
synthesize previously acquired skills and to develop a personal philosophy of
art. This would occur through reading and analyzing the literature of aesthetics and art criticism and through discussing and applying criteria of aesthetic
judgment, all within seminar types of situations.

As a number of essays demonstrate, Smith is not only an articulate
spokesperson for the arts but also an acute critic of misguided proposals for
using the arts and aesthetics in education. He has been especially concerned
about attempts to use instruction in the arts for nonaesthetic ends. Over the
years, educators have proposed a plethora of rationales to enable the arts to
gain a firmer foothold in the schools. For example, arts education has been
proposed as a way of fostering basic skills in reading, writing, and mathematics; as a means of creating a more positive atmosphere within the school;
as an instrument for meliorating social problems; as a way of improving race
relations; and so on. Although Smith would be the first to acknowledge that
instruction in the arts can lead to a host of beneficial outcomes, he argues
that not all learning outcomes are unique to the arts and offer a basis for
justifying the arts as distinctive school subjects. To focus on such nonaesthetic
goals reveals a fundamental confusion about aims and purposes and leaves
education in the arts without a distinctive role within the school curriculum.

Because educational goals not only justify practice but direct it as well,
there is also the very real danger that the adoption of nonaesthetic goals will
distort or destroy the very fabric of teaching and learning in the arts. This is
especially the case with some social-reconstructionist approaches to art education. In promoting the political agendas of special interest groups, there is
an inherent tendency for educators to focus on works of art for their ideological content, that is, to ignore those that have no pronounced ideological
message or those that promote an ideology different from the one currently
in fashion, or even to abandon the study of the fine arts altogether. For Smith,
all this would transform teaching and learning in the arts in unacceptable
ways and deprive students of the unique benefits that can only be derived
from disciplined study of the arts.

Smith is also a sharp critic of some of the more extravagant claims
made on behalf of the aesthetic in education. A number of philosophers
and curriculum theorists have likened learning in the classroom to having
an aesthetic experience, likened teaching to acting, and likened evaluating
educational phenomena to criticizing of works of art. His critiques of such
notions rest principally upon detailed analyses of the underlying concepts of
aesthetic experience, acting, and art criticism. In seeking illuminating analogies, he argues, theorists have ignored some major differences between dis-
similar phenomena. The net result of this is not only theoretical confusion,

but also unfounded and questionable prescriptions for curriculum, instruction, teacher training, and educational evaluation.

In giving this schematic overview of some of the main strands of Smith's thinking, I have, of course, overlooked much of the richness and complexity of these essays. A brief preface cannot do justice to his discussions about art as a facet of humanity, his detailed analyses of aesthetic experience, his informative overview of concepts and concept learning in the arts, and his perceptive comments about educational evaluation, to mention just some of the topics discussed in these essays. Nor is it possible to describe in detail his careful analyses of such issues as multiculturalism, elitism, and postmodernism in arts education. Moreover, readers will be rewarded by definitive accounts of the development of the concept of an aesthetic education and of curriculum trends in visual arts education during the postwar period.

Over the years, Smith's writings have been enormously influential among reform-minded educators seeking an alternative to the studio and performance-based models that currently dominate arts instruction in the schools. The source of his influence has been a comprehensive philosophy of arts education, a philosophy founded upon impeccable scholarship and careful reasoning. The essays in this volume present a compelling vision of the arts in the schools. They merit the attention of all educators concerned about the role of the arts in education and the practice of arts education in instructional settings.

—George Geahigan
Purdue University

Acknowledgments

IN REVIEWING my writings I am reminded of the good fortune I have enjoyed in carrying on conversations, either personally or through correspondence, with several of the distinguished scholars and educators of the past half century. To them I owe an immeasurable debt of gratitude for most of the ideas that inform this volume. I am further indebted to George Geahigan for his Foreword to this collection. No one in the field is more familiar with my work or able to explicate it as accurately and clearly as he has done. Through the years I have also benefited from the assistance of my wife, Christiana, the coauthor of one of the selections and whose editing skills are evident in the others. The intelligence and technical skills of Selena Douglass are also appreciated. Last but not least, the questions and skepticism of students over the years have pressed me to communicate my thoughts as clearly as I can.

Introduction

THE ESSAYS collected here present a point of view that has undergone modification with increased understanding of both aesthetic concepts and the various contextual considerations that are brought into play in understanding and appreciating works of art. Modification, however, has not affected my belief in the significant contributions that art and aesthetic education are capable of making to a satisfying life. Such life enhancement is achieved through the refinement of perception and imagination and the development of a capacity for appreciating images worthy of attention and admiration.

The use of the terms *art education* and *aesthetic education* throughout the collection is justified by the close relation between artistic and aesthetic concepts (in most theories of art and the aesthetic, they are inextricably intertwined) as well as by the frequently interchangeable meanings of the terms. To be sure, because the realm of the aesthetic extends beyond the world of art, much can be said in favor of a natural aesthetics and the aesthetics of everyday life. Still, one can argue that it is works of art that are generally sought out for their uncommon concentrations of aesthetic value. In other places I have discussed the farther reaches of the aesthetic, but in the selections reprinted here the emphasis is largely on works of art.

Precedents for the use of the term *aesthetic education* can be found in the writings of Friedrich Schiller in the late eighteenth century and Herbert Read and John Dewey in the twentieth. Yet it was Harry S. Broudy's midtwentieth-century essay "Some Duties of an Educational Aesthetics" that started me thinking seriously about the relations of aesthetic theory to artistic practice and the place of the arts and aesthetic education in general education. I became Broudy's junior colleague in the History and Philosophy of Education Department at the University of Illinois (later renamed the Department of Educational Policy Studies), and it is understandable that the junior professor would fall under the influence of the distinguished and more experienced senior professor. What followed is part of my professional history: the establishment of courses in aesthetic education; my founding of the *Journal of Aesthetic Education*; and addresses and writings that have been devoted principally to the problem areas of aesthetic education, namely, issues of justification, curriculum, teaching and learning, evaluation, and policy. One of my principal endeavors has been to discover how creative and academic disciplines can illuminate the problem areas of art and aesthetic education. The style and tone of the essays vary according to the topics and occasions for writing—an invitation, a research project, a collaborative effort, a critical examination, an editorial opinion. Although I generally maintain a positive outlook, I have been critical of ideas and tendencies that I believe are detrimental to the best interests of art and aesthetic education, among them certain developments in educational research and postmodern theorizing.

I initially considered a chronological ordering of the essays to indicate the evolution of my thinking, but this did not work very well. Hence I opted for a thematic arrangement, trusting that each essay's earlier or more recent original appearance would be apparent. I also decided that in addition to very brief synopses of the pieces, I would, where appropriate, add a few words about the persons and events that played a part in their origin. The themes of the selections range from the relationships of liberal education to arts education and those obtaining among art, aesthetics, and aesthetic education to teaching and curriculum, the arts and the humanities, and cultural diversity. All the essays have undergone editing, but only with respect to improvements in style and usage, not substance.

"Arts Education as Liberal Education" (Chapter 1), which opens the collection, exhibits many of the preoccupations that animate most of my writing. The essay came about through my friendship with Ronald Berman, a Shakespeare scholar and lately an authority on the writings of F. Scott Fitzgerald and Ernest Hemingway. I discovered that he and I shared an appreciation of the value of the arts and humanities and a concern about the growing politicizing of cultural and educational policy. This politicization was something Berman had to contend with as chairman of the National Humanities Foundation in its formative days, while I saw it manifested in the educational policies of the National Endowment for the Arts. I was invited by guest editors Berman and Philip Tate to address the significance of liberal studies for teacher preparation in a special issue of the *Journal of Education*, a venerable journal published by Boston University since 1875. The article was first presented as the Dunbar Lecture at Millsaps College, an institution known for its devotion to the liberal arts. I drew on its contents again for lectures presented at the Harvard Graduate School of Education and a Teachers College, Columbia University summer institute.

"Philosophy and Theory of Aesthetic Education" (Chapter 2) was prepared in response to an invitation from guest editor Harold Osborne to contribute to a special issue of *Dialectics and Humanism* on the topic "Art and Philosophy: Mutual Connections and Inspirations." Sadly, Osborne died before the issue saw print. Osborne was the longtime editor of the *British Journal of Aesthetics* and at the time of his death president of the British Society for Aesthetics. Although we never met, I had come to know him through correspondence, and toward the end of his career he generously contributed several articles and reviews to the *Journal of Aesthetic Education*. Along with Harry Broudy, Osborne was an early influence on my thought. After a few remarks about the differences between scientific and practical theories, the essay places its discussion in the context of a commitment to excellence in general education and then touches on four theories of aesthetic experience. The theories of Osborne and Monroe Beardsley are joined by those of Nelson Goodman and E. F. Kaelin, an inclusion that indicates the broadening of my views on aesthetic concepts (also evident in some of my later writings[1]). In the selection I go on to draw attention to the cognitive status of art, then further suggest a distinction between the proximate and prospective values of art, understood as the difference between the more immediately felt effects of aesthetic experiences and other values that such experiences can enhance.

The idea of aesthetic education has been developed on both sides of the Atlantic. The occasion for "Art, the Human Career, and Aesthetic Education" (Chapter 3) was a conference held in Wimbledon, England, at which I was privileged to present a keynote address. Alan Simpson, with whom I was to form a lasting friendship and eventually coedit an anthology on aesthetics and arts education, was instrumental in organizing the conference and in stimulating interest in aesthetic education in Great Britain.[2] It was at the same conference that I met Sir Roy Shaw, then secretary general of the British Arts Council. We discovered a common interest in the writings of Matthew Arnold and a conviction of the importance of excellence in art education. Sir Roy held the achievement of excellence to be a suitable educational objective not only for young students but also for adults, with whom he had worked in England's highly regarded adult education programs. I was later privileged to welcome him to the University of Illinois, where he spoke about his interests to faculty and students. He also responded to invitations to write for the *Journal of Aesthetic Education*. In chapter 2, after covering some familiar ground, I provide several examples of responses to different kinds of phenomena that can be interpreted as exhibiting some of the features of aesthetic experience. I then anticipate difficulties that can arise when a proposed theory of aesthetic education meets with resistance and mention the need for a philosophically sound justification of aesthetic education. The role of governments in shaping cultural policy also receives some space.

"Problems for a Philosophy of Art Education" (Chapter 4) was written in response to an invitation from Louis Lankford, a prominent theorist of aesthetic education who guest-edited a special issue of *Studies in Art Education* devoted to the philosophy of art education. In the chapter I examine a number of ostensible dichotomies with a view to determining whether they are genuinely dichotomous or whether their terms can be synthesized in new formulations. I discussed similar problems in a working paper on issues in art education that I had prepared as part of a Getty-supported project designed to identify the basic literature of discipline-based art education.

The next selection, "Concepts, Concept Learning, and Art Education" (Chapter 5), is similarly devoted to the problems of relating theory to practice and research. It entails pointing out different meanings of concept, describing the nature of concept acquisition, and indicating the relevance of a theory of meaningful learning. At the time I wrote the piece I was preoccupied with discovering the distinctive attributes of aesthetic response and thus paid less attention to the cognitive status of the art object. Yet even though I did not refer to the latter specifically, I have always proceeded on the assumption that works of art are unique manifolds of significance. Other selections in this volume, especially those in Part 3, on the arts and the humanities, should clear me of any charge of holding a formalist theory of art that rejects the notion of meaning in the arts.

The Getty Trust famously became involved in art and aesthetic education in the 1980s and 1990s, but prior to the Getty's arrival on the scene the Aesthetic Education Program of CEMREL (Central Midwestern Regional Laboratory), under the able direction of Stanley S. Madeja, was the most comprehensive effort in research and development in art education in the United States. It attracted and employed major figures and agencies in art education and related fields. The essay "The Artworld and Aesthetic Skills: A Context for Research and Development" (Chapter 6), coauthored with Christiana Smith, was presented to a CEMREL-sponsored conference on the role of the arts and aesthetics in the future. I begin by indicating the prerequisite for any research proposal, which is the need to have a set of assumptions about the nature of the enterprise in question. Describing the nature of art education involves identifying the components of the artworld and an account of the concepts, skills, and difficulties that figure in developing appreciative and critical dispositions in the young. Despite the essay's emphasis on the visual arts, educators in dance and music education found the classification of critical skills useful in charting concepts and skills in their respective domains.

"Teaching Aesthetic Criticism in the Schools" (Chapter 7) is as timely today as it was when it was written. The atmosphere of nonjudgmentalism that Paul Goodman and Robert Brustein exposed in their critique of the countercultural New Left in the 1970s is similar to the criticism of value distinctions in contemporary postmodern theorizing. In Chapter 7, having discussed types of criticism and critical standards, I provide an example of aesthetic criticism and suggest how its components can be understood.

In the 1980s a cluster of reports lamenting conditions in the schools ignited a national excellence-in-education movement. It was in the spirit of that movement that then president of the National Art Education Association, Nancy MacGregor, invited me to prepare a statement on behalf of the association in response to the movement. The result was *Excellence in Art Education: Ideas and Initiatives*. Sales of the initial volume and its sequel *Excellence II: The Continuing Quest in Art Education* (1995) reflect continuing interest in its topic.[3] Not surprisingly, the volume also generated controversy. The general complaint was that the pursuit of excellence is inherently elitist and therefore incompatible with democratic principles, a view that I of course rejected. The selection reprinted here, "An Excellence Curriculum for Art Education" (Chapter 8) is based on themes from these books and is an edited revision of a talk presented to a Teachers College, Columbia University symposium on curriculum.

In Part 3, I present my current thinking about aesthetic education and highlight a perspective from the humanities. Although I have always had an interest in the range of studies encompassed by the humanities (I taught art history for several years and have written about the relations of aesthetic criticism to humanistic understanding),[4] it was not until the advent of the Getty Trust's involvement in art education that I began to frame more systematically a humanities interpretation of aesthetic education. A stimulus was supplied by the Getty approach to art education known as discipline-based art education (DBAE), which stressed the importance of grounding the teaching of art in the ideas and methods of art making, art history, art criticism, and aesthetics. It was acknowledged that these were not the only disciplines that bear in some way on art education, but they were considered basic. It seemed to me that the supplementing of creative activities with academic disciplines in effect aligned the teaching of art with the humanities, and so I took what seemed a logical next step and worked out a connection. Making such a connection was not difficult inasmuch as the Getty stance echoed my own inclination toward the disciplines in question. For example, sections of my first published collection were organized under the rubrics of *art history*, *aesthetics*, and *art criticism*, and there was a discussion of artistic creation as well.[5]

"Aesthetic Education: A Critical Necessity" (Chapter 9) was written in response to an invitation from Ann Kuo, a leading international figure in arts education, to present a keynote address to a regional congress of the

International Society for Education Through Art (InSEA) held in Taichung, Taiwan. This occasion provided me with an opportunity to present a version of a humanities interpretation of aesthetic education that made reference to the multicultural interests of the society's members. My lead-in was a discussion about the future of the humanities written by Walter Kaufmann, who likened the reading of a classic text to a visit to a foreign culture undertaken for the purpose of experiencing cultural shock. I suggested that his analogy had implications for preparing sojourners of the art world. The overcoming of ethnocentricity is one of Kaufmann's four aims for the humanities, the other three being the appreciation of excellence, the cultivation of aesthetic vision, and the acquisition of powers of critical thinking—all topics I have discussed in essays included in this collection. The brief reference to Clifford Geertz's study of Balinese life and culture serves to illustrate differences in aesthetic considerations in Western and non-Western societies, differences to which I give more attention in the essay on cultural diversity in Part 4.

"Toward Percipience: A Humanities Curriculum for Arts Education" (Chapter 10) was the result of my association with two scholars, Albert William Levi, who for most of his career was David May Distinguished University Professor of the Humanities at Washington University, and Bennett Reimer, who at the time was John W. Beattie Professor of Music at Northwestern University. The humanities perspective was derived from Levi's redefinition of the traditional liberal arts as the humanities, which he understood as the substantive and procedural aspects of languages and literature, history, and philosophical reflection—or, as he put it, as the arts of communication, continuity, and criticism. The discussion of percipience appeared in the National Society for the Study of Education (NSSE) yearbook *The Arts Education and Aesthetic Knowing*, of which Reimer and I were coeditors. The book's theme was the cognitive revolution in arts, or as one reviewer of the volume put it, the harvesting of the cognitive revolution for arts education. In order to establish a link between Levi's redefinition and the disciplines of DBAE, all I had to do was argue that art is a special way of communicating that has a history of continuity and a literature that reflects on its values. After presenting Levi's redefinition, in the essay I sketch the contours of a humanities curriculum that features the purpose of general education, an interpretation of aesthetic experience in terms of its constitutive and revelatory values, and descriptions of five overlapping and interrelated phases of aesthetic learning. As everyone who has ever prepared a yearbook for NSSE knows, the editors came to appreciate the friendly guidance and support of Kenneth Rehage, at the time the society's treasurer. Inasmuch as the essay was written for a general-education audience and not art education specialists, I reiterate Levi's interpretation of the humanities and Beardsley's discussion of aesthetic experience, explored in other essays.

Because the visual arts are what I know best, most of the examples in my writings are about them. Occasionally, however, and with a sense of limitations, I have strayed into other aesthetic domains—in the instance of the following selection, the teaching of music. The precipitating event was an address to an international symposium held at Indiana University under the direction of Estelle R. Jorgensen. The topic of the symposium was the philosopher/teacher, with a slant toward research and teaching. The proceedings of the conference were later published as a special issue of the *Journal of Aesthetic Education* (Fall 1991), with Jorgensen as guest editor, and after that as a book (1993) published by the University of Illinois Press.

Encompassing art education within the category of the humanities is perhaps less controversial than trying to do the same for music education. In "Teaching Music as One of the Humanities" (Chapter 11), I make reference to the work of Peter Kivy, a prominent philosopher of music, who holds a contrary view. For example, Kivy believes that far from being about anything or saying anything profound, a musical composition such as Beethoven's Third Symphony (the *Eroica*) is nothing but "a magnificent abstract structure of sound: one big beautiful noise, signifying nothing."[6] Not entirely convinced, I turned to the writings of Beardsley, who had dealt extensively with the problems of meaning in music (for example, problems with evocative, expressive, and signification theories of musical meaning). In wrestling with these difficulties, Beardsley asked whether Nelson Goodman's cognitive theory of art as understanding might yield some insight into the question. Beardsley arrived at the qualified conclusion that inasmuch as music is constituted by modes of continuity, the perception of which can contribute importantly to an understanding of movement in human experience, it can make a claim to conveying knowledge. I thought that such a modest and carefully developed stance on musical meaning was sufficient for my purposes; that is, it suggested a way in which music education might be approached through a humanities-based conception of art education. Additionally, in this chapter I take account of Leonard Meyer's discussion of the sciences, the arts, and the humanities.

"Remoralization and Aesthetic Education" (Chapter 12) represents another instance of my indebtedness to Harry S. Broudy's writings. I adapt to the specific context of aesthetic education some ideas Broudy elaborated in his *Truth and Credibility: The Citizen's Dilemma*, which is one of those rare volumes that has continuing interest and relevance. Broudy points out the need for a remoralization of society and identifies resources for bringing it about. He concedes to the sciences the capacity to make warranted assertions about matters of fact but notes that such assertions, which are numberless and often conflicting, are not sufficient to allow ordinary citizens to arrive at moral judgments. Citizens therefore must increasingly seek guidance from the opinions of experts, which confronts them with the dilemma of deciding on which expert—or political leader—to trust. The citizen's choice among experts, in turn, is most reliably based on the experts' credibility, that is, what Broudy calls the experts' warranted commitment to positions vouchsafed by their willingness to take responsibility for their beliefs and actions. The credibility and warranted commitment that citizens look for in experts are also qualities that they ought to try and cultivate in themselves. In this they can be helped, Broudy argues, through the study and appreciation of exemplars of art and the humanities.

Other chapters in this collection refer to cultural diversity, for example, "Aesthetic Education: A Critical Necessity" (Chapter 9) in Part 3, in which I distinguish between types of multiculturalists. In "The Uses of Cultural Diversity" (Chapter 13) I have something different in mind. The essay, suggested by Lionel Trilling's essay "Why We Read Jane Austen," discusses how two societies, one Western and one non-Western, may nonetheless have a notion of the aesthetic to which they attach importance. Trilling found it appropriate to examine the anthropological methods that Clifford Geertz used to help understand the nature of personhood in Balinese life, a culture in which aesthetic values are a significant component of personal identity but are contrary to Western attitudes. Trilling was prompted to ask whether life seeks, or should seek, to approximate art, and he concluded that the question constitutes "a dialectic, with all the dignity that inheres in that word." I think this question is an apt one with which to close a volume that is an endeavor to find a coherent relationship of art to the human career.

A few additional words are required in order to respond to editorial suggestions made by the publisher and questions raised by readers of the manuscript. One question relates to timeliness and another to repetition of ideas. The essays selected go back to 1977 and are as recent as 1995. Given the penchant for "what's happening now" and "breaking news," it might seem that anything written more than a decade ago is beside the point and of no more than historical interest. I would be pleased if some of my work would be preserved in the chronicles of art education, but obviously I assume that the essays in this volume have contemporary relevance. As for some repetition of content, I think repetition can be a plus if it helps to reinforce an idea or approach. Moreover, the same or similar ideas receive more or less discussion depending on the context.

Back to the first question. It needs to be pointed out that the arts and humanities are spared the plight of rapid obsolescence that afflicts the natural and physical sciences. Scientific knowledge advances at such a rapid pace that it is said that textbooks must be rewritten every six months. Scientific journals, moreover, churn out research even more rapidly, and electronic forms of communication increasingly are supplanting the printed word. The dynamic of communication in the arts and humanities is more relaxed. The past continues to influence thinking on a number of contemporary problems, whereas a scientific theory once disproved is primarily of archival interest.

By way of a more specific defense of my selections, I would point out that it is precisely because higher education and the schools have lost sight of the traditional ideal of humanistic learning that such an ideal needs to be recalled and the consequences of abandoning it pointed out. The ways in which aesthetics, especially philosophical aesthetics, bears on art education, also has abiding importance. Indeed, after a period during which the notion of the aesthetic came under a cloud there has been a revival of interest in the concept of aesthetic experience, the feeling being that too much of value is lost by efforts to expunge it from our understanding of human experience. Moreover, dichotomies, merely suppositional or real, are in continuous need of analysis, which, I trust, I have shown. And because teaching anything, art included, inevitably involves concepts of one kind or another, it is useful to have a notion of what concepts are and how they figure in teaching a spectrum of skills. Once such skills are identified, research can try to establish how they can be better taught. The cognitive revolution in understanding the nature of mind and learning continues to yield results, and the conception of art education from a humanities point of view can be seen as part of and even a distinctive contribution to it. Finally, the role that aesthetic education and the humanities may play in remoralizing society is perhaps of greater importance today than it was when the essay in question was published. All these topics are discussed in the essays I've reprinted.

Such a defense, however, may not satisfy those who might think I haven't covered enough bases or covered them sufficiently or even covered the wrong ones. One reader asked why I did not pay more attention to postmodernism. I briefly discuss postmodernism as a problem for art education in Part 1, where I comment on the split between modernism and postmodernism. In that context I mention more or less invidious interpretations of postmodernism and say that the employment of the terms *modernism* and *postmodernism* as counters in ideological debates has diminished their educational usefulness. I also stated that I was not aware of any persuasive interpretation of postmodern art education. Nor do I think a persuasive interpretation is possible. Why do I say this?

Stated baldly, invidious postmodernism holds that works of art should be understood not in terms of their aesthetic properties and content so much as in the ways in which they can be understood in terms of the social and cultural conditions that produced them. Postmodern art educators further tend to politicize art and art education along the lines of radical Left thinking.

The belief is that decisions about content and teaching are determined by dominant groups in the society whose primary concern is to maintain their power and authority, which is construed as a form of oppression. It therefore becomes the obligation of instruction to expose such conditions through deconstructive analysis and to foster in students a critical attitude that predisposes them to social reform. The reigning disposition is to question the legitimacy of typically Western values, namely those of knowledge, meaning, truth, value, objectivity, and the possibility of communication itself. In other words, the culture wars carried on in the disciplines of university departments are now being waged in art education as well. A consequence is that radical reform should supercede ways of teaching art that stress the importance of aesthetic and artistic values. In other words, art education becomes just one more means for promoting social change. It has been suggested that having lost the larger ideological battle to advance Marxist tenets, adherents of postmodern theorizing now direct their energies toward undermining the structures of authority wherever and whenever they find them. I think there is some truth to this suggestion.

It is not only my heavy investment in aesthetic education that causes me to have problems with postmodern interpretations of art education. It is also because those who have seriously tried to understand postmodernism have ended up saying that the clearest thing that can be said about it is that it is a very unclear, hotly contested concept;[7] that postmodernists themselves often don't know what the term means;[8] and that because of the complexity, difficulty, and density of expression of postmodernist theory, attempts to popularize it are bound to result in serious oversimplifications.[9] Harnessing art education to social reconstruction is made even more questionable by the fact that teachers and schools are ill-prepared to undertake such a task in any meaningful sense.

Perhaps the most important failing of postmodernism is its rejection of objectivity, even as an ideal. Yet disbelief in the possibility of objective judgment makes it difficult to see how an advanced society can function. In this respect one can only conclude that postmodernism flies in the face of common life experience. As I concluded in "Problems for a Philosophy of Art Education" in Part I, I believe that the gulf between radical postmodernism and modernism is unbridgeable. A view of learning that by implication is anarchic and nihilistic is self-defeating.

I stress that my criticism is limited primarily to destructive, radical forms of postmodernism. There are also more commonsensical interpretations that, to borrow a phrase, might be termed constructive postmodernism.[10] I have no problem, as some of the essays in this volume indicate, with the study of works by underrepresented groups and cultures, as long as it does not foster the kind of particularism and cultural insularity that dissolves shared values necessary for social cohesion or weakens standards of accomplishment. My description of four types of multiculturalism in Part I may be seen as reaching for a responsible multiculturalism.

The idea of deconstruction, moreover, despite its typical uses by postmodern theorists, can perhaps be muted. I say this because it has been argued that deconstruction is merely a cautious tale that reminds us of the complex relations between language and reality, but that it does not do much more than that. Consequently, we must go on doing what we have always done, and must do.[11] I assume that this means that we may continue to believe in the possibility of rational communication and the search for objective understanding. Finally, a meeting ground between different types of criticism, cultural and aesthetic, might be prepared by an acknowledgment that serious works of art can be appreciated in several dimensions. For example, an artwork's social aspects may be judiciously given their due without suppression of the work's aesthetic values, and vice versa. That is, a less presumptuous cultural criticism would not eliminate, but rather embrace and preserve, aesthetic values, while aesthetic criticism would acknowledge that cultural and aesthetic values often intertweave.[12] The question is whether cultural criticism, or cultural studies, should supersede the development of aesthetic literacy. I think not and view with skepticism positions that commit art education to social reconstruction. This is not the place for a more comprehensive and systematic discussion of postmodernism. The term encompasses a vast literature, and all I have done here is to condense more extensive remarks I've made elsewhere.[13]

NOTES

1. See my "Contemporary Aesthetic Education," in *Encyclopedia of Aesthetics*, ed. Michael Kelly (New York: Oxford University Press, 1998), 4:93–96; and "Aesthetic Education: Questions and Issues," in *Handbook of Research and Policy in Art Education*, ed. Elliot Eisner and Michael Day (New Jersey: Lawrence Erlbaum Associates, 2004), 163–185.

2. Ralph A. Smith and Alan Simpson, eds. *Aesthetics and Arts Education* (Urbana: University of Illinois Press, 1991).

3. See *Excellence II: The Continuing Quest in Art Education* (Reston, Va.: National Art Education Association, 1995).

4. See "From Aesthetic Criticism to Humanistic Understanding: A Practical Illustration," *Studies in Art Education* 25 (Summer 1984): 238–44.

5. See *Aesthetics and Criticism in Art Education: Problems in Defining, Explaining, and Evaluating Art* (Chicago: Rand McNally, 1966). Reprinted in 2001 in the Archival Series of the National Art Education Association, with an updated bibliographical note.

6. Peter Kivy, "Music and the Liberal Education," *Journal of Aesthetic Education* 25, no. 3 (1991): 85.

7. Richard Shusterman, "Aesthetics and Postmodernism," in *The Oxford Handbook of Aesthetics*, ed. Jerrold Levinson (New York: Oxford University Press, 2003), 771.

8. Charles Jencks, *Post-modernism: The New Classicism in Art and Architecture* (New York: Rizzoli, 1987), 7.

9. David Carrier, *Journal of Aesthetic Education* 20, no. 4 (1986): 99–101. This is a review of two books on postmodernism and art education.

10. Martin Schiralli, *Constructive Postmodernism: Toward Renewal in Cultural and Literary Studies* (Westport, Conn.: Greenwood, 1999), esp. chap 3.

11. Joseph Margolis, "Deconstruction: A Cautionary Tale," *Journal of Aesthetic Education* 20, no. 4 (1986): 91–94.

12. Monroe C. Beardsley, "Art and Its Cultural Context," in *The Aesthetic Point of View: Selected Essays*, ed. M. J. Wreen and D. M Callen (Ithaca: Cornell University Press, 1982), 370.

13. See my *The Sense of Art: A Study in Aesthetic Education* (New York: Routledge, 1989), 169–80.

Culture and the Arts
in Education

Background and Vision

Arts Education as Liberal Education

THE POLITICIZING of arts and humanities education in recent years has resulted in our losing sight of the traditional humanistic point of view toward learning. In what follows I discuss the humanistic ideal, provide a interpretation of the humanities that accommodates the serious study of the arts, and sketch a K–12 excellence curriculum that consists of five phases of aesthetic development.

On the occasion of the sixtieth anniversary of the Memorial Library of Bard College, an institution noted for its dedication to liberal learning, Werner Jaeger, the great scholar of Greek culture, presented an address titled "The Greeks and the Education of Man."[1] Jaeger recalled the essence of the Greek ideal of life and its formidable influence on subsequent periods, including our own, and pondered the likely fate of the ideal. He reminded his audience that every attempt to define and estimate the value of the liberal arts and the humanities has its roots in the Greek creation of a definite conception of culture. Central to that conception was a commitment to discovering what is essentially human and what obligations such discovery entailed. In this connection he said that we are but the latest guests at the rich table of the ancient Greeks, the earliest, of course, having been the Romans, who with their idea of the humanities demonstrated the inherently educational potential of the Greek ideal. Practical thinkers that they were, the Romans distilled the essence of Greek literature and made it the core of their education.

What did the Greeks mean by *humanity*? We find that the term refers first to education, especially to the raising of children, but later it came to mean the sum total of a higher civilization or culture that was embodied in literature. And for the Greeks, *literature* implied more than verbal texts; it meant the unity of all great works, including works of art. The name given to this unity was *paideia*, which today usually translates as "general education or culture."

The Greek idea of culture, then, was not that which is held by today's anthropologist; it was highly normative and included all the creative activities of a nation. Works of poetry exemplified the ideal; they were at once sources of aesthetic pleasure, conveyers of an ethos, and the successful fulfillment of artistic intentions. Above all, a poetic work embodied the excellence of the object that was represented. Perhaps we may say that even more readily than Greek poetry a work of Greek sculpture comes to mind in which the subject of the distinctively human is quite tangible. But the same ideal pervaded oratory, history, and philosophy.

As Greek thought evolved, so did the virtues, norms, and values of *paideia*. First came heroic virtue and military prowess, then political and civic virtue, and, finally, the supreme value of wisdom, which was philosophical virtue. In other words, Greek education was not merely a socializing process in the sense understood today. Nor was it professional or specialist training. Rather, it was general education as a process of the conscious formation of the living person. In modern terms we would call this process the systematic building of a sense of self that attempts to find the correct relations of the self to others and to culture. It might be said that becoming human had an architectonic character.

A question naturally arises about the nature of the materials with which one composes a self. For the Greeks the answer to this question was gymnastics and music, which included poetry and dance as well as vocal and instrumental music. For a while poetry reigned preeminent, and Homer and the Greek dramatists provided the humanizing materials. Such works were at once enjoyable, inspirational, and educational and were intended to arouse a sense of duty and obligation. The important point is that the formulation and expression of one's humanity—the basic concern of Greek education—permeated all forms of Greek thought: poetry, musical harmony, the structure of language, rhetoric, logic, arithmetic, and geometry. If this Greek concern sounds familiar, it is because we are all Greeks, whether or not we realize it and irrespective of our race, class, or sex.

The Greek experience is important to consider for another reason: it provides a model for thinking about the relations of tradition and modernity. In Greek thinking, the past—its antiquity—was never considered sacrosanct; indeed, Greek writers subjected it to harsh criticism. But neither was it ever considered irrelevant. Jaeger remarks that in reading Greek writers, one has the impression that the past is constantly present. All criticism took as its starting point the heritage as it had been handed down. The accepted idea was that one had to work one's way through tradition and possess it before attempting to complement or transcend it. As it was with the Greeks, so it was with the Romans, the Church Fathers, the Renaissance humanists, and many others. Indeed, if Western civilization has any rhythm it is the constant rediscovery of the Greek idea of culture. "Every generation," Jaeger remarked, "has to determine for itself the point at which

Greek humanism is to be fitted into the status of contemporary civilization" (17). And in the 1950s Jaeger believed he perceived a revival of interest in doing just that.

Twenty years after Jaeger had extolled the virtues of the Greek ideal of education, Lionel Trilling, the distinguished cultural critic and teacher of literature, addressed the same topic. The occasion was an Aspen Institute for Humanistic Studies conference on the educated person in the contemporary world. Trilling was asked if he could identify any factors in the contemporary society that would make likely the emergence in the late twentieth century of a vital education related to the humanistic educational tradition. The tenor of Trilling's response is contained in the title of his address, "The Uncertain Future of the Humanistic Educational Ideal."[2]

As a longtime faculty member of Columbia University, an institution that pioneered in general education, Trilling was exceptionally well qualified to discuss the question put to him. He was not long in stating his belief

> that at the present time in American society, there are few factors to be perceived, if any at all, which make it likely that within the next quarter-century there will be articulated in a convincing and effectual way an educational ideal that has a positive and significant connection with the humanistic educational traditions of the past. (160–61)

It seemed to Trilling that all indications pointed in the opposite direction and that society would increasingly distance itself from such traditions. Yet Trilling's skepticism was tempered by his realization that the winds of American educational thought are subject to rapid shifts of direction.

He noted, for example, the history of his own university's attitudes toward liberal education. That history extended from the days of Frederick Barnard, who wanted to abolish Columbia College, to the time of Nicholas Murray Butler, who, after wanting to shorten the time that undergraduates spent "idling and dawdling" on general studies, changed his mind and said that such education might after all contribute to the generous and reflective use of leisure. There was, in other words, more to being human than professional competence; general culture also counted for something. Ultimately, the idea of general education prevailed, and Columbia College became the core of the university. After World War I, John Erskine established a two-year Great Books Program for juniors and seniors that was predicated on the assumption that the best way to become intelligent was through acquaintance with the great intellectual and artistic works of the past. Erskine's influence was felt across the country, most significantly in the Great Books idea of the University of Chicago and St. John's College. The view that only in this way could the whole person become educated gradually won acceptance.

The best citizen would be the individual who learned what great minds from the past had said about reason, virtue, beauty, and truth.

Trilling also discussed an opposing attitude about the value of a liberal education that prevailed at the time, namely, that what such an education provided was less an occasion for self-understanding and an invitation to discover the conditions of a good life than an opportunity to become an accredited member of a favored social and economic class. In short, a liberal education was viewed as enhancing one's prospects for upward mobility. What Trilling was alluding to was a characteristic ambivalence on the part of Americans toward the cultivation of the mind for its own sake. Yet for many of my generation, including those with working-class backgrounds, this ambivalence was resolved in favor of the inherent values of a liberal education. There was an unconscious yearning for the beneficent state described by Trilling. "The educated person," he wrote, "is exactly an initiate who began as a postulant, passed to a higher level of experience, and became worthy of admission into the company of those who are thought to have transcended the mental darkness and inertia in which they were previously immersed" (170). Trilling said that this assumption has always existed somewhere in the traditional humanistic ideal of education. In anthropological terms the process is known as experiencing a culture's rites of passage.

If, as Trilling indicated, attitudes toward the traditional humanistic ideal are subject to swings of opinion, is this not cause for some optimism regarding the future of liberal learning? Trilling responded to his own question by pointing to the disfavor in which the idea of initiation through ordeal was held in the mid-1970s. Such an idea presupposes not only a commitment to seek self-understanding; it also implies acceptance of the idea of the self's being shaped, formed, and fashioned by engagements with worthwhile models. Yet at the time that Trilling wrote, the idea of learning through ordeal—of disciplined encounters with difficult materials, of submitting to a shaping or forming—suggested infringements on freedom and individuality. The intention therefore became one of making the young feel comfortable in educational institutions. And so it is today, which accounts for so much grade inflation and countless support groups. It is in this context that we are to understand a Plan to Increase Student Happiness, conceived by a professor of English and comparative literature at San Diego State University. In an essay in *Newsweek* magazine she related that after many years she had suddenly discovered the secret of teaching. At the end of the second week of a semester all students enrolled in each course would receive a final grade of A. This would relieve their minds of any anxiety, and they would be free to do what they wanted the rest of the semester. To her colleagues who might object, she would say, "Hey, lighten up! Why make life difficult?"[3] But, of course, schools cannot adopt a civilizing function if they abandon a commitment to disciplined learning. It is as if young people, and some of their elders, expect institutions of learning to resemble cable television where they can effortlessly and endlessly switch from one thing to another until they find something congenial. Instead of providing a countervailing space where only carefully selected ideas and goals are systematically pursued, the schools imitate the multifariousness of mass culture and even celebrate it.

Trilling drew attention to some of the obstacles that inhibit the effectiveness of humanistic learning. At about the same time, the distinguished British philosopher Michael Oakeshott was also in Colorado, where he addressed the topic of liberal education, although in slightly different terms and accents. In an essay titled "A Place of Learning," Oakeshott's explanation of learning assumes the existence of human freedom and a mind capable of rendering things intelligible.[4] Inasmuch as human life follows no preordained course, learning to become human is essentially an adventure in which individuals must learn how to script a human career and revise it as conditions demand. Because becoming human is also problematical, human life presents a predicament that must be addressed with as much intelligence as possible.

Although learning to live and shape a human career begins in the family and its environment, in modern society schools are the primary places set aside for learning. As Trilling pointed out, learning proceeds in part through examination and sometimes adoption of the ways in which others have learned and shaped their lives. The schools are also locations where the learning of particular things proceeds under specific conditions for achievement. Moreover, to do their job effectively schools must provide a secure and stable environment; they must serve as a shelter and distance themselves from the urgencies of contemporary life. In stressing the importance of learning particular things, Oakeshott aimed to counteract the abstract rhetoric expressed in such empty phrases as *learning to improve one's mind* or *learning to think critically*. Particular things, moreover, are brought to life through a common language that makes communication possible. One of the conditions of liberal learning, then, is freedom to learn. Inasmuch as one cannot learn to understand what is distinctly human while being constantly tugged at by demands from beyond the school environment, learning requires patience, perseverance, and concentration.

Oakeshott does not use the term *paideia*, but there is a concordance with Jaeger's understanding of it. That is, learning encompasses both an appreciation of the human inheritance and the means for appropriating it, which is to say that the human inheritance is not only cultural capital but also a conversational encounter with it. Learning is thus an invitation to culture.

According to Oakeshott, culture

> comprises unfinished intellectual and emotional journeys now abandoned but
> known to us in the tattered maps left behind by the explorers; it is composed of
> lighthearted adventures, of relationships invented and explored in exploit or in
> drama, of myths and stories and poems expressing fragments of human self-
> understanding, of gods worshipped, of responses to the mutability of the world
> and of encounters with death. And it reaches us . . . as a manifold of invitations
> to look, to listen, to reflect . . . to encounter particular adventures in human self-
> understanding. (29)

Oakeshott then went on to recall the tradition of liberal learning and its twelfth- and fourteenth-century revivals. But Oakeshott's concern was not so much historical as critical and speculative. Like Trilling, he was interested in assessing the circumstances that threatened the survival of liberal learning. Writing in the 1970s, he did not believe that the tradition was already in its death throes. It still survived in pockets of resistance to the imperatives of the alternative culture. Yet the tradition seemed clearly in danger of crumbling under a number of developments that were slowly but surely eroding its foundations.

The enemies of liberal learning turned out to be those who really wanted to be helpful, those who were often caring and concerned and evinced genuinely humane sentiments. Such sentiments were often expressed in efforts to be relevant, which usually meant taking into account student interests and addressing a range of social problems. Yet what should be relevant, said Oakeshott, is the engagement of the human inheritance for what it says about self-understanding and the quest for the good life. Considered this way, the cultural heritage, as the classicist William Arrowsmith once remarked, literally trembles with relevance. Its ideas, images, myths, and stories illuminate better than anything else the perplexities and joys of human existence. Not only that; attempts to be perpetually "with it" are doomed to failure. Oakeshott's point is that to try to accommodate current fashions and address the litany of social ills besetting society is to leave no time for teaching the subject. Dancing to the tune of relevance soon becomes a *danse macabre*.

If keeping up with the tempo set by "relevance" is self-defeating, so is a commitment to socialization and general education as understood by Oakeshott. As he saw it, this kind of general education fails to pay attention to particular things. By contrast, the ideas and works of the Great Conversation are concrete, particular things and not merely tools for honing critical skills. Nor is the Great Conversation static; it is inherently dynamic and manifests both continuity and change while expressing both conservative and revolutionary values. Its repertoire changes, but an indispensable core remains. Yet the future of this core is no longer assured. The classics of the Western intellectual and cultural heritage are increasingly examined primarily for devil signs believed responsible for most of our contemporary problems.

Obviously, adventures in ideas are not all of a kind. There are adventures in the natural and social sciences, in mathematics, as well as in the arts and humanities. As my interest is primarily in the last, I will pass over Oakeshott's discussion of other subjects that are not preeminently concerned with understanding human values. To give a sample of Oakeshott's thinking, he says of literature that it consists of "the contemplative exploration of beliefs, emotions, human characters and relationships in imagined situations, liberated from the confused, cliché-ridden, generalized conditions of commonplace life and constituting a world of ideal human expressions inviting . . . the exact attention and understanding of those who read" (33).

The forces, then, that in the mid-1970s seemed to Oakeshott to be derailing the ideal of liberal learning were emphases on relevance and socialization and a misconstrued notion of general education. His plea was for the study of culture not as

> a miscellany of beliefs, perceptions, ideas, sentiments and engagements, but . . . as a variety of distinct languages of understanding, and its inducements are invitations to become acquainted with these languages, to learn to discriminate between them, and to recognize them not merely as diverse modes of understanding the world but as the most substantial expressions we have of human self-understanding. (38)

To say this, he suggests, is to hold that liberal learning is essentially education in imagination.

Perhaps because of a long-standing tendency of writers in the humanistic tradition to distinguish between making and contemplating, Oakeshott does not specifically include the creative and performing arts in the variety of languages he recommends for study. If, however, we grant the arts the status of special languages that have something of value to communicate, then they too can be subsumed under the rubric of *the humanities*. As artistic statements, works of art constitute a language that has a distinguished history of accomplishment that poses special problems of appreciation, interpretation, and judgment.

Once more, Oakeshott emphasizes that the kind of education in imagination he favors should occur in protected places and be demanding. Its prerequisites are knowledgeable teachers committed to teaching who understand what schools are for and who do not confuse the curricular with the extracurricular. Students derive pleasures of learning from disciplined mastery of difficult materials, for example, foreign languages, history, works of art, philosophy, and religion, to stay with the humanities. Their liberal education may incidentally confer membership in a special class that enhances their career prospects, but such conferral is not the essence of humanistic education. In other words, initiation into the Great Conversation serves the purposes of one's becoming what used to be called a whole person, one who can compose ideas and feelings into a coherent and significant self and career.

One might say in response to Oakeshott that however penetrating and inspirational his message, reality obtrudes upon places of learning in ways that cannot be ignored. Administrators are pressured to address a plethora of social problems; students must often take time from their studies to work; special interests insist on having their voices heard in the planning of the curriculum; the federal government ties grants to restrictions; and on and on. How would Oakeshott respond to such reservations? He would say that schools should quietly remind themselves of their primary mission and refuse to compromise. As a check on the expression of sheer impulse, demands for instant gratification, and random mental wanderings, learning must stress stability, concentration, form, discipline, excellence, creativity, and civilization. That is, instead of embracing the commonplace mind, a mind that is satisfied with itself and seeks no transcendence, places of learning must invite attention to uncommon minds and to instances of significant transfiguration of the self. Under such educational conditions the young too may create their best possible selves. These sentiments were expressed by nineteenth-century cultural critics who foresaw the problems that modern democracies would invite by failing to stress the importance of superior accomplishment and its recognition. And they have been echoed by thoughtful writers in our own time.

I have discussed the tradition of liberal learning and its humanistic ideal in terms of some of the attitudes taken toward it in the 1950s and 1970s. Decades later, the question is whether Trilling was prophetic in his judgment that little in the circumstances of the time in which he wrote suggested a recommitment to the humanistic ideal. As one who tries to keep his eye on what is happening in the culture of the schools and the culture without, and who as a journal editor has read more manuscripts about both cultures than is good for anyone's well-being, I must agree with Trilling. The traditional humanistic ideal of education is vanishing from places of learning. This means that measures must be taken if the ideal is to survive, a task that has been undertaken by the American Academy for Liberal Education.

As I have said, attempts to retain the classical ideal of learning cannot be completely oblivious to the alternative culture that not only surrounds places of learning but is also invading and occupying them. Some adjustments have to be made. Neither is it possible to ignore the rest of the world or diversity within our own society. Redefinitions of liberal learning, and especially of the arts and humanities, are in order. But contemporary definitions, insofar as they are largely antagonistic to the traditional Western ideal of culture and the civilization in which it took root, are part of the problem. And so I turn to a writer, Albert William Levi, who perceived the need for a redefinition that retained what is most valuable in the tradition. For much of his career, Levi held the position of David May Distinguished University Professor of the Humanities at Washington University.

On the occasion of a humanities–world literature seminar held in Peru, Illinois, and at about the same time that Trilling and Oakeshott were presenting their addresses in Colorado, Levi, in an address titled "Teaching Literature as a Humanity," gave a brief summary of his ideas.[5] It began with a famous story from the Talmud about a learned rabbi who upon his capture by an Islamic potentate was required under penalty of death to sum up the essence of the Jewish religion—standing on one foot, no less. The rabbi recalled the sixth chapter of the Book of Micah and said, "To do justly, to love mercy, and to walk humbly with thy God." In a similar spirit, Levi summed up the essence of the humanities by saying, "It is to think critically, to communicate successfully, and to walk proudly with thy tradition " (283).

Levi thus defined the essence of the humanities in procedural terms, as ways of doing things. But in his understanding of the humanities as encouraging civilizing skills, he was always careful to associate such skills—what he called the liberal arts of communication, continuity, and criticism—with their substantive subjects, that is, languages and literatures, history, and philosophy. In a more extended discussion Levi synthesized these two great traditions of the humanities: the tradition of the Middle Ages, which stressed the procedural aspects of the humanities, and the tradition of the Renaissance, which understood the humanities essentially as contents or subject matters.[6]

These two ways of thinking about the humanities, procedurally and substantively, provide major options for teaching the humanities today, as does Levi's synthesis. In some moments Levi leaned more toward the procedural sense: to teach the humanities is to teach them as civilizing skills. At other times he favored the substantive sense; to teach the humanities is to teach them as subjects. The decision to opt for the procedural definition of the humanities makes sense in light of the enlargement of the corpus of humanistic works now available for study. Choosing the substantive definition makes sense in efforts to counteract cultural amnesia and illiteracy.

My intention is not to recommend a specific way of teaching the humanities but to recall why it is important that in any conception of humanities education, special places of honor must be given to the liberal arts of communication, continuity, and criticism. There can be no definition that does not take them into account, for they are grounded, as Levi put it, in the very nature of our humanity and in the conditions of social life. Without them the search for personal identity, the building of a viable social structure, and the reformation of values are unthinkable. Levi understood these arts as a series of concentric circles, as if caused by pebbles thrown into a pond, each having its own intention, yet overlapping the others to some extent.

The essence of the arts of communication is the quest for human expression and response. One's language not only determines the limits of one's intellection and emotional perceptions, but in its style and nuances of meaning and implication language also constitutes a form of life; one's manner of its use reveals and betrays attributes of one's character. That is, language says much about the nature of the self and the importance of sharing experience.

The character, substance, and style of a person are further grounded in the need to discover roots, to find a place in time, in a tradition. This is the essence of continuity, or historical study. History records the accomplishments and misadventures of remote and more recent ancestors, as it will record those of our own time. Levi understood history not just as an account of causes and effects but as a reflection of human relevance and importance.

Human existence is defined in terms not only of the need for human expression and orientation in time but also in connection with the need for reasonableness, which is the function of criticism, or philosophical thinking. How else can people clarify their ideas, meanings, and values so as better to modify and improve the conditions of their own existence and that of others?

Thus teaching anything, including the arts, humanistically means bringing the liberal arts of communication, continuity, and criticism to bear on understanding and appreciating a particular subject. To teach a work of literature humanistically would be to see it as an instance of linguistic expressiveness in its temporal situation that submits to appreciation and critical reflection. If we may be permitted to subsume the nonverbal arts under the rubric of language, to see them as artistic statements, then the same can be said of any work of art. As an expressive statement, every work exists in a particular medium and has a structure and a style. These three—*medium, structure*, and *style*—are the categories or dimensions of art as communication. Every masterpiece of world art is also a human creation that is produced in time and takes its place within a larger context of tradition. It therefore has a date and was created at a certain place by a certain person in a particular social situation, usually for a certain kind of people. *Date, situation*, and *audience* are thus the categories or dimensions of art as continuity. Every work of art is also the product of a philosophy of life and is therefore implicitly or explicitly a work of criticism; it either favors or denies certain constellations of value, contains implicitly or explicitly a critical message.

Attitude, values, and *message,* then, are the categories or dimensions of art as criticism.

We may thus ask the following questions of any work of art humanistically taught: (1) What is its medium? (2) What is its structure? (3) What is its style? (4) When was it made? (5) Why was it made? (6) For whom was it made? (7) What attitudes does it express? (8) What values does it assert or deny? (9) What message does it convey? (10) What quality of aesthetic experience does it afford? (11) What was its function in the culture in which it was made? (12) What is its function in the culture of today? (13) What peculiar problems does it present to understanding, appreciation, and evaluation?

What I think is helpful in Levi's redefinition of the humanities—the humanities as promoting humanizing and civilizing skills—is his provision of a method for studying the humanities and an identification of the subjects of the humanities as languages and literatures, history, and philosophy. The definition, it seems to me, is fraught with pedagogical significance. Not only that. Levi's approach is applicable to the study of any work, past or present, of high or popular culture, Western or non-Western, although Levi usually had in mind, as I do, works of serious art and, for Americans, predominantly but not exclusively Western works. In a passage from his *The Humanities Today* that features the personal and social value of the humanities, Levi writes:

> In the case of the arts of communication this has meant the presentation of languages as forms of life enlarging a limited imagination and producing that mutual sympathy Kant took to be the defining property of social man. In the case of the arts of continuity, comprehending both history proper and the use of the classics of literature and philosophy, presented as elements in a continuous human tradition, this has meant the presentation of a common past in the service of social cohesiveness and enlarged social sensitivity. And finally, in the case of the arts of criticism, this has meant the enlargement of the faculty of criticism, philosophically conceived as intelligent inquiry into the nature and maximization of values. A humane imagination, the forging of a universal social bond based upon sympathy, and the inculcation of a technique for the realization of values then become the ultimate goals of the liberal arts.[7]

And, I would add, with appropriate qualification, of arts education as well.

So goes a case for teaching the arts as humanities within the context of liberal or general education. Granted, we tend to talk about general and not liberal education in the schools, but the ideas, values, and questions remain the same. The kind of teaching I propose is of course more applicable to the middle and secondary grades. To be sure, learning in the arts begins earlier than that, and in a number of places I have discussed both earlier and later learning in terms of five phases, which range from exposure, familiarization, and refinement of perception in the early years of schooling to historical, appreciative, and critical studies in the later years[8] In the early years, classroom learning that stresses creative and performing activities, all intrinsically enjoyable and productive of intellectual development, that is, of fostering higher-level cognitive powers, would include perceptual studies as well and introduce young students to the artworld as a cultural institution. Such learning also paves the way for historical, appreciative, and critical studies where the emphasis shifts more to the examination of the art object and its contexts. The general aim throughout is to develop and refine percipience in matters of art and culture. *Percipience* refers to the ability of persons to experience works of art for the sake of their constitutive and revelatory values, by which I mean the ways in which the experience of good and great art holds potential for shaping the self in positive ways while simultaneously yielding insight into human existence and natural phenomena. I call the five phases of aesthetic learning (1) perceiving aesthetic qualities, (2) developing perceptual finesse, (3) developing a sense of art's history, (4) exemplar appreciation, and (5) critical reflection. The implementation of such a curriculum presupposes a much stronger education in the humanities for art teachers than they currently receive and greater acceptance of such preparation by the field of arts education.

In a statement he prepared for a community college humanities project that I coordinated, Levi emphasized that it is crucial that we interpret the humanities as a demand to pause and in their light examine our own realties, values, and dedications. "The arts," he wrote, "not only present life concretely, stimulate the imagination, and integrate the different cultural elements of a society or of an epoch, they also present models for our imitation or rejection, visions and aspirations which mutely solicit our critical response."[9]

Everything, then, is directed toward preparing teachers of art and young people for such learning: the study of works of art for their capacity to stretch imagination and refine perception and provide visions worthy of scrutiny.

NOTES

1. Werner Jaeger, *The Greeks and the Education of Man*, Bard College Papers (New York: Annandale-on-Hudson, 1953).

2. Lionel Trilling, "The Uncertain Future of the Humanistic Ideal of Learning," in *Last Decade: Essays and Reviews, 1965–1975*, ed. Diana Trilling (New York: Harcourt Brace Jovanovich, 1979), 161–76.

3. D. F. Borkat, "A Liberating Curriculum," *Newsweek* 123 (1993): 11.

4. Michael Oakeshott "A Place of Learning," in *The Voice of Learning: Michael Oakeshott on Education*, ed. T. Fuller (New Haven: Yale University Press, 1989), 17–42.

5. Albert William Levi, "Teaching Literature as a Humanity," *The Journal of General Education* 28 (Winter 1977): 283–87.

6. Albert William Levi, "Literature as a Humanity," *Journal of Aesthetic Education* 10 (September/October, 1976): 46–60.

7. Albert William Levi, *The Humanities Today* (Bloomington: Indiana University Press, 1970).

8. See, e.g., Ralph A. Smith, "Toward Percipience: A Humanities Curriculum for Arts Education," in *The Arts, Education, and Aesthetic Knowing*, ed. Bennett Reimer and Ralph A. Smith, Ninety-first Yearbook of the National Society for the Study of Education (Chicago: National Society for the Study of Education, 1992), 51–69.

9. *A Contemporary Course in the Humanities for Community College Students* (NEH Grant ED-10555-74-412). James J. Zigerell, Project Director, City Colleges of Chicago, n.d.

Philosophy and Theory of Aesthetic Education

IN ADDRESSING the question of the relevance of philosophy to the theory of aesthetic education, I accept Harold Osborne's view that philosophers should examine aesthetic questions with the advancement and progress of humanity in mind, and Eugene F. Kaelin's belief that aesthetic education constitutes a proper concern of aesthetics.[1] Interest in educational matters, however, is rare in contemporary Western aesthetics. Rather, as Francis Sparshott has written, "the phrase 'aesthetic education' plays little part in aesthetics generally."[2] The matter, of course, is different with theorists of aesthetic education. They examine theory to discover how it bears on important educational issues and how it might help organize instruction. In short, educational theorists have a special interest in practical theory. But what is a practical theory?

In his discussion of human potential, Israel Scheffler explains the nature of a practical theory by distinguishing its propositions from those of a scientific theory.[3] In their drive to give truthful representations of the phenomena studied, scientists attempt to formulate systems of lawlike statements in the terminology of a given discipline. Such statements are judged by the criteria of logical coherence, explanatory power, and heuristic efficacy. In the search for more general understanding, theories become increasingly systematic, abstract, and autonomous and thus more and more remote from the terms of ordinary language and practical experience. Conversely, the propositions of a practical theory, being influenced by ethical ideals, are organized for the purpose of guiding some kind of activity, in the instance at hand the professional activities of education. Since no single discipline is adequate for purposes of describing and explaining the complex activities of education, a practical theory of education must necessarily be composite and inelegant, at least when compared to a scientific theory. Following Scheffler, we may say that a practical theory of aesthetic education applies the insights of a range of disciplines to the problems of teaching an understanding and appreciation of the arts and comparable phenomena in the natural environment, although I am concerned here principally with the study of the arts. The task at hand, then, is to indicate the relevance of the insights of philosophical aesthetics to aesthetic education by showing how philosophical speculation can inform a curriculum that takes as its aim the appreciation of excellence in art. A few preliminary remarks are in order to set the context.

THE ARTS, CULTURE, AND GENERAL EDUCATION

The decision to discuss the relationships between philosophy and aesthetic education in connection with excellence in art stemmed from an effort to provide a response to the excellence-in-education movement of the 1980s. This movement, initiated by a national commission report and a rash of other studies,[4] recalls traditional democratic ideals of excellence and equity and raises familiar questions. Can we have both democracy and excellence? Can not only the most gifted and capable but all youth attain high levels of accomplishment in the various realms of human thought and action? Can we design curricula that will set high goals and expectations while accommodating human differences in background, temperament, and outlook? Whatever the precipitating causes of such periodic renewals of interest in excellence, the concern testifies to the staying power of classical ideals.

When, however, we talk about traditional ideals of humanistic education today, we are less likely to do so in terms favored by classical writers than in those of nineteenth-century cultural criticism. For example, when Lawrence A. Cremin, the preeminent historian of American education, sought to characterize American education by saying that its peculiar genius lies in its effort to humanize knowledge, he drew on Matthew Arnold's concept of culture.[5] Arnold held that the great apostles of culture are those who bring to bear on all those matters that most concern us the best that has been thought and written, which is to say that culture not only encompasses the great touchstones of the cultural heritage but also presupposes a certain quality of mind and moral commitment.[6]

What Arnold and others like him—for example, Ortega y Gasset—foresaw was that modern democracies would have a hard time maintaining high standards without an adequate concept of culture.[7] Some of the same problems that concerned Arnold and Ortega—for example, mass democracy, political stability, the quality of life—also worry us, but our era has problems that no earlier thinker could have envisioned. World overpopulation, the gap between the rich and the poor, the pollution of the environment, the depletion of natural resources, and the existence of nuclear arms make talk about the good life sound hollow when the immediate task is simply maintaining and safeguarding life. George Steiner, moreover, goes as far as to say that some of the horrific events of the twentieth century suggest that culture in the Arnoldian sense may not after all be inherently civilizing; the converse may be true.[8] The undeniable problems of modernity and doubts about the benefits of art do not, however, condemn us to unremitting despair; they simply mean that we must be more self-conscious about what we have tended to assume uncritically. We must not allow an atmosphere of apocalyptic anxiety to cause us to lose what is good in the idea of culture. Even Steiner's pessimistic speculations are hedged in with numerous qualifications.[9]

Qualifications and doubts about culture's beneficence notwithstanding, it is reasonable to assume that serious involvement in the arts can yield worthwhile benefits, not least the transcendence of what Ortega called a commonplace frame of mind. Moreover, once cultivated, the taste for culture in its honorific sense tends to be permanent. Robert Penn Warren, the first poet laureate of the United States, points out in *Democracy and Poetry* that great art provides recurrent possibilities of experience and has the power constantly to return us to ourselves.[10]

But there is no need to go on. Given the tendency of advanced societies to reduce all values to economic interests, culture in its beneficent sense is as needful today as it ever was. Even John Dewey, whom Albert William Levi charged with some responsibility for fostering an instrumental cast of mind, came to realize this in his later writings.[11] In brief, the ideals of traditional humanistic education are perennially relevant because they feature the education of what used to be called the whole person. We honor this ideal whenever we recommend that the schools induct the young into a curriculum of common, general education that cultivates worthwhile qualities of human experience by acquainting them with various ways of knowing and experiencing.[12] Persons do not live by one form of awareness alone, and they live well only when they strive to excel and are recognized for their accomplishments.[13] In the following I discuss one of these forms of awareness, which for convenience I call aesthetic literacy.

EXCELLENCE AND AESTHETIC LITERACY

The basic question for any theory of aesthetic education turns on the qualities of mind, body, and character that should be developed through the study of the arts. Because not all the desirable qualities of experience cultivated through learning are moral virtues, I follow the lead of William Frankena, who speaks not of virtues but of excellences, and who believes that the fundamental business of education is to develop worthwhile dispositions.[14] What, then, are the dispositions, the excellences of mind, body, and character, that we should cultivate through aesthetic education? I suggest that the general purpose of aesthetic education in the schools should be the development of a disposition to appreciate excellence in art, where *excellence in art* implies the capacity of works of art at their best to intensify and enlarge the scope of human awareness.[15]

The reason for emphasizing outstanding works of art as principal objects of study, at least in the middle and secondary grades, is perhaps obvious enough, but for educational purposes it is worth referring to Harold Osborne, who during his lifetime was regarded as the dean of British aesthetics. He was also a longtime editor of the *British Journal of Aesthetics.*

> Works of art [writes Osborne] can, at their best, extend the perceptive faculties to the full without satiation and as it were demand ever increased mental vivacity and grasp to contain them. . . . Years of study and experience, half a lifetime of growing familiarity, may contribute to the full appreciation of a great work of art: the experience itself is always accompanied by a feeling of heightened vitality; we are more awake, more alert than usual, the faculties are working at greater pressure, more effectively, and with greater freedom than at other times, and the discovery of new insights is their constant guerdon.[16]

Therein lies the peculiar excellence of art—its capability at its best to energize and inform experience in special, worthwhile ways. The name usually given to such energized experience is *aesthetic experience.* In attempting to explain the character of such experience, I draw on the writings of Monroe C. Beardsley, Osborne, Nelson Goodman, and Eugene F. Kaelin.[17] I will assume acquaintance with the marks of excellence in art and will refer only briefly to those excellences discussed in Lord Kenneth Clark's *What Is a Masterpiece?*—such qualities as inspired virtuosity, intensity of feeling, masterful design, uncompromising artistic integrity, imaginative power, originality of vision, and a profound sense of human values.[18] Such excellences are characteristic not only of the artists whom Clark specifically discusses—for example, Raphael, Rembrandt, and Rubens—but also of Mozart, Beethoven, Bartók, Shakespeare, Dostoyevsky, T. S. Eliot, and many others.

Regarding excellence in art as a capacity to afford worthwhile aesthetic experience, we may say aesthetic experience itself is valuable for four reasons: for the quality of gratification it provides (Beardsley); for its stimulation of direct perception for its own sake (Osborne); for its contributions to new perspectives on the world and self, or to understanding (Goodman); and for ensuring the free functioning of the institution of art (Kaelin).

Beardsley: Aesthetic Experience as Essentially Gratifying

Monroe C. Beardsley's *Aesthetics: Problems in the Philosophy of Criticism*, first published in 1958 and updated in 1981, has been one of the most influential works in American philosophical aesthetics since John Dewey's *Art as Experience*.[19] It is a work of philosophical synthesis that sets out a systematic examination of the presuppositions of art criticism. In addition to offering an analysis of the canons of judgment that he derived from a large number of critical statements made by art, music, and literary critics, Beardsley provides an instrumental theory of aesthetic value that reveals a serious concern with the role of art in human life. His writings thus have inherent educational significance.

The conceptual problem Beardsley struggled with more than with any other is whether there is a kind of human experience that may appropriately be called aesthetic that is not only sufficiently distinct from other kinds of experience but also significant enough to warrant society's efforts to cultivate it. He was particularly interested in the possibility that works of art may be ideally suited to occasion such experience, even though other things might also possess aesthetic capacity in varying degrees. Beardsley never took his success in answering these questions for granted, and he usually expressed some dissatisfaction with his own analytical efforts. Although he modified details of his theory over the years, he held to the belief that the aesthetic value of art—its artistic goodness in contrast to its cognitive or moral value—consists in its capacity to induce in a qualified observer a high degree of aesthetic experience. Such experience is valuable for a number of its features but mainly for the special feelings of pleasure, enjoyment, satisfaction, or gratification it provides. The range of terms attests to Beardsley's difficulty in specifying just what sort of hedonic effect characterizes our commerce with art, although he came to prefer "gratification."[20]

All this classifies Beardsley's theory as a hedonistic one, but not hedonistic in any simple sense. Aesthetic gratification is neither a general state of feeling well nor similar to the kind of enjoyment that can attend the informal congeniality of friendly conversation, partisan cheering at sports events, or participation in political activities. It is precisely the kind of gratification that is derived from sensitively and knowledgeably experiencing outstanding works of art—a painting by Raphael, a piano sonata by Beethoven, a sonnet by Shakespeare.

Beardsley's last essay on aesthetic experience is contained in a collection of his writings, *The Aesthetic Point of View*, published in 1982 and edited by two of his former students.[21] In this essay Beardsley asks us to think of aesthetic experience as having as many as five features, although not all five must be present for some degree of aesthetic experience to happen. This is to say that aesthetic experience does not consist of a single pervasive quality, feeling, sensation, or emotion but rather a cluster of qualities, and it is this cluster that makes aesthetic experience both compound and disjunctive.

A compressed paraphrase could run as follows. In our aesthetic experience of an outstanding work of art, attention is fixed on an object of notable presence whose elements, formal relations, aesthetic qualities, and semantic aspects are freely entertained. One indication of the presence of aesthetic character is the percipient's feeling that things are working themselves out in appropriate and fitting ways. Another indication is diminished concern about the past and future in favor of an intense engagement with what is immediately presented or invoked by the object. Aesthetic involvement further consists in a certain emotional distancing of the object that enables the percipient to maintain control over perception and to rise above rather than to be overwhelmed by any tragic import the object may have. The effect of detached engagement does not, however, deny the possibility of percipients' feeling exhilarated by the success of their efforts to make conflicting stimuli cohere into formal patterns that are imbued with expressive qualities and human import. An experience that is notable for its feelings of object directedness, free participation, detached involvement, and active discovery may also result in feelings of personal integration and a greater acceptance and expansion of the self.

Beardsley acknowledges that aesthetic experience might well contain more or fewer features than his account of it indicates; his intention was to open up rather than to close off a line of thought. But for all that may be experienced, felt, or learned through aesthetic experience, Beardsley believes that its unique value consists in the quality of gratification it affords. Rare, he says, are those stretches of time during which the elements of human experience combine in just these ways; when they do, the state of being they constitute is one of gratified well-being. We can only agree. When in the course of a typical day do we experience the stimulation, the sense of freedom, the controlled emotional involvement, the feeling of genuine discovery, the self-fulfillment that we tend to feel during the experience of a great work of art? Constituting a significant realization of human value, such a state of mind is a distinctive form of human well-being and therefore part of a good or worthwhile life. It is through individuals' having aesthetic experiences, then, that Beardsley thinks works of art "realize their potentialities and serve us well in their fashion."

Harold Osborne: Aesthetic Experience as Intrinsically Valuable Perception

"To realize their potentialities and serve well in their fashion"—the words are Beardsley's, but they could be those of Harold Osborne, who believed that works of art serve us well by stimulating and expanding direct perception, or what he calls the powers of percipience.

What is percipience? In the *Art of Appreciation* Osborne assimilates percipience to aesthetic appreciation and experience, which he describes by saying that the aesthetic experience of a work of art involves the directing of attention over a limited sensory field, an engagement during which the field's qualities are brought into focus according to their own inherent intensity, their similarities and contrasts, and their peculiar groupings.[22] Such perception is full and complete and proceeds without the kind of editing that characterizes our practical concerns and activities. Furthermore, the mental attitude assumed during aesthetic experience is unlike that required for conceptual analysis or, for instance, the historian's rooting out of causes and effects; instead, aesthetic experience involves the exercise of integrative or synoptic vision. That is, identifying the representational contents of Picasso's *Guernica* is not the same thing as perceiving its fusion of subject, form, and expression in an act of integrative perception.

The kind of rapt attention that marks aesthetic interest also lends aesthetic experience a characteristic emotional color; its mood, Osborne thinks (perhaps questionably), approximates serenity even when the object being perceived has a dynamic character. It is further important to realize that because of the dynamic of the perceptual absorption in an object during aesthetic experience, our interest involves less a consciousness of our own feelings than an awareness of the object's properties. The demands of perceptual awareness and the obligation to see the object in its complexity also tend to discourage mere idle musings and mental associations. Aesthetic experience thus has a characteristic rigor; imagination is required to apprehend a work's qualities, but it is also held in check.

Another feature of aesthetic experience is the priority of appearance over material existence. The fact that an object is a material thing existing in the world is of less interest than the imagery the material thing presents. Such imagery is suited to sustaining awareness in the aesthetic mode because it takes us out of ourselves into new worlds. Ego consciousness, however, never completely disappears; we are always aware of being aware of the qualities and meanings of the object.

Osborne reminds us that aesthetic percipience is exercised in many areas of human life, but he thinks that works of fine art and their counterparts in nature are capable of expanding it to its fullest. To repeat, at their best works of art can extend the perceptive faculties and demand ever increasing mental finesse to contain them. Central, then, to Osborne's theory is the heightened awareness of things felt during aesthetic experience. Such experience makes persons feel more vital, awake, and alert than usual, allows the faculties to work with a greater sense of freedom and effectiveness, and offers new discoveries as a constant reward.

In his argument for the deliberate cultivation of percipience for its own sake, Osborne emphasizes that such cultivation has always been the motive for the expression of spiritual needs and aspirations. Whatever the ideology, liberation from life's material constraints for the purpose of realizing more fully and more freely one's humanity is a near-universal yearning and guiding ideal. Kenneth Clark also believed that even in a predominantly secular society the majority of people still long to experience moments of pure, nonmaterial satisfaction and that such satisfaction can be obtained more reliably through works of art than by any other means.[23] This suggests that when we talk about the uses of art we must do so in a very special sense. Reason, too, says Osborne, should be cultivated for its own sake, but it characteristically finds its fullest outlet and expansion in philosophy, logic, mathematics, and the theoretical sciences.

Nelson Goodman: Aesthetic Experience as Understanding

In the work of Nelson Goodman we confront ideas that originated in modern developments in the theory of understanding and the logic of symbolic systems. It is generally agreed that Goodman's perspective is not only novel but also has radical implications for understanding art. Speaking of the importance of Goodman's work, Sparshott likened the appearance of Goodman's *Languages of Art* to a shadow cast by a giant rock upon a dreary field, while Howard Gardner expressed the opinion that overnight Goodman singlehandedly transformed aesthetics into a serious and rigorous field of study.[24] Beardsley likewise acknowledged the enormous value of Goodman's aesthetic writings. Such encomia, even if somewhat overstated, certify Goodman's stature, and there is no question that his major thesis—that art is essentially cognitive—has encouraged educational theorists to use his ideas to put a justification of aesthetic education on firmer ground.

The central proposition of Goodman's *Languages of Art* is that art is a symbolic system of human understanding and shares with other forms of inquiry, including the sciences, the human quest for enlightenment. Condensed accounts of Beardsley's and Osborne's ideas of aesthetic experience having been provided, here is how Goodman describes our engagement with art:

> Aesthetic experience is dynamic rather than static. It involves making delicate discriminations and discerning subtle relationships, identifying symbol systems and characters within these systems and what these characters denote and exemplify, interpreting works and reorganizing the world in terms of works and

works in terms of the world. Much of our experience and many of our skills are brought to bear and may be transformed by the encounter. The aesthetic "attitude" is restless, searching, testing—is less attitude than action: creation and re-creation."[25]

In these words we detect what is shared with and what is different from the accounts of aesthetic experience given by Beardsley and Osborne. All three—Beardsley, Osborne, and Goodman—acknowledge that perception is dynamic, discriminating, and interpretive and that a person's view of the world may be transformed by aesthetic encounters. Goodman's account is distinguished by what he does and does not emphasize. Identifying symbol systems and characters within these systems has a technical meaning in Goodman's theory; it involves understanding the ways in which the characters of works of art denote and exemplify. Goodman does not think that the criterion of the aesthetic is found in feelings of gratification. And although he emphasizes that in art the primary purpose is cognition in and for itself, he does not stress cognition for its own sake in the way Osborne had chosen. Goodman stresses the role of cognition in the shaping and reshaping of worlds; in short, in his concern to provide for understanding he places emphasis on the symbolic functioning of artworks and the enlightenment they yield.

When Goodman claims that the aim of art is similar to that of science— to lead to understanding—he does not mean that works of art can be true- or-false propositions; rather, like designs generally, works of art are either aesthetically right or wrong. Nor does he think there are no important differences between art and science. Artworks characteristically have qualities that persuade us to see, hear, and read differently, detect new patterns, and make connections between things. And when this is said, some of the differences between Beardsley, Osborne, and Goodman begin to fade, although others still remain. We should also realize that Goodman's theory of art is less a detailed account of the nature of perceiving and appreciating works of art than it is an explanation of their cognitive status. What Goodman calls the symptoms of the aesthetic—syntactical and semantic density, relative repleteness, exemplification, and multiple and complex reference—are not aesthetic qualities but technical terms that refer to the functions of characters in a work of art construed as a symbolic system.[26] They explain how works of art, even nonrepresentational or strictly formal ones, denote and refer.

Eugene F. Kaelin: Aesthetic Experience as Institutional Efficacy

The aesthetic ideas of Eugene F. Kaelin, presented mainly in articles, a monograph, and *Art and Existence*, constitute yet another philosophical perspective on the arts and aesthetic experience.[27] Although Kaelin writes from a

Continental existential-phenomenological point of view influenced by Sartre, Merleau-Ponty, Husserl, and Heidegger, the benefits he attributes to aesthetic experience are similar to those described by Beardsley, Osborne, and Goodman. Works of art, says Kaelin, are good for the aesthetic experiences they provide, which in turn are good because of the aesthetic communication that occurs and the intensification and clarification of human experience. The satisfaction felt in successfully fusing the systems of counters of a work of art (that is, a work's surface and depth features) constitutes the hedonic aspect of aesthetic experience, and in this respect Kaelin's theory resembles Beardsley's. Kaelin's view of art's capacity to intensify and clarify human experience also accommodates Osborne's belief regarding an artwork's propensity to stimulate the powers of percipience for their own sake. Although Kaelin's philosophical orientation is incompatible with Goodman's, both writers value art's ability to present fresh perceptions of things. Indeed, an interesting result of comparing and contrasting aesthetic theories is the discovery that philosophical differences do not necessarily imply different benefits that are believed to be derivable from the arts.

So far as this discussion is concerned, Kaelin's aesthetics is noteworthy for its stress on human freedom and the claim that the cultivation of the capacity for aesthetic experience through schooling contributes to the free functioning of the institution of art. Aesthetic experience, in other words, has both personal and social value. A theory of aesthetic education thus helps to define the kind of individual any society would wish to produce, an individual who exemplifies the human values of tolerance, communication, and judgment and who shuns intolerance, dogmatism, conformity, and oppression.

How, according to Kaelin, does aesthetic experience exemplify such values? The answer lies in understanding the ways in which aesthetic experience originates, unfolds, and achieves closure. Kaelin describes how percipients create contexts of significance whose intrinsic values provide the material for immediate aesthetic experience. Paying attention to the presentational qualities of works of art involves perception of what is variously termed matter and form, subject and treatment, and local and regional qualities, all aspects of surface and depth relations. In short, aesthetic experience is animated and controlled by the imperatives of bracketed contexts of significance. Successful fusion of a work's system of counters results in acts of expressive response that constitute the consummation of aesthetic experience. In Kaelin's terminology, *felt expressiveness* implies a sense of fittingness or appropriateness between surface and depth counters. A case in point is his description of the counters of Picasso's *Guernica*. After pointing out and interpreting the work's various features, Kaelin writes that "so interpreted, our experience of *Guernica* deepens and comes to closure in a single act of expressive response in which we perceive the fittingness of this surface—all broken planes and jagged edges in the stark contrast of black and white—to represent this depth, the equally stark contrast of the living and the dead."[28] What Kaelin calls a single act of expressive response is what Osborne calls an instance of synoptic or integrative vision.

According to Kaelin, what then is the point of looking at notable works of art? The point is the worthwhile aesthetic experiences they are capable of providing, where worthwhileness consists of the value of aesthetic communication as well as the exercise of perceptual skills and aesthetic judgment. All this occurs in contexts of significance governed by the intrinsic values of a system of counters. Kaelin in effect offers his own version of Erwin Panofsky's belief that a work of art is essentially a humanly made object that demands to be experienced aesthetically.[29] As Kaelin writes, works of art "come to exist only in the experience of persons who have opened themselves to the expressiveness of a sensuous surface and allowed their understandings and imagination to be guided by controlled responses set up therein."[30] Everything that we prize in the traditional ideal of liberal education is present in Kaelin's account of aesthetic experience, especially the notion that disciplined encounters with excellence test, strengthen, and expand basic human powers.

Since percipients have to be willing to be guided by a work's context of significance, they cannot assess a work's value on the basis of conformance to rule or ideology. The method of phenomenological analysis described by Kaelin takes its cues from the immediate givens of a work of art and assumes that value emanates from a work's unique context of significance and not from the superimposition of interpretive frameworks that are insensitive to intrinsic values. There is no knowing in advance what a work of art will feature or what it might say about our relations to reality and to one another. Aesthetic communication is thus essentially free communication. Through acts of artistic creation and appreciation, moreover, persons can choose their future—in the first instance by creating new worlds of aesthetic value, and in the second by opening themselves to new possibilities of experience. Art thus serves Being by helping to realize human powers and potentialities that benefit both the individual and society.

SOME CONCLUDING OBSERVATIONS

In concluding, I once more recall Osborne's belief that philosophers should address aesthetic questions with the advance and progress of humanity in mind. This admonition was also heeded by Beardsley, Goodman, and Kaelin, who have also provided material for a justification of aesthetic education.

Beardsley contributes to humanistic objectives and suggests a solution to the justification problem by telling us how to distinguish superior from less excellent works, namely, by assessing the capacity of works to afford worthwhile aesthetic experiences.

Osborne contributes to humanistic objectives and the justification of aesthetic education by describing the quality of experience that excellent art is capable of engendering and contrasting it to experiences typically afforded by amusement art. He further discriminates between styles of vanguard art and prefers those that present significant new ways of viewing reality. He thinks, for example, that the art of Monet, Cézanne, Matisse, and Picasso is far more likely to endure than the work, say, of latter-day Conceptual artists.

Goodman's powerful case for art's cognitive character has the effect of diminishing the distance between the two cultures of scientific and artistic understanding. This helps to establish the seriousness of aesthetic studies in a way that should make justifying aesthetic education less difficult. As Goodman puts it, in art as in science the drive is curiosity and the end is enlightenment; the primary purpose "is cognition in and for itself; the practicality, pleasure, compulsion, and communicative utility all depend on this."[31] Under the direction of Howard Gardner and David Perkins, participants in Project Zero, a research unit founded by Goodman at Harvard University, have been investigating the dynamics of artistic cognition in the creation and appreciation of art.[32] Such work may ultimately help us to better understand how the arts might more effectively be taught.

Kaelin contributes to humanistic objectives and the progress of humanity by stressing the important role that art plays in establishing aesthetic communication among free peoples. Artistic and aesthetic encounters exemplify the human values of openness, relevance, autonomy, and freedom, all vital to the efficacious functioning of the institution of art. Only an educated and aesthetically literate society can ensure that conditions of aesthetic freedom and communication will prevail and that the institution of art will not be controlled by political considerations.

One upshot of this discussion is my realization of the utility of eclecticism, for in comparing the accounts of aesthetic experience by four theorists I found little disagreement regarding the preeminent values to be derived from contemplating works of art. Works of art at their best not only afford a fresh outlook on the world that enables us to see the familiar in an unfamiliar light; they also help us to perceive new connections between things in light of which we organize and reorganize our experience of reality. Their individual philosophical orientations, methodological assumptions, and categories of description and explanation notwithstanding, the four writers concur about art's capacity for human renewal.

I have referred to different kinds of benefits that can be realized through a serious study of the arts, but a further distinction, between proximate and prospective values, is helpful to keep in mind. Proximate values are the immediately felt qualities of aesthetic experience. Prospective values are values to which proximate values contribute, for example, percipience and imagination generally as well as sympathetic understanding. What I call proximate and prospective values Beardsley calls two kinds of inherent value, Osborne the principal and subsidiary functions of art, and Kaelin aesthetic and nonaesthetic values. One goal of aesthetic education research might be to achieve a better understanding of the connections between proximate and prospective benefits, although a firm linkage between different kinds of values is not absolutely crucial to a justification of aesthetic education. One can argue convincingly that aesthetic experience is a special form of human awareness that serves individuals in ways that other forms of awareness do not and that it therefore contributes to the actualization of worthwhile human potential. A life bereft of aesthetic capacity is a life only partially fulfilled, and it is a serious indictment of societies and their educational systems if they permit the young to pass through schooling without helping them to realize a significant part of their humanity.

By virtue of their persuasive articulation of art's various functions, all four theorists discussed provide material for a theory of aesthetic education. Such articulation is certainly one fundamental way in which philosophical aesthetics becomes relevant to a theory of aesthetic education. Although it has been said that the principal reason for formulating theories of art is to help organize instruction,[33] a larger range of considerations obviously motivates aesthetic theorizing.

A few final words. Although a theory of aesthetic education may be influenced by several different perspectives on the nature and function of art, the ideas and theories chosen will be determined in part by the individual temperaments of educational theorists and prevailing social conditions. Some educational theorists prefer a Goodmanlike justification because it seems best suited to bolster the case for arts education in the schools. Any position that promises an improvement of understanding reinforces educators' arguments in favor of their educational specialties. However, an excessively cognitive interpretation of art's function risks underplaying the importance of the feeling aspects of aesthetic experience. Simply being told what an artwork exemplifies or signifies is never sufficient. In words that cannot be repeated too often, Frank Sibley has emphasized that in art one needs to see and feel things for oneself.[34]

The four theorists in question are important also because they point to what is most characteristic about art. They all appreciate its peculiar energies and understand the ways in which works typically realize their potentialities. Such emphasis is important at a time when so much theoretical writing dwells on social and political studies of art. But when art and aesthetic education are interpreted principally in ideological terms, the central business of art is slighted. Virgil C. Aldrich has written that "the greatest art is formally expressive at once of materials on the one hand and of subject matter on the other, doing justice to both in a reciprocal transfiguration, each inspiring the other in the content of the composition."[35] Some necessary qualifications notwithstanding (not all worthwhile works of art have identifiable subject matter), this is the fundamentally aesthetic business and achievement of art. The more the subtle and precarious balance between the relations of medium, form, and content is upset, as it is with the inordinate intrusion of ideological concerns, the less likelihood a work has of achieving its full potential for expressive statement and aesthetic response.

It is not that there are no connections between the appreciation of art and social change or reform. One would think that persons of cultivated aesthetic dispositions would abhor assaults on the environment and human sensibility and thus be inclined to strive to bring about a better quality of life and higher level of culture. Developing aesthetic sensitivity, in other words, is compatible with developing a sense of social responsibility. A single-minded concern with ideology, however, corrupts the aesthetic imagination. In this regard, we would do well to recall some words of the historian Richard Hofstadter: "If there is anything more dangerous to the life of the mind than having no independent commitment to ideas, it is having an excess of commitment to some special and constricting idea." The intellectual function (and I would add the aesthetic function), he said, "can be overwhelmed by an excess of piety expended within too contracted a frame of reference."[36] Partly for this reason I have accommodated not one but four perspectives on the nature of art and its characteristic functions. To be sure, aesthetic theorists continue the search for the essence of art, to distinguish art's primary and secondary functions and to express concern over hazy speculation. I don't underestimate the value of sharply focused philosophical analysis. Still, I conclude with Morris Weitz, who said that it behooves us to entertain a variety of aesthetic theories because "their debates over the reasons for excellence in art converge on the perennial problem of what makes a work of art good."[37] I understand the theories of Beardsley, Osborne, Goodman, and Kaelin in this spirit, that is, as contributions to the critical dialogue about excellence in art and aesthetic education.

NOTES

1. Harold Osborne, "The Twofold Significance of 'Aesthetic Value,'" *Philosophica* 36, no. 2 (1985): 5–24. Eugene F. Kaelin, "Aesthetic Education: A Role for Aesthetics Proper," *Journal of Aesthetic Education* 2, no. 2 (1968): 51–66.

2. Francis Sparshott, *The Theory of the Arts* (Princeton: Princeton University Press, 1982), 484.

3. Israel Scheffler, *Of Human Potential* (Boston: Routledge and Kegan Paul, 1985), 5.

4. E.g., The National Commission on Excellence in Education, *A Nation at Risk* (Washington, D.C.: Government Printing Office, 1983); Mortimer J. Adler, *The Paideia Proposal: An Educational Manifesto* (New York: Macmillan, 1982); Ernest Boyer, *High School: A Report on Secondary Education in America* (New York: Harper and Row, 1983); John Goodlad, *A Place Called School* (New York: McGraw-Hill, 1984); and Theodore Sizer, *Horace's Compromise: The Dilemma of the American High School* (Boston: Houghton Mifflin, 1984).

5. Lawrence A. Cremin, *The Genius of American Education* (New York: Random Vintage Books, 1966), 108.

6. The oft-quoted remarks in question are from Matthew Arnold, *Culture and Anarchy* (New York: Cambridge University Press, 1969), 70. First published 1869.

7. José Ortega y Gasset, *The Revolt of the Masses*, trans. Anthony Kerrigan (Notre Dame: University of Notre Dame Press, 1985). For a comprehensive assessment of Ortega's educational significance, see Robert McClintock's *Man and His Circumstances: Ortega as Educator* (New York: Teachers College Press, 1971).

8. See George Steiner, "To Civilize Our Gentlemen," in *Language and Silence: Essays on Language, Literature, and the Inhuman* (New York: Atheneum, 1967).

9. Note especially the qualifications in Steiner's *In Bluebeard's Castle: Some Notes towards the Redefinition of Culture* (New Haven: Yale University Press, 1971).

10. Robert Penn Warren, *Democracy and Poetry* (Cambridge: Harvard University Press, 1975), 72.

11. Albert William Levi, "Nature and Art," *Journal of Aesthetic Education* 18, no. 3 (1984); John Dewey, *Art as Experience* (New York: G.P. Putman's Sons, 1958). First published 1934 by Minton, Balch and Co. See also Dewey, *John Dewey: The Later Works, 1925–1953*, ed. Jo Ann Boydston (Carbondale: Southern Illinois University, 1987), Vol. 10.

12. Some representative works stressing ways of knowing are Louis Arnaud Reid, *Ways of Understanding and Education* (London: Heinemann, 1986); Philip H. Phenix, *Realms of Meaning* (New York: McGraw-Hill, 1964); Paul H. Hirst, *Knowledge and the Curriculum* (Boston: Routledge and Kegan Paul, 1974); and Howard Gardner, *Frames of Mind* (New York: Basic Books, 1983).

13. In this connection, it is worth recalling the remarks of Moses Hadas in his *The Greek Ideal and Its Survival* (New York: Harper Colophon Books, 1966). What is memorable in the Greek experience, writes Hadas, is "the remarkably high level of their originality and achievements," a level that "premises a deeply held conviction of the importance of individual attainment. The goal of excellence, the means of achieving it, and (a very important matter) the approbation it is to receive are all determined by human judgment" (13).

14. William Frankena, *Three Historical Philosophers of Education: Aristotle, Kant, Dewey* (Glenview, Ill.: Foresman, 1965), esp. chap. 1.

15. I have expanded this view in my *Excellence in Art Education*, updated version (Reston, Va.: National Art Education Association 1987).

16. Harold Osborne, *The Art of Appreciation* (New York: Oxford University Press, 1970), 36–37.

17. The discussion of Beardsley, Osborne, and Goodman draws substantially on my lecture *Aesthetic Education in Modern Perspective* (Provo, Ut: College of Fine Arts and Communication, Brigham Young University, 1986).

18. Kenneth Clark, *What Is a Masterpiece?* (New York: Thames and Hudson, 1979).

19. Monroe C. Beardsley, *Aesthetics: Problems in the Philosophy of Criticism*, 2nd ed. (Indianapolis: Hackett, 1981). First edition published 1958 by Harcourt, Brace and World.

20. I have traced this shifting terminology in my "The Aesthetics of Monroe C. Beardsley: Recent Work," *Studies in Art Education* 25, no. 3 (1984): 141–50.

21. Beardsley, "Aesthetic Experience," in *The Aesthetic Point of View: Selected Essays of Monroe C. Beardsley*, ed. M. J. Wreen and D. M. Callen (Ithaca: Cornell University Press, 1982).

22. Harold Osborne, *The Art of Appreciation* (New York: Oxford University Press, 1970), esp. chap. 2.

23. Kenneth Clark, "Art and Society," in *Moments of Vision* (London: John Murray, 1981), 79.

24. Nelson Goodman, *Languages of Art*, 2nd ed. (Indianapolis: Hackett, 1976).

25. Ibid., 241–42.

26. The last symptom, multiple and complex reference, was added since *The Languages of Art* was published. See his note in *Ways of Worldmaking* (Indianapolis: Hackett, 1978), 67.

27. In discussing Kaelin, I draw on the following works: *Art and Existence: A Phenomenological Aesthetics* (Lewisburg: Bucknell University Press, 1970); *An Existential-Phenomenological Account of Aesthetic Education*, Penn State Papers in Art Education, no. 4 (University Park: Pennsylvania State University, 1968); "Aesthetic Education: A Role for Aesthetics Proper," *Journal of Aesthetic Education* 2, no. 2 (1968); and "Why Teach Art in the Public Schools?" *Journal of Aesthetic Education* 20, no. 4 (1986): 64–71.

28. Kaelin, "Aesthetic Education: A Role for Aesthetics Proper," *Journal of Aesthetic Education* 2, no. 2 (1968): 154; reprinted in R. A. Smith, ed., *Aesthetics and Problems of Education* (Urbana: University of Illinois Press, 1970).

29. Erwin Panofsky, "The History of Art as a Humanistic Discipline," in *Meaning in the Visual Arts* (Chicago: University of Chicago Press, 1982; first published 1955), p. 11.

30. Kaelin, "Aesthetic Education: A Role for Aesthetics Proper," 155.

31. Goodman, *Languages of Art*, 258.

32. See Goodman's *Of Mind and Other Matters* (Cambridge: Harvard University Press, 1984), chap. 5.

33. Sparshott, "On the Possibility of Saying What Literature Is," in *What Is Literature?* ed. Paul Hernandi (Bloomington: Indiana University Press, 1978), 14.

34. Frank Sibley, "Aesthetic and Nonaesthetic," *The Philosophic Review* 74, no. 2 (1965): 136–37.

35. Virgil C. Aldrich, *Philosophy of Art* (Englewood Cliffs, N.J.: Prentice-Hall, 1963), 98–99.

36. Richard Hofstadter, *Anti-intellectualism in American Life* (New York: Alfred A. Knopf, 1963), 29.

37. Morris Weitz, "The Role of Theory in Aesthetics," in *Problems of Aesthetics*, 2nd ed. (New York: Macmillan, 1970), 180.

Art, the Human Career, and Aesthetic Education

IN AN ADDRESS to the American National Art Education Association, the distinguished cultural historian Jacques Barzun remarked that "art is an important part of our culture. It corresponds to a deep instinct in man; hence it is enjoyable. We therefore teach its rudiments."[1] A discussion of the deep instinct in question was anticipated, but none followed. Instead, in his characteristic manner Barzun upbraided art educators for their tendency to inflate pedagogical language. Leaving unargued the assumption of art's answering a human propensity, however, is an example of a luxury that educational thinkers cannot afford, especially at a time when in the United States, and undoubtedly in Great Britain as well, notions of basic education that exclude the arts are much on people's minds. We are thus left with the task of discovering for ourselves the deep instinct to which art corresponds. This discussion is an attempt to make some modest progress toward this end. The results of such an effort, even if only partially successful, may help us to decide in what ways aesthetic education may be construed as basic or fundamental.

A start may be made by asking about the roles that art has played in human careers in past ages. From among the multiple functions art has performed, is it possible to detect a characteristic or preeminent function? Some clues to this function are contained in "Art and Society," an essay on the relations of art and society by the British art historian Kenneth Clark.[2] Having scanned the history of Western art for generalizations that might prove helpful in thinking about contemporary relations of art and society, Clark discussed the vital functions that art performed in the great ages of classical Greece, the Middle Ages, the Renaissance, and the nineteenth century. In the classical and medieval periods, Clark says, people looked to art because it reminded them of things of lasting importance and confirmed crucial beliefs about human fate and destiny. Even though works of art were created by a minority that reflected the values of the dominant groups in society, they were nonetheless capable of appealing to the majority because of a relevant and understandable content. Because they were based on a book of holy writ and certain formal observances and rituals, the beliefs that art confirmed during the Middle Ages were properly called religious beliefs and the function that art performed, a sacramental function. Clark believes that as later art replaced the iconography of Christianity with secular imagery, it is more accurate to speak of art as expressing not so much religious as nonmaterial beliefs. He cites the belief in nature manifested in nineteenth-century landscape painting as an example; unable to be justified by reason, it lifts the life of the senses onto a higher plane (69). The twentieth century, in turn, has its own distinctive character. In contrast to an age of faith that raised ornate cathedrals to celebrate the glory of God, our heroic materialism raises unadorned skyscrapers in which to conduct business for the benefit of shareholders. The difference, we may say, is precisely that between Chartres Cathedral and Rockefeller Center. Clark, moreover, believed that people still long to experience a kind of pure, disinterested, nonmaterial satisfaction that can be obtained more reliably through works of art than through any other means. And he conjectured that the unbelieving majority realize that they are missing what believers experience in their contacts with works of art (79).

In other words, the deep instinct to which art corresponds is identified by Clark as none other than the instinct for beauty, for a state of mind of peculiar value. What are the features of this state of mind? To be sure, when Clark uses such words as *beauty, pure, and disinterested*, he is using terms that have caused some discomfort in recent aesthetic theorizing. The experience of art, we want to say, is neither pure nor disinterested. As for beauty, with rare exception it is no longer a key concept of contemporary aesthetic writing. Granted all this, we have a fair idea of what Clark intends. When he says that the experience of art is pure and disinterested, we may take him to mean that it detaches itself in a significant way from the practical, pragmatic, or material interests that dominate our day-to-day lives. When he says that the experience of art transcends reason, we may take him as implying that, while the experience of art is certainly cognitive, it is more than reason, since it also energizes feeling. Indeed, we may assume that it is the special way in which reason and feeling are energized that constitutes the peculiar value of aesthetic experience. But what enables works of art to do this? Why, in large part, is art so often superior to nature in this respect? The answer, of course, lies not merely in the subject matter of works of art but also in their style. Characteristically, artworks are vivid images resplendent with precious materials, sensuous surfaces, artistic form, and dramatic significance. Such images demand our attention because they are *perceptually compelling*; and they are perceptually compelling because, as Harold Osborne believed, a special aesthetic motive is at work.[3] A plethora of other motives and intentions notwithstanding, it is this aesthetic motive, Osborne thinks, that unifies the history of artistic effort. It has only been in the modern period, however, that the aesthetic motive has been conceptualized and associated with our experience of art.

We may conclude, then, that the deep human instinct to which art corresponds, the state of mind of peculiar value that art is capable of inducing, the universal motive that all art exhibits, is the instinct for the creation, perception, and enjoyment of *dramatic order*. When that order is sufficiently complex and significant, it sustains not merely fleeting moments of awareness but a special kind of experience known as aesthetic experience. So conceived, the idea of aesthetic experience presupposes both an object compelling enough to sustain attention and a qualified percipient skilled enough to engage it. We may further say that the ample provision of opportunities for aesthetic experiences, for the kind of gratification occasioned by the appropriate taking of a work of art, is the preeminent or characteristic function of art, the thing that art can do better than anything else. Or, in slightly different terms, the principal role of art in the human career is to raise the level and quality of experience by giving it an aesthetic character. Once we have had an aesthetic experience, we may, of course, do other things with works of art: we may reflect on the significance of their meanings (when there are such); we may use them as moral guides (when they so lend themselves); we may even invest in them financially. We may do all these things and much more. But what makes works of art worthwhile *as art*, and not as knowledge, moral edicts, or economic investments, is their *aesthetic value*, their capacity to invite aesthetic experience of a fairly high magnitude. And while the cognitive and moral values of art are certainly not to be underestimated, especially in the case of literature, drama, and film, it is a good question, in fact a key question, whether we seek out works of art for the knowledge and moral guidance they are capable of providing or for the fresh experience they are capable of occasioning.

The assertion that works of art have the capacity to induce better, richer, more sustained aesthetic experience than anything else does not imply denying that aesthetic experience of some duration and magnitude can be occasioned by other objects, actions, and events. To gain a clearer conception of the nature of aesthetic experience, a continuum may be imagined with the perception of the simple and fleeting qualities of things at one end and at the other the perception of works of art involving prolonged and intense concentration.

We may begin with Harold Osborne's *The Art of Appreciation*, in which in the course of explaining the modern concept of appreciation that associates it with the experience of works of art, Osborne comments on the character of everyday life:

We pass our lives, strenuously or languorously, in a never-ending give and take with a partly malleable, partly resistant environment, material and human, adapting it to our ends when we can and accommodating ourselves to it when we must. Occasionally the busy flow of life's intricate involvements is interrupted as there occur sudden pauses in our practical and theoretical preoccupations, moments of calm amidst the turmoil . . . as our attention is caught by . . . the rhythmic rise and fall of susurration on a summer's day, the smoky calligraphies of wheeling birds painted on a transparent grey sky in winter, the grotesque contorted menace of an olive tree's branches, the lissom slenderness of a birch, or the sad sloppiness of a rain-crushed dandelion. Sometimes, if more rarely, we catch a glimpse of familiar things in an unfamiliar light. Commonplace objects suddenly shed their murk and enter the focus of attention. Perhaps for the first time in our memory we *see* a familiar sight.[4]

Such is the raw material of aesthetic experience, the qualitative immediacy of life itself and the ways it can impinge on awareness. Some people, however, find it difficult to respond to even the simple qualities of things. At least this seems to have been the case with a rather well known fictional character. In the *Complete Sherlock Holmes*, for example, in "The Adventure of the Copper Beeches," we come across Holmes and Dr. Watson traveling by train through the English countryside:

By eleven o'clock the next day we were well upon our way to the old English capital. Holmes had been buried in the morning papers all the way down, but after we had passed the Hampshire border he threw them down and began to admire the scenery. [Or so Watson thought.] It was an ideal spring day, a light blue sky, flecked with little fleecy white clouds drifting across from west to east. The sun was shining very brightly, and yet there was an exhilarating nip in the air, which set an edge to a man's energy. All over the countryside, away to the rolling hills around Aldershot, the little red and gray roofs of the farmsteadings peeped out from amid the light green of the new foliage.

"Are they not fresh and beautiful?" [exclaimed Watson] . . . with all the enthusiasm of a man fresh from the fogs of Baker Street.

But Holmes shook his head gravely.

"Do you know Watson . . . that it is one of the curses of a mind with a turn like mine that I must look at everything with a reference to my own special subject. You look at these scattered houses, and you are impressed by their beauty. I look at them, and the only thought which comes to me is a feeling of their isolation and of the impunity with which crime may be committed there."

"Good heavens!" [cried Watson] . . . "Who would associate crime with these dear old homesteads?"

[To which Holmes said] "They always fill me with a certain horror. It is my belief, Watson, founded upon my experience, that the lowest and vilest alleys in London do not present a more dreadful record of sin than does the smiling and beautiful countryside."

"You horrify me!" [said Watson].
"But the reason [replied Holmes] is very obvious."[5]

Holmes then goes on to explain why the beautiful and smiling countryside is so vile.

The point, of course, is not the beauty or vileness of the English countryside, but the potentially inhibiting nature of professional preoccupation. Thoughts about crime were too much with Holmes for the aesthetic instinct to surface and break through. And what a pity, for surely nature is a bountiful source of aesthetic pleasure. Consider an example taken from Pepita Haezrahi's *The Contemplative Activity*. Her model for aesthetic experience is the perception of a falling leaf:

> Our leaf falls. It detaches itself with a little plopping sound from its place high up in the tree. It is red and golden. It plunges straight down through the tree and then hesitates and hovers for a while just below the lowest branches. The sun catches it and it glitters with mist and dew. It now descends in a leisurely arc and lingers for another moment before it finally settles on the ground.

And she goes on:

> You witness the whole occurrence. Something about it makes you catch your breath. The town, the village, the garden around you sink into oblivion. There is a pause in time. The chain of your thoughts is severed. The red and golden tints of the leaf, the graceful form of the arc described by its descent fill the whole of your consciousness, fill your soul to the brim. It is as though you existed in order to gaze at this leaf falling, and if you had other preoccupations and other purposes you have forgotten them. You do not know how long this lasts . . . but there is a quality of timelessness, a quality of eternity about it. You have had an aesthetic experience.[6]

Of course, once the leaves have fallen and must be raked up, it may be assumed that aesthetic interest subsides. But we have moved a bit farther along our continuum of awareness, from a mere noticing of the perceptually interesting features of things to an instance that not only has discernible qualities but also some duration. Thoughts of raking, however, prompt us to ask just what happens when the mind shifts from one point of view to another. In an essay devoted to mapping the structure of knowledge in the arts, Harry S. Broudy conjured up the following situation:

> Suppose we observe our neighbor walking briskly down the street of a week-day morning. The walk has a certain rhythm and pace, but our perception of it is likely to be no more than a registration of clues for inferences about what our neighbor is up to. . . . Suppose now that our neighbor suddenly breaks into

a little hop, skip and jump routine. Our interest perks up immediately, forcing strange hypotheses into our minds as to what might be the cause of this unusual behavior. The walking has become expressive of something: joy, excitement, or nervousness. In any event, we now watch the scene more intently. As we do, suppose our neighbor wheels about to face us and begins a fairly simple tap dance. At this juncture we either call the police, or we become absorbed in the dance itself. The practical and intellectual attitudes will then have begun to turn into the aesthetic attitude. Our interest is in perceiving the field and the motions within it.

And Broudy goes on:

If, however, the neighbor continues the tapping indefinitely our interest flags. The field has been explored; there is no further surprise to be anticipated, no further excitement. But suppose he varies the routine; suppose the rhythms become more complicated; suppose out of nowhere music sounds with a rhythm synchronized to the dancing; suppose a female dancer appears and joins our neighbor in his act. Suppose now instead of the drab ordinary street clothing, the dancers acquire brilliant costumes and that the simple music swells to a multi-instrumented orchestra. By this time our practical concerns with our neighbor will probably have been completely submerged in our aesthetic interest. Instead of one sense many of our senses are functioning at a high rate of intensity; instead of monotony there is variation of a pattern, there is contrast of pace, male and female, light and heavy, tension and release, a building up of climax and resolution. Before our eyes, so to speak, an ordinary piece of pedestrianism has been turned into a work of art, that is, into a field designed for perceiving and for not much of anything else.[7]

Broudy further remarks that the degree of interest occasioned by works of art will be a function not only of their formal complexity but also of the nerves of life they touch. The experience of blue skies, falling leaves, and tap dancing may be refreshing and moving, but not profoundly so. But if, says Broudy, "the dance is a caricature (a sketch) of war, of death, of love, of tragedy, of triumph, our perceiving becomes serious in the sense that we are beholding an expression that is also trying to be a statement about something so important, so close to the big issues in human life, perhaps so dangerous, so revolting that we have not yet formulated language to state it clearly." Perhaps, says Broudy, such works "portray impulses and instincts that man would just as soon forget he had" (ibid.).

Broudy's illustration moves us still farther along our continuum and reminds us of an important fact: the subject of art need not be agreeable in order to induce an aesthetic response. If this were not so, the tragic in art would be beyond our enjoyment. It is therefore not surprising that E. F. Kaelin uses Picasso's *Guernica* to illustrate the notion of aesthetic awareness. In pointing out that there is more to aesthetic perception than the noticing of sensuous surfaces, Kaelin writes:

> When we respond to a shape as a representation of a bull or horse, our experience deepens: more of the world is now includable within our brackets. If we look more closely, we can identify other objects: a broken warrior, frozen in rigor mortis, his severed arm still clutching a broken sword; a mother in agony over the death of her child; a woman falling through the shattered timbers of a burning building; a flickering light; a wounded dove, its peace gone astray.

And Kaelin continues:

> Let the mind play over these images and an idea grips the understanding: the wages of war, as it is currently conducted, are death and destruction. This is no game fought between man on horse and irritated bull on a blistering Spanish afternoon. The attack occurred at night, as the light's last flicker attests. Man, woman, child, and horse are all dead or dying, suffering, or fleeing along with the dove of peace. The bull almost impassively contemplates the scene. Salvation, when things come to such a pass, must be found in his persistence and courage. The virtue of the brave bull is to resist to the end the torments of his persecutors. So interpreted, our experience of *Guernica* deepens and comes to closure in a single act of expressive response in which we perceive the fittingness of this surface—all broken planes and jagged edges in the stark contrast of black and white—to represent this depth, the equally stark contrast of the living and the dead.[8]

Kaelin's last sentence is significant; it should allay the concerns of those who think aesthetic experience is vitiated because it restricts attention to the sensuous and formal elements of art. Aesthetic experience, it must be emphasized, accommodates (when they are present) the semantic elements of art, or what L. A. Reid has called meaning-embodied and values-embodied.[9]

Formal qualities may of course be featured in some works of art. Consider, for example, what it might be like to come upon Cézanne's painting of Mont Sainte-Victoire in the Courtauld Institute of Art of the University of London. Upon first glance any number of the painting's features and patterns might be initially noticed, but at some point we might be prompted, as Meyer Schapiro was in his monograph on Cézanne, to say of the painting that

> it is marvelous how all seems to flicker in changing colors from point to point, while out of this vast restless motion emerges a solid world of endless expanse, rising and settling. The great depth is built up in broad layers intricately fitted and interlocked, without an apparent constructive scheme. Towards us these layers become more and more diagonal; the diverging lines in the foreground seem a vague reflection of the mountain's form. These diagonals are not perspective

lines leading to the peak . . . [rather they] conduct us far to the side where the mountain slope begins; they are prolonged in a limb hanging from the tree.

It is this contrast of movements, of the marginal and centered, of symmetry and unbalance, that gives the immense aspect of drama to the scene. Yet the painting is a deep harmony, built with a wonderful finesse. It is astounding how far Cézanne has controlled this complex whole.[10]

We may agree with Schapiro and say further that the perception of such fields of aesthetic value constitutes some of the finest moments of aesthetic experience in the human career.

But by making aesthetic experience central to a conception of aesthetic education, has the discussion perhaps strayed too far from the theme of this conference, "Aesthetic Education: The Place of Expression"? Not really, for aesthetic experience involves the perception of all aesthetically relevant aspects, including those qualities often referred to as expressive qualities. In the ordinary, nontechnical discourse about works of art that prevails in the classroom, there is but a negligible semantic difference between saying "This work expresses sadness" and "This work has a sad quality," or "This work has a joyous air" and "This work expresses joyousness." That is, the meaning and import of works of art apprehended during aesthetic experience can also be understood as that which these works express. Consequently, if aesthetic education programs are the place where pupils acquire the skills and attitudes for aesthetic experiencing, they are also the place where pupils learn about expression, that is, the expressiveness of works of art and other things.[11]

At this point it will be helpful to recall Jacques Barzun's remark about art's corresponding to a deep human instinct that is enjoyable. Kenneth Clark and the other writers provided clues to the nature of this instinct, clues that have preoccupied philosophical thinking about art and the aesthetic since the eighteenth century. It is now time to go beyond these clues and ask about the present status of the concept of aesthetic experience, or, more to the point, about what current conception of aesthetic experience would be useful to a definition of aesthetic education.

AESTHETIC EXPERIENCE

Particularly noteworthy is the concept of aesthetic experience articulated by Monroe C. Beardsley in a presidential address to the Eastern Division of the American Philosophical Association.[12] Beardsley, who admirably combines the best in the tradition of aesthetic theorizing with contemporary analytical thinking, concluded that experience has a significant aesthetic character whenever it possesses such features as object-directedness, felt freedom, detached affect, active discovery, and a sense of wholeness in the person under-going the experience. Space does not permit an extended discussion of Beardsley's analysis, but a few words about its pedagogical usefulness are in order.

First, educational thinkers must be skeptical of accounts of aesthetic experience that make intrinsic enjoyment or satisfaction the sole objective of aesthetic education. No matter how exalted the objects that occasion it, enjoyment cannot suffice as a convincing justification for instituting programs in aesthetic education. A further question thus needs to be asked: What makes aesthetic enjoyment so desirable that formal schooling must make provisions for it? Or, what does aesthetic experience contribute to other worthwhile values in human experience?

Beardsley's description of aesthetic experience is helpful because it clearly goes beyond mere enjoyment. An experience of felt freedom, active discovery, and a sense of wholeness can be claimed to be not only enjoyable but also *beneficial*. But in what way? Elsewhere, Beardsley has written that because the experience of art may relieve tensions and quiet destructive impulses, aesthetic experience can be a morally acceptable way to sublimate violent and aggressive drives, which is to say that aesthetic experience can be a moral substitute for violence.[13] If so, then it might also be able to harmonize conflicting tendencies within the self. Furthermore, since the undivided attention that must be paid to artworks presupposes uncommon perceptual sensitivity, it seems reasonable to suppose that aesthetic experience can also lead to an improved ability to notice things generally. If this happens, more of nature's qualities and aspects of human relationships could become accessible to persons as a result of their having studied art. In this sense art might be said to have some potentiality to cultivate emotional maturity, which though not knowledge in the propositional sense must nonetheless be construed as a significant addition to human understanding. Furthermore, works of art being the products of imagination and imagination being required to apprehend them, it may well be the case that aesthetic experience can stimulate the imagination to function more effectively in other areas of human existence. Finally, if it is plausible to hold all of the foregoing—if, that is, art can inform, excite, enrich awareness, integrate the self, and cultivate the imagination—it can also be said to be, as John Dewey emphasized in his theory of aesthetic experience, an ideal for the human career.

Although a measure of plausibility may attach to each of these alleged benefits of aesthetic experience, a justification for aesthetic education need not subscribe to all of them. A judicious selection might stress three major benefits: the refinement of perception, the stimulation of imagination, and the presentation of ideals of human possibility. It seems reasonable to suppose that by developing perceptual sensitivity to works of art, aesthetic education can contribute toward a more inclusive perceptual sensitivity that notices the subtler aspects of things. And there can certainly be no harm in suggesting that the energizing of mind that occurs during aesthetic experience simultaneously stretches the imagination. Finally, although artistic import is not propositional knowledge, the variety of images, meanings, and values in works of art may cast significant light on the human career and its potentialities.

To sum up at this point: aesthetic education can be understood as activities that involve awareness of many things: blue skies, falling leaves, sunlit farmsteads, tap dancing, and the entire range of artistic expression. If I have concentrated on works of art, it is, once again, not because the aesthetic enjoyment of a large number of other phenomena has been ruled out; it is because works of art are the preeminent loci of aesthetic qualities and dramatic order, the places where we tend to find the most highly concentrated and compact fields of aesthetic value. And when beset with problems of selection, it is wise to choose representative and powerful examples of the thing in question. A raised level and quality of experience—the general goal of aesthetic education—will be attained only if we educate young minds and sensibilities through objects that have the power to enlarge their aesthetic capacities.

Having presented a conception of aesthetic education grounded in an aesthetic motivation and suggested that an important function of art is to engender high levels of aesthetic experience, I now ask, What are some difficulties anyone wishing to adopt a similar position might encounter?

A first difficulty could be posed by the aesthetically indifferent art of the 1960s and 1970s, often referred to as Conceptual art or Anti-art. Such art self-consciously sets itself against the idea that a work of art is something to be valued for its aesthetic properties. Would not, then, such art have the effect of rendering anachronistic, or perhaps even miseducative, the view of aesthetic education espoused here?

Two things can be said about such art. First, as the art critic Harold Rosenberg has put it, Conceptual artists have indeed often tried to deaestheticize art. He used a statement by the sculptor Robert Morris to characterize Conceptual art, and it may stand for countless other examples. For his metal construction *Litanies*, Morris had the following "Statement of Esthetic Withdrawal" executed before a notary public: "The undersigned, Robert Morris, being the maker of the metal construction entitled Litanies, described in the annexed Exhibit A, hereby withdraws from said construction all esthetic quality and content and declares that from the date hereof said construction has no such quality and content. Dated: November 15, 1963/Robert Morris."[14]

A put-on? Probably so, but the pervasiveness of Conceptual art cannot be ignored. To be sure, by asking us to regard things with greater self-consciousness, Conceptual art may be said to perform one of the conventional functions of art, but with an important difference. Works of this sort not only direct attention away from themselves to the *idea* of art, they also tend to be contrivedly dull and banal. Thus Conceptual art may invite us to think about art in general, but not very searchingly. Nor does it do much to sustain or energize awareness. Its worthwhileness is therefore arguable. How much significance should be attached to something that tries to denature aesthetic experience and eliminate all difference between art and life? If there is nothing in such art for the viewer, why should the viewer care about it?

Second, the argument for aesthetic education and the conception of art's function on which it is based are not collapsed by counterexamples of aesthetically indifferent art inasmuch as Conceptual may be but a moment in the history of art. Indeed artists are once more embracing aesthetic form and exploring different kinds of illusion and imagery. Looking back, we might say that Anti-art has been a very effective teacher. By dismantling art part by part it made us once more aware of what art is. It also helped create a yearning for the restoration of the aesthetic qualities that had been withdrawn. By preaching aesthetic abstinence, Conceptual artists prepared the ground for a renewed aesthetic appetite.

Yet another difficulty may arise from the discovery that art historians—whose field is one of the important sources of background knowledge for aesthetic experience—do not hold aesthetics in high esteem. If much of modern art seems indifferent to traditional aesthetic values, a good number of art historians seem indifferent to aesthetic theorizing (including, one would assume, to theorizing about aesthetic education). H. W. Janson, for example, once remarked that, by and large, aesthetics does not figure in the work of most art historians.[15] And James Ackerman made a special point of saying that he avoided the use of the term *aesthetic* in his writings.[16] Such remarks from reputable art historians would appear to carry weight; the question is how much weight and whether they can be countervailed. Part of the problem may be purely verbal: let two parties understand how they are using a term, say, *aesthetic value*, and the issue may dissolve. Another part of the problem may lie in the biases of specialists, in their belief, for example, in the self-sufficiency of their disciplines. For counterbalance, one may point to art historians who do acknowledge the relevance of aesthetics. It was Erwin Panofsky, foremost among distinguished art historians, who characterized works of art as humanmade objects demanding to be experienced aesthetically.[17] All art, whether good or bad, he said, has aesthetic significance that should be heeded by art historians. Furthermore, the citations from Kenneth Clark and Meyer Schapiro suggest that talk of aesthetic experience and quality comes naturally enough for at least some art historians. In short, indifference to aesthetic theory by some art historians should not encourage indifference to art history on the part of aesthetic educators. Certainly,

the concepts and results of both aesthetic and art-historical inquiry are helpful in teaching critical appreciation. Such concepts ultimately function tacitly during the experience of art, something Kenneth Clark may have had in
mind when he said that "if I am to go on looking responsively I must fortify
myself with nips of information . . . and the value of historical criticism is
that it keeps the attention fixed on the work while the senses have time to
get a second wind."[18]

Finally, the concept of aesthetic education described here may be faulted
for its silence on the issue of ideology. How valid this objection is depends
on how the term *ideology* is understood. If it is taken to refer to the semantic
elements of artworks, that is, to their meanings, then the criticism can be
deflected, for aesthetic experience encompasses the apprehension of whatever artworks mean, communicate, or express. This does not imply that ideological content should be taken as the essence of art; nor is it being advocated
that art ought to promote a particular ideology in any vulgar sense. Ideological content is simply one element among others to consider in perceiving
works of art. To be sure, it may be said that aesthetic education is inescap-
ably ideological because all thinking is ideological; all thought springs from
ideas and convictions about the individual and society, knowledge and value,
and so on. In this case, there is an obligation to state the ideology one pro-
fesses. Also central to the notion that art is inevitably ideological is the de-
nial of the possibility of objectivity, the import of which is that we can never
achieve unbiased knowledge about ourselves and the world. It is this sense
of ideology that animates much critical theorizing. In short, the term *objectivity* having become a red flag, its mere mention often incites hostile reaction. It is also clear that the use of the term has given rise to numerous
misconceptions about its meaning in various fields of inquiry. David Best
has pointed out some of these misconceptions in an article in the *British
Journal of Aesthetics*.[19] The work of Michael Polanyi, of which L. A. Reid
and Harry S. Broudy have made good use, is also relevant in that Polanyi
appreciates both the personal element in knowledge and its consensual character, thereby combining subjectivity and objectivity.[20] Space does not permit expanding on the subject, but perhaps enough has been said to suggest
lines of further discussion.

AESTHETIC EDUCATION AND POLICY

By way of indicating some contrast to the point of view presented in this
chapter, a few observations are offered about the direction in which thinking about arts education is developing in one prominent sector of society in
the United States. That direction is the one characterizing the outlook and

mentality of officials and agencies involved in guiding governmental financial aid to the arts. These observations are not made with a view to pointing out parallels that are believed to exist between the United States and Great Britain. The intent, rather, is to suggest that accounts of what goes wrong in one country can serve as cautionary tales.

Public support for the arts in the United States has had a short and distinctive history. One of the peculiar features of this history has been a reluctance to base support for the arts on commonly shared assumptions about aesthetic value or a national cultural heritage. This has resulted in government spending on the arts and arts education being justified on the basis of the alleged social and economic usefulness of the arts. As for the economic argument, it is said that government-funded programs and institutions will create jobs, attract new industries, and increase tourism in the districts of elected representatives. As far as the social uses of the arts are concerned, the arts are said to have, among other things, the capacity to reduce crime and juvenile delinquency, animate the aging, build ethnic identity, relieve alienation, and rehabilitate criminals. In other words, arguments for government support for the arts are straightforwardly political. It is thus not surprising that the process of awarding grants has become increasingly politicized. The task of getting and distributing funds for the arts has been entrusted to the National Endowment for the Arts, an agency that has effectively allied itself with a number of key foundations, cultural organizations, and state arts councils to create an influential cultural network. Through its prestige and power to disburse grants, and thereby to confer status on grant recipients, the arts establishment has already significantly encroached on art programs taught in the schools and is bidding to become an even stronger influence in the decade just begun. That is to say, the case being made for aesthetic education by many educators is becoming similar in substance, sentiment, and rhetoric to the ideology of the cultural establishment. Realizing that this is the way to secure funds, many are only too happy to endorse a vigorous yet incautious instrumentalism (in contrast to the modest and cautious instrumentalism I've described) regarding art's economic and social functions. It is not too much to say that art is being promoted in the cultural establishment and by like-minded others as a kind of powerful patent medicine good for whatever ails individuals, the schools, and the body politic. We read that art can humanize the gray fortresses of learning, help teach basic skills, integrate a compartmentalized curriculum, reduce the early school-leaving rate, and much, much more.[21]

An impression gained from reading Janet Minihan's study of state subsidies to the arts in Great Britain is that the British do better in defining cultural and educational relations.[22] If so, it would be worthwhile to study the British way, for the politicizing of arts education in the United States runs counter to the appreciation of art's true potencies and the distinctive contribution it can make to the human career.[23] This is not to imply that there is nothing praiseworthy in the government's support of the arts in the United States. Its thinking about arts education has just got off on the wrong track. In contrast, then, to the dreary politicizing of the arts and arts education, in this chapter I have tried to put aesthetic education in proper educational perspective.

NOTES

1. Jacques Barzun, "Art and Educational Inflation," *Art Education* 31, no. 6 (1978), published concurrently in the *Journal of Aesthetic Education* 12, no. 4 (1978). Also in *Art in Basic Education*, Occasional Paper 25 (Washington, D.C.: Council for Basic Education, 1979).

2. Kenneth Clark, "Art and Society," in *Moments of Vision* (London: John Murray, 1981).

3. Harold Osborne, *Aesthetics and Art Theory: An Historical Introduction* (New York: E. P. Dutton, 1970), 23.

4. Harold Osborne, *The Art of Appreciation* (New York: Oxford University Press, 1970), 20–21. Chapter 2, "Appreciation as Percipience," was reprinted in *Aesthetics and Problems of Education,* ed. Ralph A. Smith (Urbana: University of Illinois Press, 1971).

5. Arthur Conan Doyle, *The Complete Sherlock Holmes* (New York: Doubleday, n.d.), 1:322–23.

6. Quoted by Osborne in *The Art of Appreciation*, 25.

7. Harry S. Broudy, "The Structure of Knowledge in the Arts," in *Aesthetics and Criticism in Art Education*, ed. Ralph A. Smith (Chicago: Rand McNally, 1966), 34–35.

8. Eugene F. Kaelin, "Aesthetic Education: A Role for Aesthetics Proper," in *Aesthetics and Problems of Education*, 154.

9. Louis A. Reid, *Meaning in the Arts* (New York: Humanities Press, 1969). Cf. "Meaning in the Arts," in *The Arts and Personal Growth*, ed. Malcolm Ross (New York, London: Pergamon Press, 1980).

10. Meyer Schapiro, *Paul Cézanne* (New York: Harry N. Abrams, 1952), 74.

11. For further discussion, see John Hospers, ed., *Artistic Expression* (New York: Appleton-Century-Crofts, 1971). In thinking about the concept of expression, it is well to keep in mind what Hospers calls the process, properties, communication, and evocation senses of the term.

12. Monroe C. Beardsley, "In Defense of Aesthetic Value," *Proceedings and Addresses of the American Philosophical Association* 52, no. 6 (1979): 741–42.

13. Monroe C. Beardsley, *Aesthetics: Problems in the Philosophy of Criticism* (New York: Harcourt, Brace and World, 1958), 573–76.

14. Harold Rosenberg, *The De-definition of Art* (New York: Horizon Press, 1972) 28.

15. H. W. Janson, "The Art Historian's Comments," in *Perspectives in Education, Religion, and the Arts*, ed. Howard E. Kiefer and Milton K. Munitz (Albany: State University of New York Press, 1970), 295. Cf. Monroe C. Beardsley, "Reply to Professor Janson," *Metaphilosophy* 1, no. 1 (1970).

16. James Ackerman, "Toward a New Social Theory of Art," *New Literary History* 4, no. 2 (1973): 330.

17. Erwin Panofsky, "The History of Art as a Humanistic Discipline," in *Meaning in the Visual Arts* (New York: Doubleday Anchor, 1955), 11.

18. Kenneth Clark, *Looking at Pictures* (New York: Holt, Rinehart and Winston, 1960), 16–17.

19. David Best, "The Objectivity of Aesthetic Judgment," *British Journal of Aesthetics* 20, no. 2 (1980).

20. For an explanation of how science achieves consensus of opinion, see Polanyi's "The Republic of Science: Its Political and Economic Theory," in *Knowing and Being: Essays by Michael Polanyi*, ed. Marjorie Grene (Chicago: University of Chicago Press, 1969).

21. The views of this establishment are conveniently encapsulated in its "magnum opus," Arts, Education and Americans Panel, *Coming to Our Senses: The Significance of the Arts for American Education* (New York: McGraw-Hill, 1977). For my criticisms of this report, see *Teachers College Record* 79, no. 3 (1978); and the *Journal of Aesthetic Education* 12, no. 1 (1978). Cf. my "Policy and Art Education: Some Fallacies," *High School Journal* 63, no. 8 (1980).

22. See Stuart Hampshire, "Private Pleasures and the Public Purse," *Times Literary Supplement*, 13 May 1977; a review of Janet Minihan's *The Nationalization of Culture: The Development of State Subsidies to the Arts in Great Britain* (New York: New York University Press, 1977).

23. For a description of how the arts became politicized in the 1970s, see Ronald Berman, "Art Versus the Arts," *Commentary* 68, no. 5 (1979). At one point, Berman writes that "the social functions of art were emphasized in their variety, the debates suggesting that art displaced adolescent violence and anomie, encouraged craftsmanship, discouraged crime, and offered new opportunities for employment. Art was an alternative to drug addiction, an auxiliary to prison rehabilitation, and a solution to the problem of old age. Exposure to art might relieve inner-city tensions and possibly improve the tone of the adversary culture" (47).

Problems for a Philosophy of Art Education

G IVEN THE DIFFERENT senses of *philosophy*, I begin with the basic distinction between the procedural and substantive interpretations of philosophy—philosophy as rational critical analysis and philosophy as systems of ideas—and stress the procedural sense. The topics and issues are presented as ostensible dichotomies. The enclosing of "versus" within quotation marks is intended to suggest that in some instances no dichotomy really exists. In other cases a reconciliation of the ideas implied by the terms of the dichotomy may prove more difficult or even impossible, and then the quotation marks can be mentally deleted.

ESSENTIAL "VERSUS" PERSUASIVE DEFINITIONS OF ART

Since the publication in 1956 of Morris Weitz's "The Role of Theory in Aesthetics,"[1] there has been a continuing interest in the question of art's definition in both philosophical aesthetics and art education. Weitz argued that efforts by theorists to define art in the classical Aristotelian sense, that is, in terms of a real, true, or essential definition, were logically self-defeating inasmuch as the concept of art is open-textured and therefore not amenable to such definition. Therefore, attempts to know that, by definition, something is a work of art are destined to fail. The question of something's status as art is a decisional matter, not a factual one. This means that art is characteristically defined in terms of what the definer believes is valuable.

In effect Weitz says that all definitions of art are persuasive, honorific, programmatic, or value-laden definitions. They contain recommendations to attend to certain features of art for the sake of the benefits they can yield.[2] Weitz advised that, once the problem of definition is properly understood, it behooves theorists to be generous toward traditional theories of art. "What is central and must be articulated in all the theories," he wrote, "are their debates over the reasons for excellence in art—debates over emotional depth, profound truths, natural beauty, exactitude, freshness of treatment, and so on, as criteria of evaluation—the whole of which converges on the perennial problem of what makes a work of art good" (153). Weitz's counsel is both wise and timely inasmuch as contemporary theoretical writing in art education reveals little interest in traditional definitions of art and criteria of excellence.[3]

Because some writers in art education seem to think that Weitz was saying that art cannot be defined at all, the question has been raised of whether the philosophy of art education even needs a definition of art. Before one addresses this question, it should be pointed out that Weitz did not have the last word on the problem of defining art. A substantial literature challenged his basic premises. It claims that his analysis was inconclusive and even imprudent in assuming *a priori* that no correct or true definition of art could be formulated. Critics pointed out that there are alternative ways to define the essence of art, for example, in terms of intention, characteristic function, and institutional contexts.[4] The fact is that the search for the essence of art goes on. Although the literature on definition cannot be summarized here, it can be conveniently examined in Stephen Davis's *Definitions of Art.*[5]

For all that can be said on behalf of the philosophical quest for the essence of art, it is acceptable, I think, for a philosophy of art education to regard definitions of art and art education as persuasive or programmatic definitions, as recommendations to draw attention to worthwhile aspects of art. Theorists of art education should be encouraged to entertain such definitions because they are essentially, as Weitz claimed, arguments about what counts as excellence in art and art education. An essential definition, it should noted, may also be a persuasive definition and vice versa; hence the distinction between the two is not hard and fast.

PROCESS-CENTERED "VERSUS" PRODUCT-CENTERED AESTHETIC LEARNING

Another ostensible dichotomy in the theory of art education is typically phrased as "process 'versus' product." Should teaching aim at the development of aesthetic understanding primarily through studio activities or through appreciative, historical, and critical studies? Or through both making and responding? Answers to these questions will depend on one's vision of art education, which in turn will be influenced by more or less explicit assumptions about the nature of a good or worthwhile life. Getting clear about the issues involved, however, is difficult because adversarial fervor tends to avoid key questions. What follows will sound familiar but bears repeating in this context.

Although process theorists tend to differ in major respects in their theoretical premises, the outcome they seek is basically the same: it is the development of certain powers of mind that can be developed by involving the young in artistic activities. As one process theorist, Howard Gardner, has put it, "The heart of any arts-educational process must be the capacity to handle, to use, to transform different artistic symbol systems—to *think with* and *in* the materials of an artistic medium. Such processes can occur only if artistic creation remains the cornerstone of all pedagogical efforts."[6] Although Gardner's interpretation of arts education derives largely from a range of disciplines, it is essentially a psychologist's perspective. His theory of multiple intelligences and its significance for teaching art is one way of thinking about art education, and it constitutes a refinement of process theories that many in the field have found congenial.[7] Its limitation is that it fails to do justice to historical and critical studies that, I think, call for greater emphasis at this moment in history.

An alternative to theories that center interest on process and creative activities is a product-centered conception. Although it acknowledges a role for creative activities in the development of aesthetic understanding, it does not consider them to be the cornerstone of teaching and learning. Rather, it argues that value resides principally in the completed work of mature artists. Albert William Levi and Ralph Smith's humanities-based interpretation of discipline-based art education is a case in point.[8] This approach to curriculum encourages learners to value both the constitutive and the revelatory powers of works of art, which is to say the potential that works of art have for both shaping the human personality in positive ways and providing insight into human experience and other phenomena. Although this interpretation of art education is grounded in the insights of cognitive psychology, it is basically a traditional humanities view of teaching that derives its objectives and pedagogy from the ideas and practices of art history, art criticism, and aesthetics. Perhaps it is possible for a comprehensive philosophy of art education to combine the principal features of both process- and product-centered conceptions of aesthetic learning. Decisions about which is core and which periphery will, however, influence matters in one direction or another.

Ideally, a philosophy of art education should adjudicate wisely among the several components of what may be called the aesthetic complex: the creation of artworks, which raises questions about the nature of artistic intelligence; the character of artworks, which raises questions about their nature, meaning, and value (that is, ontological, epistemological, and axiological questions); response to artworks, which raises questions about perception, interpretation, appreciation, and judgment; and the history of art, which raises questions about context, tradition, and style.[9] How much attention should be given to each component would be determined by what theorists and teachers believe is needed at a particular moment in the history of the field. In recent years, critics of an overemphasis on artistic production and the image of the child as artist have produced a literature that seeks to broaden the scope of aesthetic learning.[10] These efforts, however, are resisted by educators who think that supplementing aesthetic activities with historical and creative studies will devalue what they believe is most important about aesthetic learning.[11] Accordingly, the dichotomy is likely to be with the field for some time. There seems to be no way of resolving it to everyone's satisfaction.

INSTRUMENTAL "VERSUS" NONINSTRUMENTAL USES OF ART

The purported instrumental "versus" noninstrumental dichotomy can be stated in different terms, for example, extra-aesthetic "versus" aesthetic functions of artworks, extrinsic "versus" intrinsic values, utilitarian "versus" nonutilitarian uses of art, and so forth. In one sense art education is always instrumental, a means subserving a subject, a content, a human value, a way of knowing. The subject served by art education is, of course, art. The content to teach it derives from a variety of related disciplines and human experiences. The peculiar value of art is aesthetic value, and art's way of knowing is aesthetic knowing. Yet the questions of how to address works of art and what works of art do for persons and society are strategic ones.

Noninstrumentalism is the belief that works of art should be valued intrinsically for their inherent values. Yet, as noted, the notion of inherent values is ambiguous. Nothing can really be valued for its own sake inasmuch as all human acts satisfy some individual interest or social need. In one well-developed theory, works of art are valued for their capacity to provide degrees of aesthetic experience. They are thus instrumental to providing such experience. Yet the chain of instrumentality does not stop there. The having of aesthetic experiences may contribute to other values that a society prizes. They may not only quiet destructive impulses and achieve a greater integration of the self; they may also refine perception and stretch the imagination. And if aesthetic experiences can have these effects, they may further be an aid to mental health, foster mutual sympathy and understanding, and provide an ideal for human life.[12]

A very different sense of art's instrumentality is found in some contemporary policy making and research. There, art's utility is to be understood not so much in connection with the benefits just mentioned as in relation to the use of works of art and artistic activities as a means to achieve in quite a direct way a number of nonaesthetic objectives, for example, the improvement of the basic skills of reading, writing, and calculating and the ameliorating of social problems. Thus we read that a study of the arts can ameliorate race relations, abate school violence, and lower the drop-out rate.[13] In short, artistic activities and works of art are understood to have significant motivational power and social problem-solving significance. But valuable as such uses of art may be, it has to be asked whether they should substitute for the study of art as a distinctive subject with its own content, procedures, and values. Is art not more than a teaching aid, a motivational device, a social tool, a therapeutic activity? Does it not consist of unique and significant accomplishments that exemplify some of the finest and most profound expressions of humankind? If this is denied, I believe there is no justification for art education.

That art education continues to be justified on the basis of its efficacy in achieving nonaesthetic objectives indicates that the field of art education continues to be confused about its basic aims and purposes. For example, the pianist and cultural critic Samuel Lipman called *Coming to Our Senses*, which is commonly referred to as the Rockefeller Report, a monument to such confusion.[14] *Towards Civilization*, a report on arts education issued by the National Endowment for the Arts—although not without the flaws of all such reports—is in effect an antidote to *Coming to Our Senses*.[15] The same is true of the idea of discipline-based art education insofar as it includes the study of art for its distinctive history of accomplishment.[16]

Yet another instrumental use of art assumes that art should serve explicit political goals. Casting aside Weitz's wise admonition to heed the value and usefulness of traditional theories of art and their arguments about artistic excellence, this instrumentalist conception would press art education into the service of achieving the goals of special interest groups. It is quite clear that a politicized art education will be an art education that differs sharply from the ways it has been conceived since the mid-twentieth century. And there is a question whether it should be called *art* education.

Given, then, that all definitions of art education are in some sense instrumental and programmatic, the distinction between instrumental and noninstrumental values is not rigid, but it is one that needs to be better understood.

HIGH CULTURE "VERSUS" POPULAR CULTURE

The terms of this ostensible dichotomy are perhaps not best suited to describe the issues involved. Not only are works of high culture sometimes popular; so-called works of popular culture sometimes succeed in attaining the status of high culture. Moreover, what is one era's popular art sometimes becomes another era's high culture. All this has been said before.

What really lies behind the distinction are the assumptions, first, that different degrees or magnitudes of excellence can be detected in artistic performances and, second, that by virtue of their form and expressive import certain works have greater potential for inducing worthwhile experiences than do other works. Works of high culture are renowned for this capacity. Yet the recommendation to encourage and recognize excellence in art and art education is a matter of concern to those who prefer to deemphasize value differences and who regard as elitist any effort to promote the appreciation of excellence. For art educators of this latter stripe the ideal seems to be folk or community art that celebrates everyday activities, rituals, and ceremonies. Dewey, of course, also argued for a greater interdependence of art and society in order to offset what he considered the excessive worship of museum art. Yet Dewey dedicated *Art as Experience* to a museum director noted for his connoisseurship, and the volume contains illuminating discussions of fine art. It is, of course, not necessary to adopt a view that stresses the creation and appreciation of relatively autonomous works of art to the exclusion of another that favors a communitarian interpretation of art's function. Unfortunately, however, art educators are expected to chose the latter approach while the study and enjoyment of revered masterworks has been made to seem an elitist and inherently undemocratic activity.

Yet the case for high culture and the cultivation of an appreciation of its masterworks at appropriate levels of instruction is grounded in beliefs that are difficult to dispute. Stuart Hampshire has indicated why. He has said that there is a tradition of great art that is worth preserving and transmitting; that there are people (artists, historians, critics, educators) who care about this tradition and whose judgments are the best guides to artistic excellence that we have; that works of high culture are inestimable sources of intense enjoyment, gratification, and humanistic insight; and that such works are significant constituents of national pride and unity.[17]

What is central to the acceptance of the works of high culture is also what is central to the acceptance of excellence generally—outstanding human performance. Indeed, a volume of substantial length would be required to list and describe the ways in which Americans value and reward excellence in many fields. Moreover, encouraging excellence of one kind or another is a major institutional practice of virtually all professional organizations. What cannot be argued away is the existence of great art and the fact that it is great because of the way it magnificently transfigures the commonplace.[18] The criteria of greatness are, moreover, no mystery. They encompass incomparable artistic finesse, the extraordinary capacity to provide high degrees of aesthetic gratification, and stature, this last term implying the significant human values that masterworks individually express.[19]

I have given some space to the case for high culture because its premises are those that are being questioned. The premises of populism, however, go largely unchallenged inasmuch as they are believed by its advocates to be more consistent with democratic principles. And, of course, populism has its virtues. Populists keep defenders of high culture from becoming too impressed with themselves and remind them that the arts of everyday living make legitimate claims on our attention. Populists further show a genuine regard for the interests of young people, for many of whom popular culture is an unquestioned good. Populists further tend to cast a wide net over the whole world of art and point out that the Western distinction between high and popular culture is not universally shared. No doubt populists also think that there are traditions of popular culture worth transmitting, that popular culture has its experts and scholars who are the best guides we have to its significance, and that popular culture is also a source of national pride. American popular culture is, after all, widely admired throughout the world. All this can be said in behalf of populist thinking, although I am not aware of any well-developed theory of populism in the field of art education. The major claim for popular art seems to be that it is closer to the interests of students.

Perhaps, however, the problems could be couched in terms of cultural equity, namely, that all art forms of all groups deserve study in the schools irrespective of whether they satisfy conventional criteria of quality. Seemingly attractive, this approach would present insuperable practical difficulties in selecting works for study. Should, for example, the interests and preference of students outweigh the judgments of their more mature and experienced teachers? Do not the cultural heritage of a society and the mature judgments of experienced professionals count for something? Thus the question persists of whether conventional criteria of excellence should be lightly cast aside in choosing content for instruction.

The problems are partly philosophical and partly social and political. Resolving the issues they raise will depend not only on what are thought to be the inherent values of works of high culture and works of popular art, but also on a great deal of empirical evidence. The usefulness of the distinction between high culture and popular culture thus depends on the meanings assigned to the terms in the purported dichotomy.

CULTURAL PLURALISM "VERSUS" CULTURAL PARTICULARISM

The terms of this dichotomy are, I think, irreconcilable, and thus the quotation marks should probably be removed. What is meant by cultural pluralism and cultural particularism is brought out in a number of writings by Diane

Ravitch.[20] Her discussion of cultural particularism, or what she also calls cultural centrism, is especially important because of her criticism of cultural separatism (with apologies for introducing so many *isms* into this discussion). Cultural particularism is descriptive of any separatist movement that rejects pluralism and multiculturalism, but its principal exponents tend to be African American historians and writers. In testimony and in a number of articles, Ravitch has been pointing out that for certain contemporary Black writers, fundamental values no longer reside in cultural pluralism, universalism, and a richly varied common culture; rather, these writers subscribe to separatist values grounded in beliefs in biological determinism and cultural predestination.

The aim of an Afrocentric curriculum is to build a sense of security and self-confidence in Black youth, whose chances for success in society are thought to be lowered by studies that do not sufficiently recognize their history and cultural achievements. To counter this situation, indeed to transform it, Afrocentrists are strongly critical of the European cultural heritage of Western civilization; hence the pejorative use of the term *Eurocentric* to designate ideas and values that are considered inherently racist, sexist, and elitist. The political objective is to weaken the hegemony of Western principles by decentering such values in American schooling. But by rejecting cultural pluralism, multiculturalism, universalism, and a common American culture, particularism, says Ravitch, invites and fans social conflict. There is no question, in her view, about the need to correct and expand the historical record as far as the cultural contributions of members of minority groups are concerned. But an alternative education that explicitly promotes an ethnocentrism grounded in notions of racial superiority, cultural predestination, and filiopietism was bound to be challenged.[21]

In this connection some earlier observations by Mary Ann Raywid have proved to be prescient.[22] She perceived the dangers of trying to tie personal identity to ethnic origin and the potential of such a tendency for engendering social divisiveness. She also expressed concern that the new emphasis on ethnicity might well prove dysfunctional and maladaptive for minority children, who must find a place in society in which skill, competence, and achievement count for more than ethnic origin—a point also made by John Wilson in his analysis of the relations between art, culture, and identity.[23] Raywid thus called for new social groupings in which members would have common and special interests, all the while acknowledging that ethnic values and modes of expression could be perpetuated and developed within subgroups.

Ravitch in effect updates Raywid. She points out that particularist thinking ignores important differences within cultures that result from intermarriage and linkages across groups. These differences make untenable the division of the population into five ethnic groups, a scheme that has been proposed by particularists (African American, Asian American, European American, Latino/Hispanic American, Native American). Such divisions ignore the universality of human accomplishment and assert that only members of an individual's ethnic group can serve as models or heroes. By way of contrast, Ravitch refers to a Black woman runner who said she admired Baryshnikov because of his magnificent bodily discipline, an accomplishment that was relevant to her own chosen activity. Baryshnikov's skin color or ethnic origin didn't matter.

Most of all, Ravitch finds particularists blameworthy for their denigration of the tradition of liberalism, whose modern origins date from the period of the Enlightenment. In scorning Eurocentricity, particularism in effect abjures liberalism's commitments to reason and rationality, which are values that are central to the ideals of modern democratic societies. She finds equally reprehensible the tendency of particularists to regard any criticism of their ideas as racist. Ravitch explains that there are good reasons for Americans to retain close relations with Europe. The roots of many of the social, moral, cultural, political, and religious traditions of the United States are to be found there; a majority of Americans are of European descent; and English remains the principal language of the country. Collectively, these facts and many others make for a common culture that has been richly influenced by contacts with other cultures and that it has been the goal of schooling to transmit.

It is not that Ravitch is hostile to pluralism. She acknowledges that the United States is a multicultural society, and her work on a multicultural history curriculum for the state of California is more than ample evidence of her convictions. Yet she sees serious pedagogical problems with a policy of multiple centrisms. She is most alarmed at what she calls the politicizing of truth. She states that truth is not a function of power, dogmatic theories, and unchecked relativism. Rather, it is a continuing search that leads to the constant revision and correction of knowledge. She suggests that an educational system increasingly committed to separatist thinking might even undermine public support for the schools. Why should a society subsidize attitudes that are intentionally divisive?

To recall the basic choices: either a richly varied common culture that stresses shared and universal values or a plethora of ethnic enclaves and special interest groups each bent on pressing rights derived from past and present injustices and inequities. Typically, Americans reject extremist thinking, and so one expects particularism will in all probability be ultimately renounced. But until then it will remain a source of social conflict and thus the dichotomy and the important issues it raises deserve serious study.

POSTMODERNISM "VERSUS" MODERNISM

The terms have no stable meanings and there is no consensus regarding their origins or manifestations. For example, Jacques Barzun, in *The Use and Abuse of Art*, in which he describes how art and attitudes toward art have changed over the past 150 years, states his belief that modern *times* began about 1450 with the Renaissance; the modern *era* about 1789 with the French Revolution; modern *manners* about 1890–1914, or the turn of the last century; and *contemporary* times from 1920 on.[24] Central to Barzun's analysis is an explanation of the forces that both created the avant-garde and brought about its demise. This is a sensible way to think about modern history: modern and contemporary times.

Ihab Hassan, by contrast, believes that Postmodernism is prefigured by Mannerism, Romanticism, and Modernism.[25] This would locate the origins of Postmodernism in the seventeenth century. To claim, moreover, that Freud, Marx, and William James, among others, are the major influences on Postmodernism is to say nothing that could not also be said of their influence on Modernism. What is more, Postmodernism can be understood not only as a reaction to Modernism but also as an extension of it. For still others Postmodernism consists simply of the stylistic tendencies that followed those of Modernism—in the way, for example, that the stylistic tendencies of Postimpressionism followed those of Impressionism. Perhaps this is what Jacques Maquet had in mind when he stated that there are two Postmodernisms: one that radically rejects Modernism and another that rejects radical rejection.[26] Any discussion of Modernism and Postmodernism must, therefore, be somewhat arbitrary, a matter of stipulative definition.

Perhaps some initial clarification can be gained by first considering one meaning of Modernism. For example, the entry for *Modernism* (there is none for *Postmodernism*) in the revised and expanded edition of the *Dictionary of Modern Critical Terms* reads:

> Modernist art is, in most critical usage, reckoned to be the art of what Harold Rosenberg calls "the tradition of the new." It is experimental, formally complex, elliptical, contains elements of decreation as well as creation, and tends to associate notions of the artist's freedom from realism, materialism, traditional genre and form, with notions of cultural apocalypse and disaster. Its social content is characteristically avant-garde or bohemian; hence specialized. Its notion of the artist is of a futurist, not the conserver of culture but its onward creator.[27]

The entry goes on to say that Modernism expresses not one aesthetic or style but many. It encompasses Postimpressionism, Expressionism, Futurism, Vorticism, Dadaism, and Surrealism. In this respect it is misleading to say, as is often done by Postmodernists, that the Modernist aesthetic is essentially formalistic, because this would exclude too many styles and works containing semantic content.

The ambiguity inherent in the meaning of *Modernism* is revealed when it is realized that the term denotes both a perennial and a time-bound tendency. As a perennial phenomenon, it relates to all those moments in the history of art when artists attempted to be modern, to be of their time. Thus, in departing from some of the conventions of medieval art, Renaissance art can be said to have been modern, which is how Barzun meant it. As a time-bound concept, Modernism refers to the era of the avant-garde in the twentieth century.

Now, if we accept the view that Modernism consisted of a reaction to the aesthetic clichés of nineteenth-century official culture, which is to say the official art of the academic salons, then, as Fowler says, its artists were future oriented. Hilton Kramer, however, in *The Age of the Avant-Garde*, observes that another strand of Modernism looked back as well as forward in its effort to forge new aesthetic values.[28] If Dada artists were the epitome of revolutionary thinking, artists such as Braque and Picasso reflected the continuity of artistic culture and were committed to renewing its deepest impulses. They believed that a tradition had to be mastered and felt before it could be altered, added to, or extended. "The impulse to act as the creative conscience of a usable tradition was," Kramer writes, "as much a part of the avant-garde scenario . . . as the impulse to wage war on the past" (12).

If the emergence, career, and fate of the avant-garde are central to understanding Modernism, then Postmodernism can be understood as a state of culture in which the avant-garde not only has lost its traditional function but, in an important sense, no longer exists. What must be kept in mind, however, is that there are varieties of Postmodernism. In architecture, Postmodernism can imply a rejection of the internationalist aesthetic of twentieth-century architecture in favor of an often irreverent and playful eclecticism. Or, as Charles Jencks points out, it can stand for a free-style classicism that favors the reintegration of Modernist ideas with Western traditional humanism.[29] Given this interpretation of Postmodernism, it is a distortion to equate Postmodernism with a radical critique of Western intellectual, cultural, and aesthetic traditions. Jencks's analysis, moreover, sounds similar to the dialectic of Modernism described by Kramer, and in fact both writers appeal to T. S. Eliot's essay "Tradition and the Individual Talent" to support their interpretations. Kramer suggests that the Postmodern turn, to borrow Hassan's phrase, occurred around 1960 when artists and cultural institutions endorsed a camp mentality and legitimized kitsch. He characterizes this attitude and type of art as reveling in comic absurdity and the facetious.

Much more needs to be said on the subject, of course, and it would help if there were some well-worked-out interpretations of Postmodernism in the field of art education, but I am aware of none. Enough has been brought out, however, to cast some doubt on the usefulness of Modernism and Postmodernism for theoretical discussion. For the most part the terms function as counters in ideological debate. Is there, then, a philosophical problem here? Not insofar as the use of *Postmodernism* mainly records stylistic preferences or an attempt to be modern. In philosophy and literary theory, by contrast, fundamental questions about the nature of reality, truth, language, meaning, intention, and value arise. I think, however, that a theory of art education can skip over most of these developments, notably deconstruction, whose premises, when carefully analyzed, would deny any educative value to the arts.[30] But that argument cannot be pursued here. The meanings of terms of the dichotomy are complex and confounding and therefore must be used with care.

QUANTITATIVE "VERSUS" QUALITATIVE EVALUATION

The terms are once more inherently ambiguous and, like some others discussed above, tend to be used as counters in debates about the nature of educational assessment and research. The ambiguity becomes readily apparent when it is realized that an assessment, say, of mastery, can be both quantitative and qualitative at the same time. Usually, *quantitative evaluation* refers to methods of assessment that rely on statistical measures of overt behavior in the performance of learning tasks. Such measures rule out inferences regarding the effects of interior mental activity, that is, memory, conceptual frameworks, allusionary bases, and so forth. In contrast, qualitative assessment provides estimates of the effects of instruction on a learner's cognitive structure—the ways in which, for example, the mind accommodates and assimilates new information.

Qualitative assessment further refers to field studies of education that go beyond the assessment of learning outcomes. Drawing on ideas and methods of the social sciences and the humanities, it favors interviews, case studies, and observations of educational milieus. It requires not only extensive knowledge of subjects and schools in addition to observational skills, but also literary finesse in reporting observations. Because acquiring and refining such knowledge and skill takes years of practice, qualitative evaluation is no task for novices.

One of the surprising developments in qualitative theory—surprising in both the model presented and the favorable reaction accorded it—is its increasing use of aesthetic criteria. For example, learning has been said to be structurally equivalent to aesthetic experience, teaching similar to acting, and educational criticism analogous in important respects to aesthetic connoisseurship and art criticism. These perspectives have yielded some interesting observations, but at least one model, the connoisseurship model of educational criticism, has, I think, been elaborated beyond reasonable bounds, with some correspondingly questionable consequences.

As I have suggested, educational criticism at its best is the result of mature experience and good judgment of the sort, for example, that informs Theodore Sizer's *Horace's Compromise*.[31] Yet educational criticism runs the risk of becoming too self-consciously artistic. For example, Sarah Lawrence Lightfoot's *The Good High School* features "portraits" of character and culture in which her literary skills tend to divert attention from the educational phenomena being portrayed.[32] This example, as I see it, provides a key to a fundamental problem in the connoisseurship model of educational criticism. Their denials notwithstanding, proponents of this model have in effect transformed teaching, learning, and schooling into artistic performances and venues in order to justify the relevance of the concepts of connoisseurship and the principles and techniques of art criticism. What is more, when, as is being done, these aesthetic stances toward educational phenomena are combined with the techniques of the humanistic social sciences, particularly with the thick descriptions used by anthropologists, the connoisseurship model becomes too complex and unwieldy.

That Elliot Eisner's connoisseurship model has been well received in certain educational quarters must be acknowledged, but the possibility must also be entertained that its acceptance has more to do with unhappiness with standardized testing as a significant measure of learning than with the substance of the model. Doubts, for example, have been expressed about Donald Arnstine's equating learning with aesthetic experience. Working from a well-developed concept of aesthetic experience, Monroe Beardsley writes in discussing Arnstine that "the best educational experiences will seldom, if ever, be the best aesthetic experiences. And, of course, vice versa."[33] And the notion that teacher education can be likened to the training of actors was questioned by several writers who have examined the assumption.[34]

In truth, the topic of the relations between aesthetics and general educational theory deserves little more than an occasional essay or commentary, or, at most, a collection of speculative essays.[35] It would also help if, as Beardsley has pointed out, writers did not confuse whatever aesthetic decorative dimensions schooling may have with structural equivalencies between aesthetic and educational activities. Finally, there is the all-too-common error of calling things by their wrong names. *Connoisseurship* is simply a misnomer for the tasks described by the model. Such analogizing to the aesthetic realm is yet another symptom of what Barzun terms the Art Era and its tendency to see too many things under the aspect of art.

Undoubtedly there are philosophical problems associated with educational evaluation. But to repeat, the task for educational theory is fruitful conceptualization and analysis. Obviously, not all meaning and significance relevant to assessment can be captured in numbers. But that does not imply that educational criticism should be modeled along the lines of art criticism. Matthew Arnold, the quintessential school inspector of the nineteenth century, intuitively understood this. As Richard Hoggart points out, his reports on schools were literal, straightforward, and unvarnished.[36] His literary talents were reserved for his letters, poetry, and cultural criticism. Although the terms of the dichotomy may not be inherently contradictory, the idea of qualitative evaluation raises issues that need further scrutiny.

The problems I have discussed are not likely to go away. Some of them are distinctively philosophical in the sense that they concern issues arising in efforts to define art. Such questions require careful analyses of concepts to clear up as much confusion as possible, for example, the ambiguities inherent in the notions of instrumental and noninstrumental value and quantitative and qualitative evaluation. Still other problems require separating distinctively philosophical questions from social and political issues. This involves doing philosophy in its more ordinary sense of critical reasoning and thinking. Some problems are enduring, while others are more typical of specific periods. In certain instances the dichotomies in question can be collapsed and in Deweyan fashion their terms integrated into a new formulation. In other instances the dichotomies are irreconcilable. Given the complexity of some of the issues, I have been able to do little more than set an agenda for further work.

NOTES

1. Morris Weitz, "The Role of Theory in Aesthetics," in Joseph Margolis, 3rd ed. *Philosophy Looks at the Arts* (Philadelphia: Temple University Press, 1987).

2. For a discussion of the similarities between the logic of the concept of *art* and the logic of the concept of *education*, see Israel Scheffler, *The Language of Education* (Springfield, Ill: Charles C. Thomas, 1961), 31.

3. A similar observation has been made by Anita Silvers in "The Story of Art Is the Story of the Test of Time," *Journal of Aesthetics and Art Criticism* 49, no. 3 (1991): 211–24.

4. The aesthetic theories of Monroe Beardsley and Nelson Goodman feature the functions of art while those of George and Arthur Danto stress institutional and contextual considerations.

5. Stephen Davis, *Definitions of Art* (Ithaca: Cornell University Press, 1991). Cf. Ralph A. Smith, ed., *Aesthetics and Criticism in Art Education: Problems in Defining, Explaining, and Evaluating Art* (Chicago: Rand McNally, 1966).

6. Howard Gardner, "Toward More Effective Arts Education," *Journal of Aesthetic Education* 22, no. 1 (1988): 163–64.

7. Howard Gardner, *Art Education and Human Development* (Los Angeles: Getty Center for Education in the Arts, 1990).

8. Albert William Levi and Ralph A. Smith, *Art Education: A Critical Necessity* (Urbana; University of Illinois Press, 1991). This is the first volume in the five-volume Getty-supported series Disciplines in Art Education: Contexts of Understanding.

9. See the introduction to Alexander Sesonske, ed., *What Is Art?* (New York: Oxford University Press, 1965).

10. See, e.g., Elliot W. Eisner, *Educating Artistic Vision* (New York: Macmillan, 1972); Edmund B. Feldman, *Becoming Human Through Art* (Englewood Cliffs, N.J.: Prentice Hall, 1970); Laura Chapman, *Approaches to Art Education* (New York: Harcourt Brace Jovanovich, 1982); and Ralph A. Smith, *The Sense of Art: A Study in Aesthetic Education* (New York: Routledge, 1989).

11. See, e.g., John Michael, "Studio Experience: The Heart of Art Education," *Art Education* 33, no. 2 (1980): 15–19; and Larry Schultz, "A Studio Curriculum for Art Education, *Art Education* 33, no 6 (1980): 10–15.

12. See Monroe C. Beardsley, *Aesthetics: Problems in the Philosophy of Criticism*, 2nd ed. (Indianapolis: Hackett, 1981), 573–76.

13. Arts, Education, and Americans Panel, *Coming to Our Senses: The Place of Art in American Schools* (New York: McGraw-1977).

14. Samuel Lipman, "The NEA: Looking Back and Looking Ahead," *The New Criterion* 71, no. 1 (1988): 6–13.

15. National Endowment for the Arts, *Towards Civilization: A Report on Arts Education* (Washington: D.C.: National Endowment for the Arts, 1988).

16. See Ralph A. Smith, ed., *Discipline-Based Art Education: Origins, Meaning, Development* (Urbana: University of Illinois Press, 1989).

17. Stuart Hampshire, "Private Pleasures and the Public Purse, "*Times Literary Supplement*, 13 May 1977, 579. Cf. Ralph A. Smith, *Excellence in Art Education: Ideas and Initiatives* (Reston, Va: National Art Education Association, 1981), chap. 4.

18. I borrow the phase from Arthur Danto, *The Transfiguration of the Commonplace* (Cambridge: Harvard University Press, 1981).

19. Harold Osborne, "Assessment and Stature," *British Journal of Aesthetics* 24, no. 1 (1984): 3–13.

20. Diane Ravitch, "Multiculturalism in the Curriculum," *Network News and Views* 9 (March 1990): 1–11; "Multiculturalism: E Pluribus Plures," *The American Scholar* 59 (Summer 1990): 337–54; "Multiculturalism: An Exchange 60 (1991): 272–76.

21. Arthur Schlesinger Jr., *The Disuniting of America: Reflections on a Multicultural Society* (Knoxville, Tenn: Whittle Books, 1991).

22. Mary Ann Raywid, "Pluralism as a Basis for Educational Policy," in *Educational Policy*, ed. J. F. Weaver (Danville, Ill: Interstate, 1975), 87–89.

23. John Wilson, "Art, Culture, and Identity," *Journal of Aesthetic Education* 18, no. 2 (1984): 89–97.

24. Jacques Barzun, *The Use and Abuse of Art* (Princeton: Princeton University Press, 1974).

25. Ihab Hassan, *The Postmodern Turn* (Columbus: Ohio State University Press, 1987).

26. Jacques Maquet, "Perennial Modernity: Forms as Aesthetic and Symbolic," *Journal of Aesthetic Education* 24, no. 4 (1990): 47–58.

27. Roger Fowler, ed., *A Dictionary of Modern Critical Terms*, rev. ed. (New York: Routledge and Kegan Paul, 1987), 151.

28. Hilton Kramer, *The Age of the Avant-Garde* (New York: Farrar, Straus and Giroux, 1973).

29. Charles Jencks, *Post-modernism: The New Classicism in Art and Architecture* (New York: Rizzoli, 1987).

30. M. J. Wilsmore, "Against Deconstructing Rationality in Education," *Journal of Aesthetic Education* 25, no. 4 (1991): 99–113.

31. Theodore Sizer, *Horace's Compromise: The Dilemma of the American High School* (Boston: Houghton Mifflin, 1984).

32. Sarah Lawrence Lightfoot, *The Good High School: Portraits of Character and Culture* (New York: Basic Books, 1983).

33. Monroe C. Beardsley, "Aesthetic Theory and Educational Theory," in Ralph A. Smith, ed. *Aesthetic Concepts and Education* (Urbana: University of Illinois Press, 1970), 3–20.

34. Ayers Bagley, ed., *Teacher Education as Actor Training*. Paper prepared for the annual conference of the Society of Professors of Education, University of Minnesota College of Education, 1974.

35. See Ralph A. Smith, ed., *Aesthetic Concepts and Education* (Urbana: University of Illinois Press, 1970).

36. Richard Hoggart, *An English Temper* (New York: Oxford University Press, 1982), 87.

The Artworld and Art Education

Concepts, Concept Learning, and Art Education

THE CYCLICAL nature of trends in educational thinking makes the present moment conducive for renewed emphasis on teaching concepts. Those who have been observing educational tendencies have probably noticed similarities between certain aspects of the contemporary scene and the brief period in the early 1960s when Jerome Bruner's little book, *The Process of Education*, set educators to thinking about cognitive development and teaching basic principles and concepts.[1] I recall the time well. I was just beginning to teach art history and was stimulated to ask what might be meant by teaching its basic concepts and ideas. It was not long before I became steeped in the philosophy of art history and quickly discovered that art history is a function of historians' working assumptions and methodological principles. Walter Abell's discussion of the critical traditions of art history and the attributes of art and causal factors associated with each tradition did much to clarify matters for me, as did the general philosophical preoccupation at the time with the concept of explanation.[2] By the mid-1960s, however, the educational climate had changed. So-called affective, open, informal, or alternative education was upstaging more cognitive approaches to learning. It was not, of course, an exclusive trend, for the discussion of cognitive processes continued to be carried on in learned books and journals. The wheel has continued to turn, and it is now basic education that is preoccupying policy makers and educators. The present emphasis on the basics echoes the early 1960s primarily in its demand for accountability and a semblance of orderliness. The basics of today, however, do not feature the basic concepts and structures of disciplines so much as certain foundational skills involved in reading, writing, and mathematics. The accent on minimal competency explains why the rhetoric of excellence of the earlier period has not been revived. One hears that even the Council for Basic Education is not altogether happy with the back-to-basics movement. Still, everything considered, there is probably less resistance to the notion of concept learning today than there has been in some time.

THE CONCEPT OF CONCEPT

Any effort to address the role of concepts in art education must clarify what the term *concept* means. Unfortunately, there is no generally accepted definition. In *The Opening Mind*, Morris Weitz writes that "concepts have been construed as universals, definitions, innate ideas, images, thoughts, conceptions, meanings, predicates and relations, abstract objects, abstracted items, extracted common features, neutral entities, and as habits, skills, or mental capacities."[3] He concludes that the concept of *concept* is in truth a family of concepts. This situation dictates caution by anyone entertaining ideas about concept learning in art education, but it also permits some latitude. For example, one need not adopt the entire family but only those of its members that are relevant to one's purpose.

The preference here is for the last three meanings mentioned by Weitz, namely, habits, skills, and mental capacities, a choice influenced by an interest in how individuals acquire and use concepts. What is more, the appropriate use of a concept can be regarded as the best evidence of a person's having learned that concept, which is a significant point pedagogically. As far as having a concept is concerned, P. L. Heath writes that

> to have a concept "x" is (with some exceptions) . . . (a) to know the meaning of the word 'x'; (b) to be able to pick out or recognize a presented x (distinguish non-x's, etc.), or again to be able to think of (have images or ideas of) x (or x's) when they are not present; (c) to know the nature of x, to have grasped or apprehended the properties (universals, essences, etc.) which characterize x's and make them what they are.[4]

"To be able to pick out" or "to have grasped or apprehended" are capacities that may also be construed as skills. And skills, in contrast to some capacities and abilities that may be innate, are amenable to instruction. All this is to say that the development of a pedagogically promising concept of *concept* should be one that permits defining concepts in terms of skills.

So much for suggestions regarding how concepts might be understood. The question that concerns us here is, What place do notions of having concepts, of concepts-in-use, and of concepts-as-skills have in art education?

CONCEPTS IN ART EDUCATION

It is difficult to support the contention that concepts play an important role in art education without having a vision of the field. I hold steadily in mind as the overarching purpose of art instruction the effort to develop in students a capacity for reflective percipience in matters of art and culture. In other words, the desired outcome of art and aesthetic education is a trained perceptual capacity that prompts questions regarding the relation of concepts and aesthetic perception. How, for example, do concepts function in aesthetic situations?

Although it will be maintained that concepts function in the aesthetic situation in a distinctive manner, they arise in much the same way as they enter any other experience; they constitute filters that make perception possible. For what persons are able to perceive depends largely on the concepts they have, which is to say, on the distillations from past experiences that compose what is often termed their *apperceptive mass*. In order for aesthetic experience to be as rich as possible, a person's general background of knowledge must contain concepts specific to aesthetic contexts. The concept of a work of art will serve as an illustration. Unless students have some concept of a work of art, it is unlikely that their response to works of art will be as appropriate as that of one who has such concepts. The point of having the concept, as John Wilson has indicated, is that "the pupil has something to cling onto; he has the concept of a work of art, and he can know what sort of thing to do with cases which he has not met before."[5]

Here we discover once again the equation of having a concept with the ability to use it. Thus if we were to insert the expression *work of art* into the formula provided by Heath for having concepts, we would conclude that for a student to have the concept that *work of art* implies, in addition to knowing the meaning of the term, the ability to grasp or apprehend, if not necessarily the "universals" or "essences" of art, at least relevant properties, namely those elements, complexes, relationships, qualities, and meanings that constitute works of art. In order to do this, students must have learned the concepts that refer to an artwork's manifold of properties. And it would also be worthwhile if students knew not only how to perceive an artwork's manifold of properties but also how to describe, analyze, interpret, characterize, and assess them, in which case the critical concepts pertaining to these activities would also have to be acquired. Possessing a number of aesthetic and critical concepts and knowing how to use them properly represents an accomplishment that should qualify as the possession of perceptual/critical skills. Add to that what should be obvious. Because skills are actualized in performance, the teacher wishing to assess a student's aesthetic progress would be ill-advised merely to ask for definitions of aesthetic concepts.

To summarize: a major objective of art education is the acquisition of the capacity for reflective percipience, which I understand to be the capacity for the aesthetic appreciation of works of art. Because aesthetic perception of any complexity is guided by and depends on aesthetic and critical concepts, developing percipience involves teaching aesthetic/critical skills.

Although there may be nothing uncommon in the way concepts enter the aesthetic situation (as background and guide for perception), their function within aesthetic experience is distinctive. This function is the result of the kind of interest that governs aesthetic experience. In ordinary experience, concepts and perceptions characteristically subserve some utilitarian or intellectual interest. John Dewey marked the difference between aesthetic and nonaesthetic experience with the notion of residue. Cognitive experiences leave a residue in the form of knowledge and concepts that become useful either immediately in present experience or in some future experience. Aesthetic experience, by contrast, is less future oriented; it exhausts itself in the here and now and is sought for the sake of immediately enjoyed perceptions.[6] The notion of enjoyed perceptions is important, for the refined, sensitive perception of the properties of artworks that becomes possible for persons with the requisite aesthetic skills is experienced as highly gratifying. This gratification is often referred to as the *experience of aesthetic value*, or as *aesthetic value realized in experience*. This should help us understand the difference between the function of concepts in ordinary and in aesthetic situations. In such situations, concepts are instrumental to intellectual or practical ends; in aesthetic situations, concepts are instrumental to a value experience.

This difference highlights the essence of my view of art and aesthetic education. Other positions in art education may stress other aspects. For example, a strong cognitive claim is frequently made for the arts. The belief is that the arts can provide students with unique knowledge and understanding about themselves and the world in which they live. I admit that my hospitality to concepts in art education may make it seem surprising that I do not recommend this approach. My reasons are not based solely on the epistemological problems involved in assigning cognitive status to works of art. Even if one is willing to concede that some works of art may convey knowledge in some sense, one would still not have identified a property distinctive of art. The unique feature of works of art and other aesthetically worthwhile things are that they reward careful, skillful attention and provide a special gratification that ranks high among life's values. This is what art, irrespective of other functions and artists' intentions, does best, and what art can do best should be the principal concern of art education.

Some reinforcement for a number of the points I have made may be found in *Experience and the Growth of Understanding*, by the British philosopher D. W. Hamlyn. Toward the end of his discussion Hamlyn says that his analysis of cognitive development might be misconstrued as insisting that fresh knowledge and understanding can only be acquired in certain ways. He mentions aesthetic appreciation as a counterexample. Although it may involve understanding, knowledge, and know-how, it does not aim to *understand* the object as such. It may simply be a matter of seeing things that were not noticed before. This can often be achieved by taking up the right point of view, by attending to the right features of objects, or by seeing something under the right concept. Hamlyn concludes that "an ability to see something in a certain way [is] . . . a form of skill and can accordingly be acquired through learning."[7]

Acquired in what way? Having set forth the relationships between aesthetic concepts, aesthetic/critical skills, aesthetic appreciation, and aesthetic gratification, I now turn to the problem of how aesthetic and critical concepts are learned and how consequently they may be taught.

MEANINGFUL LEARNING: A THEORY
OF CONCEPT ACQUISITION

The idea of meaningful learning was originally presented in David Ausubel's *Educational Psychology: A Cognitive View*.[8] Published in the late 1960s, when so-called affective education held sway, the book's argument went relatively unnoticed. It did catch my attention, however, especially Ausubel's sensible remarks on motivation and his recommendation that educators might do well to eliminate the inherently ambiguous term *affective* from their vocabulary. Later, I was also attracted to Joseph D. Novak's *A Theory of Education*, in which Novak presents a theory that discusses the relevance to education of Thomas Kuhn's and Stephen Toulmin's recent work in epistemology and philosophy of science and Ausubel's theory of meaningful learning.[9]

In *The Structure of Scientific Revolutions* Kuhn centers his discussion on paradigms, paradigm shifts, normal and revolutionary science, and related topics.[10] In *Human Understanding* Toulmin derives a theory of human understanding from an evolutionary model.[11] The model is an attempt to explain the evolution of human understanding through examinination not just of the historical growth of thought within intellectual populations and their characteristic concepts and procedures but also of the ways in which concepts and procedures change and the various factors that influence such change. What Novak took from Kuhn and Toulmin was the way in which paradigms guide and control collective intellectual activity, how they emerge, evolve, and then, gradually or suddenly, are replaced by new paradigms. Novak noticed an analogy between scientific paradigms that guide scientific inquiry and the evolution of and change in conceptual frameworks in individuals described in Ausubel's theory of meaningful learning. That theory was, in fact, to become the major consideration of Novak's book. A brief summary follows, although it is developed further, with some slight changes in emphasis and language, in the second edition of Ausubel's *Educational Psychology*, coauthored by Ausubel, Novak, and Hanesian.[12]

Following Ausubel, Novak's theory relies on a theoretical construct termed a *conceptual framework, cognitive structure, or conceptual hierarchy*. Being a construct, such a framework has less to do with brain physiology than with a heuristic device that lets us understand and guide concept acquisition. It does, however, make assumptions about unobservable interior processes that puts the theory in opposition to certain behaviorist premises. In Novak's view, the individual is assumed to possess a cognitive structure consisting of hierarchically ordered concepts that are a person's representations of sensory experience. Although it is difficult to gain a precise image of such a framework, it is nonetheless possible to ask how it develops, how concepts are acquired, and whence their origin.

A person's cognitive framework is said to grow through the process of meaningful learning during which new information is related to a relevant concept already present in cognitive structure. In other words, new information, when learned meaningfully, is assimilated; and in the second edition of Ausubel's work the preference is for the phrase *assimilation of learning*. Since assimilation occurs when a new item is ordered to, or subsumed under, a relevant concept within cognitive structure, that concept is termed a *subsuming concept* or a *subsumer*. Subsumers are those concepts in a person's cognitive framework that have the capacity to assimilate new items; they represent the framework's potential for cumulative growth and expansion, which is one aspect of an evolutionary nature of cognitive structure that should make it attractive to educators.

Evolution, however, is not merely a matter of amassing concepts. Assimilation is an interactive process during which mutual modification takes place between the new and the old. When a new concept is assimilated by a subsumer, the subsumer itself undergoes some change; for example, it may become more differentiated in terms of detail and specificity. The subsumer, in other words, improves its capacity for still further assimilation of information. Simultaneous with the acquisition of new knowledge, adjustments and realignments occur within stored information. The continual refinement of the conceptual structure has two noteworthy effects. First, because of the subtle modifications of the old by the new, items learned meaningfully are seldom retrieved precisely in the form in which they had been learned. Second, with progressive differentiation, new linkages are frequently established between the subsumers themselves. A previously learned concept may be recognized as an element of a larger, more inclusive concept and thus achieve a new potency. This sort of learning, which does not depend as much on the assimilation of new information as on recognizing new connections between items already known, is termed *superordinate learning*.

Skipping many details, the important point is that through meaningful or assimilation learning, students not only acquire new information but, because of the concurrent development of their conceptual frameworks, also increase their capacity for further learning. This contrasts to rote learning, in which new information tends to be stored in cognitive structure in an arbitrary, unrelated fashion. Items learned by rote, however, do not in large part contribute to the framework's evolution and, lacking firm anchorage, tend to be quickly forgotten.

But what is the origin of the concepts that get assimilated in meaningful learning? They can be generated by learners themselves through concept formation, a learning style characteristic of early childhood (though not confined to it) in which young children develop their concepts by testing hypotheses and generalizing from specific instances, although one assumes that this is not done in a highly self-conscious or rigorous sense. In assigning concept formation largely to the earlier years of childhood, Novak and Ausubel differ from the curriculum theorists of the 1960s who tended to follow Bruner in emphasizing the learning of basic ideas and concepts via inquiry and discovery methods. In contrast, the theory of meaningful learning points out the potential wastefulness of time inherent in the exclusive use of the discovery method. Learning is not made meaningful simply because students discover concepts by themselves. Meaningfulness depends on how firmly a new concept gets anchored into cognitive structure and on the differentiation and superordinate learning it helps facilitate once assimilated. The point is that the theory of meaningful learning assumes that by school age, children possess a sufficient number of subsumers to commence reception learning.

Reception learning is another name for meaningful learning and concept assimilation. This is not, however, to say there is anything passive about it, as the participation and attention of learners are essential. Teachers, moreover, are challenged by the fact that a person's cognitive framework is not mental flypaper to which concepts simply adhere or a magnet that attracts any concept in its vicinity. This circumstance poses at least three separate tasks for teachers. First, since meaningful learning occurs only in the presence of relevant subsumers within the learner's cognitive structure, teachers have to make special efforts to ascertain what subsumers learners already possess. Second, because new information has little chance of being learned meaningfully when it is presented thoughtlessly or haphazardly, teachers must organize it in such a way as to make learning more likely. In the terminology of meaningful learning theory, teachers should attempt to build cognitive bridges between new information and old by means of advance organizers. Such organizers are the more general and inclusive concepts of a discipline or subject and serve as a bridge to more detailed understanding. Teachers therefore must identify those concepts of a subject or discipline that promise to be effective advance organizers while also being suited to the subsumers already present in the cognitive structures of students. A third task for teachers consists of facilitating superordinate learning, that is, helping students become aware of new connections and relations between things they already know. The successful application of the theory of meaningful learning to the practice of art education depends, of course, on well-trained, skillful teachers, but the merits of assimilation learning make it well worth the extra effort.

MERITS OF THE THEORY

The theory of concept acquisition deserves attention because it does justice to both the structure of a subject (advance organizers and the hierarchy of general to lower-order concepts) and the cognitive structure of students (their evolving cognitive frameworks). Emphasis on structure, however, should not obscure the appreciation of contextual variety and flexibility that the theory permits. Although it emphasizes active reception learning, the theory is, within limits and in appropriate contexts, compatible with other learning and teaching styles. The importance of concept formation in early childhood acknowledges the continued significance of constructive activities in preschool and the lower grades. It is at these levels that a modest number of basic aesthetic and critical concepts can be formed, that is, generalized and abstracted during the students' manipulation of materials. Without a small stock of these subsumers it would be very difficult, if not impossible, to commence formal instruction in the use of aesthetic and critical concepts later on. Freedom, spontaneity, and discovery thus play a part in superordinate learning. Although teachers must make certain that students apprehend increasing numbers of linkages between subsumers already in their cognitive structures, and may often help by pointing them out, much of superordinate learning probably occurs in the form of sudden insights.

Meaningful learning theory has the additional advantage of coping with the problem of understanding how what has been learned gets used. Popular opinion has it that formal schooling is a waste of time when people forget or do not use the knowledge and skills they had learned in school. These complaints can be countered by adding meaningful forgetting to meaningful learning. Meaningful learning, it will be recalled, is a fairly good hedge against forgetting. But even items once learned meaningfully are not retrievable indefinitely. Yet while they may be lost to memory they are not completely obliterated. Recall that an item learned meaningfully modifies a subsumer by expanding its capacity for further assimilation and that it also changes slightly the nature of stored information. These modifications appear to be quite permanent. Even when a certain concept drops out at the lower end of the framework the differentiations it helped bring about still remain. To put it more simply: because in assimilation learning the acquisition of new information also expands the capacity of the cognitive structure for more learning, that expanded capacity tends to persist even after particular items are forgotten. Therefore, the person who once learned aesthetic concepts meaningfully but can no longer recall many of them is not in the same position as the person who never learned any such concepts in the first place. Similarly, we do not expect students to go through life engaging artworks in precisely the fashion they practiced during their art and aesthetic education studies, that is, through the methodical application of critical skills and discourse using aesthetic concepts. What we do expect is that students will have acquired the richly differentiated cognitive structure necessary for gratifying aesthetic appreciation.

Another merit of the theory of meaningful learning lies in its ability to serve as a unifying matrix for research in art education. When grounded in a comprehensive learning theory, research ceases to explore discrete, unrelated problems and instead examines what must be known in order to transform learning theory into a practicable classroom approach.

SUGGESTIONS FOR RESEARCH

It should be recalled that the theory of meaningful learning was formulated with the problems of teaching the natural and social sciences in mind, but Novak thinks it is appropriate for certain aspects of humanities education as well. We are nonetheless justified in being skeptical of this belief until we examine just how well the model is suitable for art and aesthetic education. There is also the crucial matter of ascertaining the concepts (subsumers) that students already possess and the methodology for doing this. Reliable generalizations about different student populations would further be welcome, and some recent work in aesthetic development may be providing some of the answers. Such studies may be interpreted as saying that at certain ages children tend either not to possess or are unable to use properly certain fairly basic aesthetic concepts.[13] In terms of assimilation theory, this suggests that the formal teaching of critical and aesthetic concepts should probably be deferred until a reasonable number of relevant subsumers have become available in the cognitive structures of learners.

Much work would also be needed in the mastery of aesthetic concepts. Especially important to understand are those that are distinctive of individual art forms, those that cut across the arts, and those that best serve as advance organizers. Also important is determining the degree of mastery sought. The research problem is thus not confined to deciding which concepts are suitable for different stages of aesthetic development; researchers must also keep in mind the levels of mastery that can reasonably be expected at various stages. The notion of degrees of mastery, moreover, is consonant with the conception of an evolving cognitive structure. A low degree of mastery, for example, a relatively crude and inflexible use of an aesthetic concept, suggests a poorly differentiated cognitive framework.

Finally, clues to possible research projects can also be found in art history and art criticism. We know that persons who possess traditional observational concepts, that is, the aesthetic and critical concepts stored in cognitive structure, have less difficulty in perceiving new phenomena in art.[14] Faced with the problem of introducing students to new and different styles, we might ask how this can be done. In this connection we might do well to study writers who have in fact helped bring about shifts in public taste and appreciative capacity. How did Heinrich Woefflin teach us to see the differences between Renaissance and Baroque styles, or Roger Fry, Meyer Schapiro, Harold Rosenberg, Sidney Greenberg, and Leo Steinberg the character of modern and postmodern art?

Some technical understanding of cognitive structure and concept formation notwithstanding, there should not be insuperable difficulties in developing meaningful learning in art education. Certainly there is nothing to fear from it, and under certain definitions it is quite compatible with traditional purposes of art education. Moreover, since texts in art education take some notion of concept learning for granted, the notion of concept learning is really not novel.[15] The purpose of recommending concept learning as a topic for research in art education has been to suggest a theory, or variations of a theory, that could help to unify thinking and research in the field.

NOTES

1. Jerome Bruner, *The Process of Education* (Cambridge: Harvard University Press, 1960).

2. See, for example, Ralph A. Smith, ed., *Aesthetics and Criticism in Art Education: Problems in Describing, Explaining, and Evaluating Art* (Chicago: Rand McNally, 1966), esp. Part 3.

3. Morris Weitz, *The Opening Mind* (Chicago: University of Chicago Press, 1977), 25.

4. P. L. Heath, "Concept," in the *Encyclopedia of Philosophy*, vol. 11, ed. Paul Edwards (New York: Macmillan, 1967), 177.

5. John Wilson, "Education and Aesthetic Appreciation: A Review," *Oxford Review of Education* 3 (1977): 202.

6. John Dewey, *Art as Experience* (New York: Minton, Balch, 1934), 55.

7. David W. Hamlyn, *Experience and the Growth of Understanding* (London: Routledge and Kegan Paul, 1978), 122.

8. David P. Ausubel, *Educational Psychology: A Cognitive View* (New York: Holt, Rinehart & Winston, 1968).

9. Joseph D. Novak, *A Theory of Education* (Ithaca: Cornell University Press, 1977).

10. Thomas H. Kuhn. *The Structure of Scientific Revolutions* (Chicago: University of Chicago Press, 1962).

11. Stephen Toulmin, *Human Understanding*, vol. 1, (Princeton: Princeton University Press, 1972).

12. David P. Ausubel, Joseph D. Novak, and Helen Hanesian, *Educational Psychology: A Cognitive View*, 2nd ed. (New York: Holt, Rinehart and Winston, 1978).

13. See Michael Parsons, Marilyn Johnston, and Robert Durham, "Developmental Stages in Children's Aesthetic Responses," *Journal of Aesthetic Education* 12, no. 1 (1978): 83–104.

14 For suggestions about the uses of metaphor in teaching new observational categories, see Hugh G. Petrie "Do You See What I See? The Epistemology of Interdisciplinary Inquiry," *Journal of Aesthetic Education* 10, no. 1 (1978): 30–43.

15 See the section on curriculum in Ralph A. Smith, ed., *Aesthetics and Problems of Education* (Urbana: University of Illinois Press, 1971).

The Artworld and Aesthetic Skills:
A Context for Research and Development

A NY EFFORT to set an agenda for research and development in aesthetic education must rest on a conception of the enterprise in question. Accordingly, this discussion presents a direction for aesthetic education that (a) is defensible educationally speaking and (b) takes into account the larger context of aesthetic instruction. That context is the cultural life of the nation, or to borrow a term from contemporary aesthetic discourse, the artworld.[1] Such a project entails taking a careful look at some current realities in both the artworld and education.

THE ARTWORLD AND POLICY CONSIDERATIONS

It will be useful to think of the artworld under two aspects: the abstract and the concrete. Abstractly, the artworld is one of the domains of value—of aesthetic value, to be precise. What follows proceeds on the unargued assumption that the aesthetic domain is intrinsically worthwhile and ranks high in the hierarchy of values (though one should be on guard against the overzealous who tout the aesthetic as a panacea for all educational and social ills).

Concretely, the artworld can be identified as a sector of society. As such it has a number of components, some of which are clearly established within its territory, while others spring up along its flexible boundaries. These constituent parts can be conveniently categorized as artists, artworks, audiences (or the art public), and what has been called *aesthetic auxiliaries*.[2] Only the last item requires some explanation. Aesthetic auxiliaries are the personnel, including volunteer workers, of what is variously known as the cultural establishment, the cultural complex, or the cultural-services field. This, in turn, is composed of all the institutions, departments, councils, committees, foundations, and the like that in some way or other serve the arts, as well as museums and galleries; theatrical, opera, and ballet companies; conservatories; arts academies; colleges of art; and a host of others.

Whether this congeries can be directed by a general policy, and whether national guidelines are even desirable in a society such as ours, are questions the discussion will not address. But while there is no overall policy for the artworld, there are more than enough policies within it that are reflected in the programs, statements of objectives, declarations of purposes, and directives of the various institutions. Critical observers of this vast complex have concluded that such policies are often ill-conceived individually, at cross-purposes collectively, and generally devoid of theory.[3]

It would be futile to try to frame a philosophical justification for what is being done in the artworld as it is presently constituted. Yet it should, in principle, be possible to achieve a minimal consensus among those in the artworld who are principally responsible for shaping policy. This agreement is conceivable because it involves no loss of independence of action, commits no one to anything not already being done, and has a generally ennobling effect; but, most important, it would provide a conceptual handle on the artworld. It goes something like this: All members of the artworld, in their many different ways, ultimately contribute to the preservation and enhancement of aesthetic value and hence to the promotion of the aesthetic well-being of society. Some of the terms introduced need further explanation.

Beginning with *aesthetic value*, it will not do to leave the vague impression that aesthetic value resides just anywhere in the artworld or is diffused generally throughout it. What is wanted is a firm grasp of what aesthetic value is and how each component of the artworld (artists, artworks, audiences, aesthetic auxiliaries) is related to it. Artists, of course, create the very basis for aesthetic value because works of art are the principal loci of aesthetic value. But it must be understood that aesthetic value belongs to artworks only as potentiality that awaits actualization in human experience. Aesthetic value, then, is best thought of as a property of an object as well as a quality of the appreciating subject's experience. This view of aesthetic value is not without ramifications, of which three are mentioned: (1) In practical terms it can help deliberations on how best to manage *aesthetic wealth*, for artworks locked away in vaults and private collections and poorly attended performances represent so much unrealized value potential.[4] (2) In theoretical terms, a conception of aesthetic value as both potential and real may qualify as a simplified version of the capacity definition of aesthetic value,[5] according to which the aesthetic value of an object is estimated by its capacity for engendering and sustaining aesthetic experiences of appreciable magnitude. (3) In societal terms, aesthetic value as herein defined both explains and justifies *aesthetic well-being* as a worthy policy objective. That is, society can have no more legitimate aim for its policies than improving the quality of experience of its members. If aesthetic value is actualized in each instance in which the experience of a percipient and members of society have numerous occasions for experiencing high levels of aesthetic value, then a general state of aesthetic well-being prevails.[6] Consequently "aesthetic well-being" as quality of experience is a defensible objective.

A necessary task is an examination of the relationship to aesthetic value maintained by the constituents of the artworld and also to aesthetic well-being. Artists and artworks have been considered; they furnish the fundamental *conditions* for aesthetic well-being, but seldom more. For in a large and complex society, artists usually have to rely on others to bring artworks and the art public together. It is up to the cultural-services field to create aesthetic *opportunities,* that is, occasions for aesthetic experiences. This is difficult and, because it contributes to aesthetic value, it is also a worthy objective that allows members of the cultural establishment to retain a vestigial dignity throughout all the frenzied marketing, managing, collecting, and exhibiting activities that lend the artworld its appearance of a thriving, even booming, enterprise.

We have talked about conditions and opportunities for aesthetic well-being; what about its reality? Artists, artworks, and aesthetic auxiliaries have been discussed; what remains for audiences? Theoretically, as was already pointed out, audiences attending to works of art are actualizing aesthetic value in experience. In practice, however, it is questionable that very much of this is happening, and this despite gratifying statistical increases in the numbers of persons observed at cultural events. A careful look at current realities advocated at the outset encompasses the state of the art public. When this is done, some disturbing phenomena might be noticed. That persons are eager for art and expect something special from it is plain. Yet the art public is often bewildered, bemused, seldom critical, and rarely outraged. The art public can thus be characterized as strangely docile in its acceptance of just about everything done in the name of art—or in the name of anti-art for that matter. This bespeaks an inability to cope with aesthetic phenomena, an incapacity for aesthetic judgment, and perhaps an indifference to what art is or should be. In short, what one finds today is a large and eager audience for the arts, but not a *discerning* public. But such a public is required to bring about a satisfactory level of aesthetic well-being. Shakespeare's audiences, we are reminded, helped to make Shakespeare great.

Two things should now be clear. First, the aesthetic-value capacity of an art object must be matched by the percipient's ability to actualize it. Aesthetic well-being is not assured by ushering large numbers of people into the presence of artworks. If persons are not properly prepared for the experience, they will derive little benefit from it. This leads to the second point, namely, that the preparation of a discerning public for the arts is a task for aesthetic education in the public schools. No other segment of the artworld itself is really adequate to it. (Museums and arts councils, for example, usually engage in educational activities of some sort or other, but they reach far too few persons for the desired impact.)

To sum up, it was claimed that the entire artworld as well as each of its member institutions receive their ultimate social justification from the role they can play in bringing about a satisfactory degree of aesthetic well-being. However, since their contributions to aesthetic well-being depend on the cooperation of a discerning public, they also have a vested interest in solid programs of aesthetic education. Therefore, no matter who frames aesthetic or cultural policy, or for which cultural institution, all such policy makers would do well to take cognizance of and plan support for aesthetic education. If the foregoing be accepted, then a strong societal case exists for aesthetic education.

AESTHETIC EDUCATION AND SOME THEORETICAL CONSIDERATIONS

A societal demand for any kind of education does not always translate smoothly into a good *educational* justification. Although it is generally agreed that public schools should make good citizens of students that prepare them to live in society, the particulars of such a mandate are in dispute. (Citizenship in what kind of society—as it now is, or as it will be when students reach adulthood? In our defective or in a better society? If the latter, according to whose blueprint?) Many thoughtful educators resist the entire notion that whenever society is found to need certain types of persons the schools are automatically charged to produce them forthwith. These educators argue that the schools' first concern should always be with the individual's needs, not with fitting the person, coglike, into some preexistent structure. Happily, this difficulty does not arise here, for in the present argument for aesthetic education, social and personal benefits coincide. True, society needs a discerning public for its artworld, and it gets it from aesthetic education. But the discerning public is composed of individuals capable of participating in the aesthetic realm—a value realm. This means that the members of a discerning art public would have been taught ways of meeting one of the most important needs of each individual— how to enrich life through value experiences.

AESTHETIC APPRECIATION AND SKILLS

Before arguing more directly for the merits of a skills approach to aesthetic education, it may be well to identify possible sources of resistance to it.

First of all, many strongly held convictions about the nature of art and aesthetic experience could be somewhat difficult to accommodate to the notion of skill. There may be concern, for example, that the insertion of skills into the aesthetic situation would significantly alter aesthetic experience by depriving it of immediacy, spontaneity, and pleasure. Yet this would constitute a misunderstanding, for it was never intended to *reduce* aesthetic experience to the drill-like exercises of a skill. Aesthetic experience, once more, is a value experience, and value is ultimately vouchsafed by valuing—that is, by prizing and enjoying on the part of the subject. What was insisted on is that aesthetic gratification differs from the more directly and easily available sensuous pleasures in that it *presupposes* a skill; its full measure is simply unavailable to the untutored. Therefore, while there may be less *immediacy* of response, the delay necessitated by the skillful probing of the aesthetic object will purchase a deeper, more informed response and with it the possibility of greater, more intense gratification.

Second, one has to reckon with the tendency to disparage "mere" skills as the poor attainments of those who cannot hope to master an art or a science.[7] The fact is that there are many sophisticated mental and perceptual skills the expert performance of which demands more from the practitioner than dexterity, rote, and repetition. It is hoped that the skills of aesthetic appreciation will come to be classed among these once their nature is better understood.

But what are the specifically *educational* advantages of regarding aesthetic appreciation as involving a species of skill?

1. Harold Osborne defines a skill as "a cultivated capacity for performance of a sort which involves following a set of rules." But he is also careful to point out that skills depend to some extent on latent knowledge that cannot be completely specified and that practitioners may follow more rules than they are conscious of or could ever make explicit.[8] Hence it can be granted that there may be somewhat more to a skill than can be imparted through instruction, an admission that might mollify those who would condemn any skills emphasis as erring on the side of the mechanical and cut-and-dried. Still, the fundamentals of a skill can, in principle, be taught, and this because there is a set of rules to be followed. Therefore, if the operations involved in appreciative encounters with aesthetic objects can be analyzed into something resembling a set of rules, steps, and procedures, the concept of skill would not be misapplied to aesthetic appreciation and the hope for teachability would not be misplaced. Furthermore, students' and teachers' verbal accounts of the deployment of their perceptual skills in the course of exploring an aesthetic object can certainly qualify as certain kinds of performance. To sum up, the singular advan-

tage of a skills approach to aesthetic appreciation lies in the presumption that systematic instruction is possible.

2. Not only can the skills of aesthetic appreciation be taught; there are also good reasons for believing that they can be taught by methods that would meet the first of the above-mentioned requirements for acceptability, that is, a clear-cut connection between classroom activities and overall objectives. This claim is not being expanded on just now, as the final section of this discussion contains some suggestions for research that should help support it.

3. A skills approach to aesthetic education might further result in improved teacher confidence. Educators who perceive themselves as being engaged in teaching basic skills of any kind generally have a better sense of what they are doing, where they are going, and how students are progressing along the way than those in pursuit of intangibles such as "making students more sensitive and truly human" or "giving students a sense for beauty."

4. It is also worth considering that a larger population may be reached, since the skills of aesthetic appreciation should be capable of being taught to practically anyone with unimpaired sensory equipment. This is not to say that all students will reach the same level of skill, but more of them will probably derive satisfaction and permanent benefit from a program oriented toward appreciative skills than from one geared primarily to fostering talents in the creative and performing arts. To put it differently, a skills approach to aesthetic education may assure a greater measure of carryover into the adult lives of students and will thus make formal schooling more effective for more individuals. Few persons have sufficient artistic gifts to join the artworld as creators or performers, but appreciable numbers can join the art public. This last point, however, needs to be qualified by further reflections.

5. The notion of aesthetic skills is also helpful for clarifying the previously mentioned second requirement for an acceptable method for aesthetic education. It was stated that aesthetic education should abjure educationally suspect means in reaching its goals. This was intended to refer to all those ways of teaching that might make authentic value choices difficult, if not impossible, for the student. Conditioning and indoctrination come readily to mind, but one also wonders about preachment and exhortation, as well as ceaseless propagandizing for art. All this could easily have the effect of inclining persons to attend cultural events because they feel they ought to, rather than from a genuine desire for aesthetic experience. Whether these are perceived as being serious problems depends very much on how teachers interpret their authority. But, serious or trivial, these difficulties cannot arise with a skills approach. Although conditioning may

be difficult to undo, habits hard to shake, and dispositions troublesome to erase, skills can simply be permitted to die from neglect. And this is a choice individuals ought to be free to make. (It is also an option most persons exercise more than once in their lives with respect to skills they find unrewarding to keep up.) Aesthetic education will have done all it should attempt to do for students when students can demonstrate acquaintance with the aesthetic domain and facility in aesthetic skills; when, in other words, students know where to look for aesthetic value and how to realize it. It is strictly an individual decision whether or not, in later adult life, time is spent in aesthetic pursuits. Chances are, though, a decision favoring aesthetic experiences will be made. A program to endow students with the skills of aesthetic appreciation can be expected to recruit new members for the art public simply because it helps remove the greatest barrier between persons and artworks: the feeling of inadequacy, incompetence, or embarrassed ignorance about art.

Basic questions for educational policy are not only whether aesthetic education can be justified in terms of the needs of individual students or what its ends should be. There are also questions about what should be taught and by which methods and procedures. There are two, possibly three, requirements that an acceptable method for aesthetic education should fulfill: (1) It must be demonstrably related to projected outcomes. (This ought to go without saying but apparently does not; for, as those acquainted with the general nature of aesthetic education programs know, the connection between activities and outcomes is often nebulous.) (2) It must not rely on educationally suspect means. In value education this means anything that would tend to deprive students of the freedom of choice and critical inquiry, thus making their value preferences inauthentic. (3) It should avoid embarrassing the profession and infuriating the taxpaying public. This is another item that should not have to be mentioned but is, in view of the many inanities proposed and practiced under the rubric of *aesthetic education*.

How, then, to teach? The clue lies in the aesthetic-value situation itself. The situation involves, as it develops, an artwork and a well-prepared percipient; or, to put it differently, an object with aesthetic-value capacity and an individual with the capability to realize it. It only remains to give some specificity to that capability. It consists, first of all, in knowing how to approach an artwork, what point of view to take toward it, what kind of interest to manifest in it, and what other sorts of interest to suspend or suppress. More important, it implies knowing which properties of the object to probe for aesthetic value and which to ignore, and how and in what sequence to do all this. In the aesthetic situation, one may say, individuals—though in a dispassionate and contemplative frame of mind—are perceptually very active; they are engaged in the *act* of appreciation (apprehending plus prizing). Individuals perform certain critical/perceptual operations on the object—in short, they practice a *skill*. Therefore, it can now be proposed that the proper method for aesthetic education is *teaching the basic skills of aesthetic appreciation*.

6. A final advantage of a skills approach to aesthetic appreciation is its capacity as an antidote to certain culturally and educationally harmful ideas about art, for example, the retreat from aesthetic judgment known as *nonjudgmentalism*. Its genesis, various manifestations, and especially the brand of aesthetic theory that supports it are beyond the scope of this discussion. But the possible consequences of nonjudgmentalism for aesthetic education, its objectives as well as its day-to-day conduct, should not be ignored.

Nonjudgmentalism accepts the proposition that there are not, in fact cannot be, any absolute standards—and not even very good proximate ones—on which to base aesthetic judgments. Because aesthetic judgments cannot be rationally defended, they are held to be arbitrary in the sense of being expressions of purely personal, subjective preferences or likings. Responsible criticism in the arts (nonjudgmental criticism, that is) should therefore describe but not evaluate. If people insist on making judgments, they must understand, and must make clear to others, that they are not estimating how good or poor a work is, but are telling the world how much they like or dislike it; in other words, they would be making statements about themselves and their feelings, rather than about the art object.

This outlook poses dilemmas for the teacher of aesthetic education. For example, what kinds of artwork should be exhibited to students? If nothing can be definitely established as aesthetically superior, the distinction between high and popular art is pure snobbery. Can artworks even be said to be better than other artifacts or natural objects? Does not the teacher's selection of an object for display represent an attempt to impose the teacher's preference on students, since it cannot be more than a reflection of the teacher's taste?

Questions such as these and the mentality they betray force a choice on aesthetic educators. The easy alternative is to join the retreat from judgment. But then aesthetic education would have to give up any pretense of promoting aesthetic well-being by educating individuals to discernment (which should certainly include ability to separate the good from the inferior). The more difficult alternative, that of pleading the case of aesthetic evaluation, can be made to appear more manageable by recalling what aesthetic skills are to be taught for: the actualization in experience of the aesthetic value an object *possesses* as a capacity. Aesthetic value, depending on an object's perceptual qualities and their arrangement, is, in that sense, objective, not a product of the subject's whims or feelings. Furthermore, since value is actualized in a critical/perceptual performance employing skills, experiencing subjects should, in principle, be able to communicate their value determination and the way they reached it to others who also have the skill.[9] It is quite possible for people with the appropriate skills (for perception as well as for aesthetic discourse) to reach substantial consensus on such matters, and to do it in a way that makes it more than agreeing to like the same thing. Thus, the value that is in the object as potential is realized in experiences that are by no means condemned to being purely private and unsharable. In sum, teachers have no reason to fear that they may be corrupting students through the imposition of values that actually are no more than private, subjective, esoteric, and therefore indefensible preferences.

If they wished, teachers could justify the choice of classics or masterpieces by reference to what is required for teaching a skill. A skill is taught by guided practice, but also through performances by the teacher for purposes of demonstration. One of the objectives of such demonstrations is to acquaint students with the full scope of the skill, with the level to which they can hope to perfect it. But a demonstration of a high level of aesthetic skill demands an aesthetic object that brings the entire range of that skill into play. Such an object would most likely be a masterpiece of art, an acknowledged classic that is complex, many layered, subtle, and a great challenge to the percipient's skills.[10]

NOTES

1. Arthur Danto, "The Artworld," *Journal of Philosophy* 61, no. 19 (1964): 571–84. The discussion borrows from that part of Danto's analysis where he speaks of the artworld as part of the ambience of response to art. Such a sense implies a knowledge of art's history and theory and extensive aesthetic experience. This sense of an artworld fits well with some uses made by educational theorists of Michael Polanyi's work. See, for example, Harry S. Broudy's "On 'Knowing With,'" in *Philosophy of Education*, Proceedings of the Philosophy of Education Society, ed. Harold B. Dunkel (Edwardsville, Ill.: Philosophy of Education Society, 1970). That is, it might be said that one "knows with" a sense of an artworld. Or, as Polanyi might say, a sense of an artworld consists of subsidiaries that bear on the focal meaning of a work of art. See Michael Polanyi and Harry Prosch, *Meaning* (Chicago: University of Chicago Press, 1975).

2. The term, along with some other notions, is taken from Monroe C. Beardsley's "Aesthetic Welfare, Aesthetic Justice, and Educational Policy," *Journal of Aesthetic Education* 7, no. 4 (1973): 49–61. For purposes of this discussion, his analysis has been condensed and, in some instances, the terminology modified.

3. This judgment may appear too dogmatic, but a persuasive defense of it is made in Jacques Barzun's *The Use and Abuse of Art* (Princeton: Princeton University Press, 1975). Originally presented as the A. W. Mellon Lectures in the Fine Arts, 1973, at the National Gallery of Art, Washington, D.C.

4. Beardsley, "Aesthetic Welfare, Aesthetic Justice, and Educational Policy," 52.

5. Beardsley, "The Aesthetic Point of View," in *Perspectives in Education, Religion, and the Arts*, ed. H. E. Kiefer and M. K. Munitz (Albany: State University of New York Press, 1970), 219–37.

6. That is to say, at any given moment the state of aesthetic well-being within a society is a function of the number of aesthetic experiences being had and their magnitudes.

7. For example, the discussion of skill learning in R. M. W. Travers, ed., *Second Handbook of Research of Teaching* (Chicago: Rand McNally, 1973) is devoted entirely to the study of physical movements in controlled laboratory experiments.

8. Much of the discussion of appreciation as a skill is taken from Harold Osborne's *The Art of Appreciation* (New York: Oxford University Press, 1970).

9. *In The Art of Appreciation*, Osborne writes: "When the capacity for appreciating works of art is brought under the heading of connoisseurship . . . as a category of skill, this is tantamount to denying that it is merely an expression of personal preference, a matter of individual likes and dislikes. . . . For that is a cognitive skill, purporting to apprehend and discriminate qualities residing in the object of attention, qualities which can be recognized and tested by others who have the skill" (15).

10. For a discussion of critical visual concepts and critical argument, see Monroe C. Beardsley's *Aesthetics: Problems in the Philosophy of Criticism* (New York: Harcourt, Brace and World, 1958), 168–77, 454–89.

Teaching Aesthetic Criticism in the Schools

THE PRESENT MOMENT is not propitious for examining the problems of teaching criticism in the schools. The emergence of mind-blowing cults of instant sensation and militant anti-intellectualism has resulted in a considerable downgrading of the value of critical analysis. Indeed, it seems we are well into a cultural trend that heaps ridicule on intellectual integrity and professional judgment of practically any kind.[1] The revolt against authority is especially intense in the aesthetic domain, and because the practice of responsible art criticism is obviously tied to reflective judgment, it will be necessary to get some bearings on the aim of criticism in an open society before suggesting a concept of art criticism that is teachable in the schools.

THE AIM AND NATURE OF CRITICISM

The ultimate aim of criticism in an open society is the criticism of life in the furtherance of humane values. To be sure, this is a revered and perennial aim of criticism, but the temper of the times demands its reiteration. Another way to put this aim is to say that criticism strives to assert a measure of control over the quality of thought and feeling in a society. It is an exception to the general revulsion against authority that we still honor this function of criticism in scientific and technological domains. We do not want bad theories and bad engineering, and we are particularly insistent on maintaining better-than-minimal health standards, the safeguarding of which is not entrusted to amateurs. Yet this function of criticism is resisted in the aesthetic domain. Here, just about anything goes. But then, it might be asked, what's wrong with that? In a highly specialized society should not there be at least one sphere of human activity in which persons can freely express their ideas and opinions?

These questions are not without point, and I have no intention of being high-handed and dismissing them. At the same time I think it must be acknowledged that aesthetic opinions are not always consistently held. It is not uncommon to hear persons assert in one context that art is a matter of personal taste or that all beauty is in the eye of the beholder and in another, say, the movies, to unequivocally deplore excessive violence and sex. Standards, then, are often expressed; not everything is thought to be a matter of personal opinion. The appeal to aesthetic standards in numerous judgments, moreover, implies a belief that works of fine art (which exhibit exemplary aesthetic values) do in some important way figure in the quality of life. And there is an impressive body of critical opinion that holds that art is in fact a prime molder of human aspiration that expresses vivid and persuasive images of human possibility.

If the ultimate aim of criticism is the criticism of life in the furtherance of humane values, the task for educational theory is to frame objectives of criticism in such a way that they arm the young with concepts and skills that can transfer to postschool behavior. The expectation is not, of course, a high level of professional critical performance; that, after all, is a lifetime goal for professional critics. The concern should be with a level of performance that is capable of achieving an intelligent interpretive perspective, what might be called quasi-professional competence.[2] I think a concept of criticism that divides into two basic sets of activities—into what may be called *exploratory aesthetic criticism* and *argumentative aesthetic criticism*—can develop the kind of critical performance envisioned here as one appropriate outcome of aesthetic education.

Exploratory criticism is an aid to and a means of sustaining aesthetic experience. Aesthetic argument, by contrast, is critical communication carried on in behalf of a given critique; that is, having both aesthetically experienced a work of art and provided an estimate of its goodness (or badness), we communicate our account and defend it if challenged. In other words, each of these two types of criticism performs a distinctive function.

EXPLORATORY AESTHETIC CRITICISM

Such criticism refers to techniques and procedures that are helpful in realizing the aesthetic value of works of art. The central task is to ascertain an object's aesthetic aspects as completely as possible. Judgment in the sense of ascribing merit or pronouncing a verdict is temporarily suspended in favor of as full a view as possible. Because the complexity a work of art cannot be immediately apprehended, repeated and sustained viewing are required. One must probe and scan a manifold of elements, sense their intensity and dramatic character, see aspects in one light and context, and then in others, and so forth. In the early stages of aesthetic learning such exploratory activities will be practiced much more consciously than later when, by bent of critical habit, objects can be rendered intelligible more quickly.

It should be underlined that although critical activity can be methodized and guided by some general principles, there are no hard-and-fast critical rules that, if patiently followed, will guarantee that all that can be seen in a work of art will in fact be experienced. As an aid, however, criticism is of considerable assistance and can be divided into the overlapping phases of *description*, in the sense of relatively straightforward noting of the more literal aspects of objects; *analysis*, which attends carefully to the interrelations of sensuous elements noted in description; *characterization*, which marks the peculiar nature of a work's aesthetic qualities; and *interpretation*, an effort to construe overall meaning.

Exploratory aesthetic criticism does not imply strong evaluation. Although a critical sense is not completely absent even in straightforward description, some critical decisions must be made about what is worth singling out for attention. Nonetheless, there is an important difference between an effort intended to achieve a relatively neutral and objective account of a work's properties, which may serve as the basis for strong evaluation or critical verdicts, and aesthetic argument that has already formed a judgment and is concerned to communicate and defend it.

Description

In the effort to discern as completely as possible the nature of a work of art, it is helpful to identify and name its major components. An exhaustive inventory is not called for, although it is well to remember that in art small things can make big differences. Such identifying and naming should include not only elements of subject matter but also an object's major areas or formal divisions. The noting of representational and formal aspects may enable later analysis and characterization to decide whether subject and form are congruent or in conflict, relations that may affect overall interpretation of meaning and assessment of merit.

It is difficult to specify in advance what a person needs to know in order to see a work effectively, but we can assume that in the case of serious works, a knowledge of art history and aesthetic theory will stand one in good stead. A good guide in this respect is Kenneth Clark, who in *Looking at Pictures* writes that "if I am to go on looking responsively I must fortify myself with nips of information . . . and the value of historical criticism is that it keeps the attention fixed on the work while the senses have time to get a second wind."[3] That Clark dedicated the volume to Roger Fry testifies as well to the utility of aesthetic theory. In different terms, what Clark appeals to is what Arthur Danto has called a sense of an artworld, an extensive knowledge of the cosmos of art.[4]

Descriptive knowledge is often disparaged because appreciation courses tend to get arrested at this level. I suspect that this charge is not always well founded, but doubtless it attests to confusion about the kinds of knowledge that are relevant to understanding and criticizing art. Instruction that stops with literal description obviously falls short of indicating what is singularly important in works of art. But this is not being proposed here; description is but a phase that leads on into more distinctively aesthetic territory.

Analysis and Characterization

The activity of analysis involves discerning much more closely the ways in which elements noted in description dispose themselves into a variety of forms and patterns. Formal analysis can be quite complicated and demanding, but there is no escaping it in the case of complex artistic artifacts.[5] How much of it should be done at a certain age or grade level is a relevant pedagogical question. Doubtless it should be used cautiously in the elementary grades lest the young become too self-conscious about the mode of attention that typifies analysis.[6] Used skillfully, however, analysis can lead even young minds to synoptic vision.

Analysis, though, cannot proceed for long without noting the dramatic character of an element or relationship. Relationships are always certain kinds of relationships: elements clash or fuse harmoniously, appear in mutual or uncertain accord, attract or repel. Analysis thus involves the characterizing of elements and relations. And with the introduction of the term *character-ization* we may note a problem with critical language, if only to explain the way critical terms are being used here. Consider the statements "X elements jar" or "X elements harmonize." Such language could imply a value judgment that X is good or bad because elements jar or harmonize. Or such statements may simply be nonnormative descriptions. In other words, a critical statement can sometimes be both a description and an evaluation. Such vagaries of language usage should not, however, divert attention from the fact that common practice distinguishes description and evaluation. A few words are now in order about the properties of characterizing terms.

Setting aside noncontroversial descriptive terms whose referents are relatively clear (for example, "The still life contains a pipe, playing cards, and vase" or "The film is in color and about romantic love"), there are terms taken from nonaesthetic contexts that are used in aesthetic situations to note the character of works of art. It is thus one thing to say that elements are square, equidistant from one another, or converge toward the horizon line, but quite another to say that they are strong, forceful, antagonistically engaged, or cast about in an atmosphere of free-floating anxiety. Whether certain elements are forceful or antagonistically engaged can be legitimately disputed, and more than one characterization of the same elements may be acceptable. But unless a work of art is radically ambiguous it is unlikely that its pervasive quality can be both, say, turgid and lyrical. As in judging people, it is, of course, possible to be mistaken about an object's qualities, as I think the writer was who said that from Mondrian's late 1930 compositions "there emanates a mathematical harmony that has the delicacy of precision instruments, the sensitivity of radio activity, and the power of Diesel engines."[7]

A second property of characterizing terms is what was earlier called their occasional evaluative import: "X is graceful or disjointed" may convey a value judgment that X is good or bad because graceful or disjointed. But it may also simply assert a nonnormative description of an object's quality. When there is doubt about the meaning of critical statements, there are a number of things that can be done. For example, one can engage in closer contextual analysis or ask artists, if they are available and willing to talk about what they intended. And even if they are they may not always be helpful.

Another point about such terms is their widespread use in critical talk. It is occasionally thought odd that human qualities are ascribed to inanimate material things, but this practice is in fact quite natural, and it would be sterile discourse indeed that tried to get along without it.[8] The displacement of sensory impressions from one sense modality is called synesthesia; it implies that works of art can look and feel the way human experience does.[9] In numerous instances there seems no good reason to doubt it.

Interpretation

Analysis and characterization phase into interpretation of overall meaning; it represents a kind of summary judgment arrived at by calling on all the pertinent knowledge, experience, and sensitivity a critic can muster. Although overall interpretation depends on the variety of local meanings discerned in the work, interpreting is not simply adding them up to get the right meaning. There is no system of aesthetic arithmetic. Meyer Schapiro's interpretation of Cézanne's Card Players as an "image of a pure contemplativeness without pathos," for example, grows out of local interpretations of the main figures whose "intent but not anxious" moods, "gravity of absorbed attitudes," "intense concern," and "progressive stabilization and detachment" are apparent.[10] Putting these interpretations together is no mere additive process. Rather, local meanings fit or accord well with larger ones, and it is a highly cultivated sense of aesthetic fittingness rather than a keen feel for discursive logic that is operative in aesthetic interpretation.[11]

In brief, there can be variability among logically compatible interpretations of the same work; the sticky issue arises in the case of logically incompatible interpretations. Cézanne's *Card Players* cannot be interpreted to mean both "pure contemplativeness without pathos" and "turbulent agitation without chaos." One meaning must be wrong, for the work is not that indeterminate or formless. The possibility must be held open, however, that new experience may turn up an even better interpretation.

Interpretation in its usual use delivers the meaning of a work of art. Meaning may also be construed as the *content* of a work in distinction from its materials, form, and subject matter.[12] Content, that is, emerges from the interanimation of materials, subject matter, and form. In such subjects as Michelangelo's sculpture *Captive* or Delacroix's *Jacob Wrestling with the Angel,* subject matter and materials have been transfigured into dramatic images of primordial struggle.

ARGUMENTATIVE AESTHETIC CRITICISM

Up to this point, exploratory criticism (description, analysis, characterization, interpretation) has been suggested as a set of techniques a learner can use to perceive an object as completely as possible. Once an object has been carefully described, analyzed, and so forth, an appraisal of its worth or goodness has also been made, or is at least one is strongly implicit in the detailed explorative account. The language of exploratory criticism, in other words, is typically normative. As indicated earlier, we describe, analyze, and characterize, and at the same time, prize, appraise, and estimate.[13] Nonetheless what criticism does in trying to render an object visible or aesthetically meaningful is different from what it does in backing up interpretations and evaluations.

What it does in the latter case is aesthetic argument, which as stipulated here assumes that a critical evaluation of an object has already been made. If asked to justify an evaluation, a responsible critic ought to be able to argue in favor of it. This can be done by *redescribing, reanalyzing,* and so on, what has already been noticed. The attempt is to persuade others that the object is in fact reasonably seen, heard, or taken in the way the interpretation and judgment have stated. This may be done with quite an armament of verbal and nonverbal critical techniques. Indeed, the resources a critic can use are practically limitless. Verbally, a critic can resurvey the same area with interesting variation, that is, point out once again both nonaesthetic and aesthetic features and how they are linked, vivify with simile and metaphor, compare and contrast, reiterate and variegate, and so on. Nonverbally there can be reference to a repertoire of bodily gestures and facial expressions that can also be effective tools of persuasion.[14]

CRITICISM IN ACTION

Schapiro's account of one of Cézanne's paintings of Mont Sainte-Victoire illustrates the range of aesthetic criticism. After commenting on the importance of this mountain peak in the artist's life—Cézanne, it is said, repeatedly painted it to help externalize his own strivings and desire for repose—Schapiro compares it, as critics are wont to do, with other paintings by Cézanne of the same subject, and in doing so says:

> The stable mountain is framed by Cézanne's tormented heart, and the peak itself, though more serene, is traversed by restless forms, like the swaying branches in the sky. A pervading passionateness stirs the repeated lines in both. Even the viaduct slopes, and the horizontal lines of the valley, like the colors, are more broken than in the picture in New York. The drawing and brushwork are more impulsive throughout. Yet the distant landscape resolves to some degree the strains of the foreground world. The sloping sides of the mountain unite in a single balanced form the dualities that remain divided, tense, and unstable in the observer's place—the rigid vertical tree and its extended, pliant limb, the dialogue of the great gesticulating fronds from adjoining trees that cannot meet, and the diverging movements in the valley at the lower edge of the frame.

And he continues:

> It is marvelous how all seems to flicker in changing colors from point to point, while out of this vast restless motion emerges a solid world of endless expanse, rising and settling. The great depth is built up in broad layers intricately fitted and interlocked, without an apparent constructive scheme. Towards us these layers become more and more diagonal; the diverging lines in the foreground seem a vague reflection of the mountain's form. These diagonals are not perspective lines leading to the peak, but, as in the other view, conduct us far to the side where the mountain slope begins; they are prolonged in a limb hanging from the tree.

He concludes:

> It is this contrast of movements, of the marginal and centered, of symmetry and unbalance, that gives the immense aspect of drama to the scene. Yet the painting is a deep harmony built with a wonderful finesse.[15]

What do we have here? It may, I think, be called an instance of aesthetic evaluation and argument.[16] Schapiro has explored the painting's qualities, estimated the degree of its excellences, and presented readers with an account they themselves may use in attempting to realize the aesthetic value of the painting. It is aesthetic argument in the sense that it is highly evaluative and persuasive; the account invites the reader into this remarkable field of aesthetic value. What, more specifically, is the content of Schapiro's critical account?

First, a description that noted merely representational elements—the mountain peak, foreground area with viaduct, house, prominent tree, valley opening to the right—would obviously fail to highlight what is most worth seeing in Cézanne's painting as a work of art. It is not until some of its very special qualities and relations are indicated and characterized that we begin to perceive the manner in which the painting's sensuous elements are interestingly disposed, or to see the painting's vivid qualities by virtue of such dispositions. Thus Schapiro indicates the variety of ways in which surface design and design in depth unite organically. He explains, for example, how the distant background tends to resolve the strains and dualities of the foreground activity. He invites viewers to see the "majestic" mountain peak, "traversed with restless forms, like the swaying branches in the sky," a "passionateness" pervading the repeated lines in both, and limbs from trees that, though not touching, can nonetheless be seen as a "dialogue of the great gesticulating fronds." And he sums up by saying that the resolution of formal analogies and oppositions gives an "immense aspect of drama to the scene."

If one examines Schapiro's critical statements carefully, one sees that they provide support for the belief that evaluative statements about a work's aesthetic goodness can often be backed up with statements about its degree of formal unity, complexity, and dramatic intensity.[17] That is, there seem to be presupposed in Schapiro's appraisal of Cézanne's painting certain aesthetic standards such as organic unity, complexity, and dramatic intensity; or to put it in slightly different terms, the qualities Schapiro singles out are special embodiments of such critical criteria. And it is believed by certain theorists (for instance, Beardsley) that the standards of unity, complexity, and intensity are in fact used to a considerable extent by the community of critics, although they do not necessarily get applied in rulelike, rigid fashion.

What must be discerned in a critic's account if one is interested in discovering the standards deployed is not only the object (or parts therein) that have been rated or evaluated but also the reasons for saying something is good or excellent (or the opposites of these). The norms or standards to which critics appeal may be contained in or implied by the stated reasons. For example, a critic may say, "X is good because of its tightly structured form" (in which case, the standard appealed to is unity), or, "X is good because of the great variety of detail" (complexity), or, "X is good because it is delicate and graceful" (degree of intensity). More frequent are overall assessments that incorporate a number of these ratings, reasons, and norms. For instance, a judgment might read, "Although it is structured rather loosely, X is good because its abundance of finely articulated details gives it an air of grace and delicacy." Here we see that the reasons for praising the work are unity, complexity, and intensity. Or, as Schapiro could have said about the aesthetic space of *Mont Sainte-Victoire*: "The great depth, though seemingly without constructive scheme, assumes dramatic significance when its relational elements are seen to be intricately fitted and interlocked." Once again, the trinity of distinctively aesthetic standards appealed to by critics tends to be unity (for example, "X is well organized, is formally perfect, and has an inner logic of structure and style"), complexity ("X is subtle, imaginative, and rich in contrasts"), and intensity ("X is vivid, forceful, and full of vitality" or "X is tender, delicate, and ironic").[18]

It is pedagogically helpful to isolate the major components of a critical evaluation.[19] In a complete appraisal, it is possible to isolate (1) the object of evaluation, or value object; (2) the rating of the value object with a value term; (3) the reason why the object has a certain value; and (4) the standard, which is explicitly stated in or implied by the reason (3). To the extent to which a reason (3) and a standard (4) are present, they provide support for the critical judgment (2).

Consider once more Schapiro's account of Cézanne. The value object (1) is obviously the painting *Mont Sainte-Victoire*. A general rating or value term, that is, (2), like *good* or *great* is not used by Schapiro, although he does use *marvelous* at one point. The reason, namely, (3), at least in part, why the painting is marvelous has to do with its "immense aspect of drama." What kind of critical reason is "immense aspect of drama"? We cannot be absolutely certain, of course, but it seems to imply the aesthetic standard of intensity, and thus we may place "intensity" at (4). If Schapiro had said, "The landscape is marvelous because of its remarkable intensity," then the aesthetic standard appealed to would have been contained in instead of implied by his stated reason.

A single critical standard is, of course, not always sufficient to support an evaluation, and a final verdict will usually embody a careful weighing of merits and demerits as measured by a number of standards, not only distinctly aesthetic norms but also cognitive and moral ones. In selecting works for study in schools it would be well to select works valuable for aesthetic and cognitive and moral reasons.

It may be noted that I have made no reference to the role of creative activities in developing critical capacities. Such activities obviously have a place. It is highly likely that the aesthetic value of works of art can be more effectively realized if one has had some experience in making art. The early years and elementary grades are the time, I think, to get this kind of feeling for the shape, sound, and touch of things, along with, to be sure, some "nips of information." What we are learning about the intellectual development of the child seems to accord with this suggestion. It is during the early years that the young are forging those cognitive powers and concepts that in later years they will refine and come to understand more formally.[20] The secondary grades (7–12) and the years afterward are the ideal time for the kind of aesthetic education I have discussed. Perhaps we may call the early years of infant, primary, and elementary schooling years a time for developing knowledge and skills that later will function tacitly in acts of aesthetic criticism.

NOTES

1. The anti-intellectualism and antiprofessionalism of certain styles of New Left protest referred to are well discussed by Paul Goodman and Robert Brustein in *Beyond the New Left: Confrontation and Criticism*, ed. Irving Howe (New York: McCall, 1970). Monroe C. Beardsley also has some good comments on the new psychedelic impresarios in "Aesthetic Experience Regained," *Journal of Aesthetics and Art Criticism* 28, no. 1 (1969): 10–11. Also see Daniel Bell's "The Cultural Contradictions of Capitalism," *Public Interest* 21 (Fall 1970), reprinted in a special double issue of the *Journal of Aesthetic Education* (January/April 1972) devoted to the topic "Capitalism, Culture, and Education."

2. A conception of general education that builds interpretive perspectives on significant domains of human experience may be found in Harry S. Broudy, B. Othanel Smith, and Joe R. Burnett, *Democracy and Excellence in American Secondary Education* (Chicago: Rand McNally, 1964), chaps. 3, 4.

3. Kenneth Clark, *Looking at Pictures* (New York: Holt, Rinehart and Winston, 1960), 16–17.

4. Arthur Danto, "The Artworld," *Journal of Philosophy* 61, no. 19 (1964): 571–84.

5. The classical analysis of form is DeWitt H. Parker's *The Analysis of Art* (New Haven: Yale University Press, 1926), chap. 2. Also see D. W. Gotshalk, *Art and the Social Order*, 2nd ed. (New York: Dover, 1962), chap. 5; Monroe C. Beardsley, *Aesthetics: Problems in the Philosophy of Criticism* (New York: Harcourt, Brace, 1958); chaps. 4, 5; and Thomas Munro, *Form and Style in the Arts* (Cleveland: Press of Case Western Reserve University, 1970).

6. Charles L. Stevenson, "On the 'Analysis' of a Work of Art," *Philosophical Review* 67, no. 1 (1958): 44–45.

7. Charmion Wiegand, "The Meaning of Mondrian," *Journal of Aesthetics and Art Criticism* 2, no. 8 (1943): 70.

8. Frank Sibley, "Aesthetic Concepts," *Philosophical Review*, 68, no. 4 (1959): 421–50; and "Aesthetic and Nonaesthetic," *Philosophical Review*, 74, no. 2 (1965): 135–59. Both articles contain systematic discussions of aesthetic judgment and critical activities.

9. E. H. Gombrich, "Visual Metaphors of Value in Art," in *Aesthetics and Criticism in Art Education*, ed. Ralph A. Smith (Chicago: Rand McNally, 1966),

174–75. See also Carroll Pratt, *The Meaning of Music* (New York: McGraw-Hill, 1931), 150–215.

10. Meyer Schapiro, *Paul Cézanne* (New York: Harry N. Abrams, 1952), 88.

11. For a discussion of the relation between micro and macro meanings, see Monroe C. Beardsley, *The Possibility of Criticism* (Detroit: Wayne State University Press, 1970), 44–61.

12. Virgil C. Aldrich, *Philosophy of Art* (Englewood Cliffs, N.J.: Prentice-Hall, 1963), chap. 2. Aldrich suggests that the question of meaning in art is best paraphrased as "What are we to look for in the work of art?" (92).

13. Aldrich says that "actually, description, interpretation, and evaluation are interwoven in live talk about art, and there is a delicate job distinguishing them. But for philosophy of art it is possible to make some useful distinctions in view of some real logical differences in the living language. So we picture description at the base, grounding interpretation, which is on the next level up, and evaluation, which is on top" (ibid., 88–89).

14. Sibley, "Aesthetic Concepts."

15. Schapiro, *Cézanne*, 74.

16. It might also be called a verbal report of aesthetic exploratory criticism. The report, however, is highly evaluative and persuasive and as such may also be construed as an argument for seeing the painting in the manner indicated by Schapiro. This is a somewhat special use of argument but one that I think is permissible. Another critic who took issue with Schapiro's account would reasonably do it by providing his or her own account of the painting. This is the way critics argue with one another. For an instructive essay on the role of persuasion in aesthetic argument, see Brian S. Crittenden, "Persuasion: Aesthetic Argument and the Language of Teaching," in *Aesthetic Concepts and Education*, ed. Ralph A. Smith (Urbana: University of Illinois Press, 1970), 227–62.

17. Beardsley, *Aesthetics*, chap. 10; and "The Classification of Critical Reasons," *Journal of Aesthetic Education* 2, no. 2 (1968): 55–63.

18. Beardsley, *Aesthetics*, 462.

19. In setting out the components of critical evaluation, I recall the method of charting classroom evaluative ventures used by Othanel Smith and his associates in *A Study of the Strategies of Teaching* (Urbana: Bureau of Educational Research, University of Illinois, 1967), 163.

20. See Ralph A. Smith, "Psychology and Aesthetic Education," *Studies in Art Education* 11, no. 3 (1970): 20–30, and Charles W. Rusch, "On Understanding Awareness," *Journal of Aesthetic Education* 4, no. 4 (1970): 57–79.

An Excellence Curriculum for Art Education

RETURNING TO Morningside Heights to talk about the arts and aesthetic education at Teachers College, Columbia University's symposium on arts curricula was a special pleasure. It was, after all, in the early and late 1950s—that so-called quiet decade—that my interest in the arts was stimulated by studies on both sides of West 120th Street and by frequent journeys into the artworld of Manhattan. Friday afternoons were the times reserved for visiting galleries and museums. Rosenberg's on East Seventy-ninth Street was the usual starting point, after which I wended my way downtown, making sure that I didn't miss the Sidney Janis and Betty Parsons Galleries before ending up at the Museum of Modern Art, which was simply the most exciting place of all for one reared in a dreary industrial valley in western Pennsylvania. Weekends were reserved for the Met, the Frick, the new Guggenheim, and the Cloisters.

The decade of the 1950s is deeply engraved in my memory and thinking. And for good reasons. Recall that the 1950s were a time when modernism was in bloom and New York City was becoming the center of the international artworld. Everywhere cultural studies were expanding and enjoying a new popularity, especially as the decade wore on. At Columbia, Meyer Schapiro was exciting graduate students with his perceptions of both Romanesque and Postimpressionist art, Howard Davis was revealing to appreciative undergraduates the excellences of Northern and Italian Renaissance painting, and Lionel Trilling was remarking the capacity of literature to counteract the abstractness of ideological thinking. Across the way, Lawrence A. Cremin, not yet president of Teachers College or the preeminent historian of American education that he was to become, was anticipating his interpretation of American education in Arnoldian terms, that is, as the effort to interpret and humanize knowledge in such ways that it could be brought to bear on all those matters that most concern us, a task that Richard Hofstadter in *Anti-intellectualism in American Life* explained will never be an easy one in a democratic society. Not only that; by the end of the decade Jacques

Barzun, in *The House of Intellect*, was cautioning that a modern society must be increasingly concerned with the anti-intellectualism not so much of those who have been the recipients of a mediocre education but of those who have received the very best education.

Passage through the Teachers College Fine Arts Education Department made me aware that there is more to art education than discovering the first cast shadow in the history of painting or detecting the hand of Hubert or Jan van Eyck in that great masterpiece of early Flemish painting *The Ghent Altarpiece*; one must also contend with the problems of aims and justification and curriculum design.

The 1950s now bear a conservative label, but for a young person in the big city with some intellectual and cultural curiosity there was more excitement than could be handled. If the decade was quiet, it was only in contrast to the noisy and boisterous decades that followed. The effect of the 1950s on my thinking explains why I cannot view some subsequent events and tendencies with equanimity. The resurgence of ideological thinking, the failure of higher education to resist the assault on intellectual standards, and the postmodern flattening of cultural values make the 1950s seem not only a quieter time but a saner one as well.[1]

More clearly than before I now realize that the 1950s made an Arnoldian of me, pure and simple. I too believe, with Matthew Arnold, that the true apostles of equality are those who take for granted that the only ideal for a democratic society is one that prizes excellence and the pursuit of the best possible self. Far from being an elitist ideal in any maleficent sense, it is one that wants for the large majority what heretofore had been the privilege of the minority and for the attainment of which universal education and schooling are the means.

What Arnold was talking about in the nineteenth century is what we have been hearing so much about in recent years, a commitment to excellence and equity. This means that we are experiencing a rare Arnoldian moment in educational thinking; and it was because of this realization that I accepted an invitation to write a response to the current excellence-in-education movement on behalf of the National Art Education Association. The result was a book titled *Excellence in Art Education: Ideas and Initiative*, whose theme is democracy and art education.[2] I will discuss a few of the book's propositions that should help us to see aesthetic education in future perspective and to perceive problems more effectively during a period when arts education curricula are in transition.

The first proposition of *Excellence* states that a commitment to excellence in art education is a commitment to general and common education from kindergarten through the twelfth grade. Education is general when it consists of learning appropriate for nonspecialists and common when students learn roughly the same concepts and skills and take similar units of work with, to be sure, some opportunity to pursue personal interests. Although *Excellence* follows the lead of current reports and stresses the secondary years, a commitment to excellence at the secondary level is meaningless unless a concern for quality animates the entire curriculum, the early as well as the later years. A concern for quality should in fact pervade the whole school setting, from the classroom to the principal's office. Talking about excellence in art education, then, implies talking not only about the qualities and meanings of outstanding works of art and the worthwhile experiences they can afford but also about an attitude toward accomplishment in general. Such an attitude has a long and venerable history dating back to classical antiquity. In *The Greek Ideal and Its Survival*, the distinguished classical scholar Moses Hadas wrote: "What the world has admired in the Greeks is the remarkably high level of their originality and achievements, and this high level premises a deeply held conviction of the importance of individual attainment. The goal of excellence, the means of achieving it, and (a very important matter) the approbation it is to receive are all determined by human judgment."[3]

In saying that a commitment to excellence implies a commitment to common, general education, in *Excellence* I also assert that art deserves study as a subject in its own right, as a domain that is characterized by distinctive purposes, concepts, and skills. I emphasize that art, one of the supreme achievements of humankind, an achievement whose power for affecting thought and action has been remarked since antiquity and whose potency is especially attested by totalitarian societies in their determination to control it, demands its own curricular time and space.

Such a view is consistent not only with a number of recently published reports, studies, and manifestos—for example, Mortimer Adler's *The Paideia Program*, John Goodlad's *A Place Called School*, Ernest Boyer's *High School*, and Theodore Sizer's *Horace's Compromise*—but also with a substantial literature of educational theory.[4] What is significant about this literature is that it argues that art should be a basic subject of the curriculum.

Little is accomplished, however, by saying that art should be studied as a subject in a program of general education and be committed to excellence without specifying in more detail what this means. In *Excellence*, I suggest that the general goal of art education is the development of a disposition to appreciate the excellence of art where the excellence of art assumes both the capacity of works of art at their best to intensify and enlarge the scope of human awareness and experience and the peculiar qualities of artworks whence such a capacity derives. I accordingly devote a chapter to the nature of excellence in the senses indicated.[5] So far as some of the inherent values of art are concerned, it can be argued that works of art have potential not just for stimulating direct perception and imagination but also for affording a high degree of aesthetic gratification and degrees of humanistic insight. They possess such potential by virtue of what Kenneth Clark in his volume on masterpieces calls inspired virtuosity, supreme compositional power, intensity of feeling, masterful design, uncompromising artistic integrity, imaginative power, originality of vision, and profound sense of human values. He mentions such works as Giotto's *Lamentation over the Dead Christ*, Raphael's *School of Athens*, Rubens's *Descent from the Cross*, Rembrandt's *Night Watch*, Courbet's *Funeral at Ornans*, and Picasso's *Guernica*, although numerous others, both Western and non-Western, could be mentioned as well.[6]

A second proposition of *Excellence* states that striving to appreciate excellence in art means study in a number of contexts in which students learn to perceive art, to understand it historically, to appreciate it aesthetically, to create it, and to think about it critically.[7] Such contexts, in turn, suggest a range of teaching methods that include, among others, the direct imparting of information and coaching in aesthetic and critical skills. The ideas and concepts taught in these various contexts constitute the organization or, if you will, the structure of knowledge of art education. Contexts, however, are not to be casually juggled. An excellence curriculum is committed to sequential learning. Such a curriculum suggests that aesthetic learning generally should follow a sequence of studies consisting of introductory units, historical units, appreciation units, studio and performing units, seminar units, and, when feasible, cultural service units—that is, eleven units distributed over six years, grades seven through twelve. If all the arts currently taught at the secondary level could be reorganized and made part of an excellence curriculum, such a recommendation would not be as utopian as it might initially seem. Nor, once again, is it novel; it is an ingredient of a number of philosophies of secondary education published over the past two decades.

In *Excellence* I argue that sequential learning is important because of the need to build systematically a sense of art with which one thinks and feels when encountering and experiencing works of art.[8] Such a sense is developed first of all from a preliminary idea of art. Then follows the historical study of art, an appreciation in depth of selected classics and masterpieces, studio and performing exercises that refine a feel for the qualities and powers of works of art, the critical analysis of puzzling topics and issues, and, when possible, work in cultural organizations in order to experience some of the institutional realities of the world of art.[9] Having undergone such a sequence of studies, students should be prepared to encounter art with a degree of autonomy and independent judgment and be able to experience the peculiar values of art at levels commensurate with their learning and experience.

One example of what *Excellence* understands by sequential learning will be sufficient. In explaining the features of masterpieces, Clark points out that of all the marks of artistic greatness two are especially important: he speaks of "a confluence of memories and emotions forming a single idea, and a power of recreating traditional forms so that they become expressive of the artist's own epoch and yet keep a relationship with the past."[10] What Clark is emphasizing is the significance that artistic genius assigns to continuity as well as innovation. In other words, one cannot properly engage a masterpiece unless one sees how elements of the old have been transmuted in the creation of a new compelling image. This is no less true of a good film or work of architecture than it is of a painting or work of sculpture. Once more, studying art sequentially in the contexts mentioned serves the objectives of historical awareness, aesthetic appreciation, and critical judgment—the three major dispositions called into play in experiencing works of art. Creative and performing activities help refine and strengthen these dispositions. We can say, therefore, that the successful completion of an excellence curriculum enables students to walk proudly with their cultural tradition, to appreciate the special character of aesthetic communication, and to reflect critically on aesthetic values.[11]

Once the purposes and objectives of an excellence curriculum are understood, curriculum evaluation falls into place. Assessment will center on whether proper objectives have been set and things are moving in the right direction, in the proper sequence, as it were, and whether evidence is available that relevant dispositions are being developed. In brief, this is how in *Excellence* I address the curriculum questions of what, when, how, and how well.

It should also be apparent that *Excellence* sees the schools, and mainly the public schools, as the principal institution in which the young pursue aesthetic learning. There can, of course, be points of contact with other cultural institutions, most obviously with museums when possible. *Excellence* also recommends when possible the potential value of a cultural service unit. From a policy standpoint, however, there should not be inordinate investment in nonconventional educational institutions; ultimately, the case for art education will be made by knowledgeable teachers of art in the schools.

A third proposition of *Excellence* states that in the preparation of art teachers, more time must be devoted to substantive work in the humanities, in particular to historical, philosophical, and critical studies of art. In taking seriously the more academic interest in art that is representative of current writing about art education, *Excellence* raises for discussion and debate the question of whether we are adequately preparing secondary teachers of art to handle new academic responsibilities and, if not, whether we need to design new patterns. For example, should the training of secondary teachers of the arts adopt the pattern of English, history, mathematics, and foreign language departments, in which prospective teachers of these subjects acquire mastery of subject matter not in colleges of education but in schools of humanities and colleges of liberal arts and sciences? Further, might not newly designed fine arts education units be created in such schools and colleges that would be responsible for coordinating study in the humanities and other liberal subjects with colleges of education? Colleges of education would, of course, continue to provide work in educational theory. I do not recommend the dismantling of colleges of education.

But if we are talking about excellence in art and art education; if we are stipulating the importance of historical, appreciative, and critical objectives; if we are in effect construing the study of art more academically; if we are thinking about a fundamentally different conception of instruction at the secondary level, then it follows that teachers should be prepared in a different atmosphere. If, however, art education departments can transform themselves and develop good working relations with schools and departments of humanities, new settings and mailing addresses will not be necessary. Nor is it obvious that colleges of liberal arts and sciences want additional responsibilities. Yet they have accepted such responsibilities in other fields of instruction.

The suggestion to move toward a more humanities conception of art education at the secondary level and to prepare teachers in new settings may be one of the more controversial aspects of *Excellence*. The suggestion, however, is just that, and it is intended to open up a line of discussion. The major consideration in entertaining these suggestions is whether new patterns of teacher preparation will ultimately improve learning about art in the schools and whether they will attract qualified young people to the field.

Yet another question raised by *Excellence* is whether art educators can ignore the observations made by John Goodlad in his study of the schools. Granted that there are numerous good programs and teachers of the arts in the schools today—presumably the Rockefeller Brothers Fund and the Getty Center located some of them—we cannot simply discount the general state of disarray in the teaching of the arts, which he characterized as excessive "playing, polishing, and performing" at the expense of the study of art as a cultural object.[12] While students report that they enjoy art classes, they also think that such classes are easy and unimportant. Goodlad, a frequent and welcome contributor to the conferences and literature of arts education, has too much credibility to be dismissed. So in *Excellence* I asked that we take notice of the disarray Goodlad described. One fact we cannot overlook is that many young people today are finding other professional fields more attractive to enter than education, and this includes arts education. To say that the survival of the field of arts education depends on change is doubtless to put too ominous an interpretation on the current situation, but neither should we pretend that there are no problems.

A fourth proposition of *Excellence* states that a commitment to excellence implies an acknowledgment of the claims of traditional as well as contemporary culture. I have emphasized the importance of building formally, systematically, and sequentially a sense of art with which one thinks about and experiences works of art. An intelligent encounter with a work of art presupposes a rich apperceptive mass made up of numerous items, but most of all of a sense of art and art history. This in itself would seem to justify developing a sense of art history. Even artists who self-consciously repudiate history do so with a strong sense of what they are reacting against. But there are comparatively few such artists. Others tell us that traditional art is important by their constantly returning to it for ideas, inspiration, and models. We think of Cézanne in the nineteenth century recalling Poussin of the seventeenth and Picasso in the twentieth recalling practically all previous eras, not least the Classical one. Such tendencies as Neorealism and Neoexpressionism are reinterpretations of the recent past. We nonetheless continue to read that the study of the past is irrelevant and that there is something wrong with acquainting the young with the finest achievements of their cultural heritage. Perhaps such things are said because of what Clark himself acknowledged— that traditional art was in large commissioned by the dominant groups in the society for the purpose of celebrating the values of such groups, whether sacred or secular.[13] But it is not only by virtue of this fact that traditional works of art are believed to be irrelevant; they are also said to be inaccessible to members of working-class cultures and ethnic groups who purportedly resonate to different beliefs and values. In short, the view is occasionally expressed that the pursuit of excellence is inconsistent with the promotion of democratic values, even that the current excellence-in-education movement is a trumped-up strategy to oppress minority groups and stamp out student creativity. Such charges imply that the pursuit of excellence is immoral; instead of studying the cultural heritage people should be given the kind of culture they want.[14]

But what is forgotten, Clark points out, is that despite the circumstances of the creation of much art, records clearly reveal that it was often enormously enjoyed by the large majority. We can read, for example, of how the residents of Sienna in the early fourteenth century rejoiced in the completion of Duccio's great altarpiece, the *Maestá*, and how the occasion was marked with great festivity and processions through the city streets.[15] For a contemporary example of civic pride being expressed by the majority in works of high accomplishment from the past, we can refer to the reaction of the residents of Reggio di Calabria in the south of Italy to the discovery of new classical figures, the so-called Warriors of Riace, in their village's offshore waters. Had these figures been merely third- or fourth-rate sculptures, less attention would have been paid to them and probably no competition with Florence would have occurred for their permanent display, with Reggio di Calabria winning out. High cultural achievement, in other words, is a continuing source of pride to any city, nation, or civilization.[16] We also do well to recall what Hannah Arendt said about art in her study of the human condition: works of art gloriously transcend both the periods and the eras in which they were created and the functions they were once intended to serve.[17]

To give one example of the power of art to transcend its time and purpose, in *Excellence* I cite the case of Nelson Edmonson, who asked why he, an agnostic, could appreciate not only the formal qualities but also the expressive meaning of much traditional religious art. Taking as a case in point the Byzantine icon titled *Vladimir Mother of God*, which depicts Mary and the Christ Child, he recalls the role that icons perform for the faithful: they relate to the goal of receiving grace and the fulfillment of God's prophetic vision. But whatever its religious meaning and function, Edmonson remarks that for him the icon "manifests mankind's remarkable creative ability to focus in one potent image, and thereby raise to a shared consciousness, the common human condition of suffering alleviated by love." He then goes on to say that persons of all beliefs or of no belief can thus experience "a sense of being an integral factor in a larger human drama, of having, as it were, an extended historical companionship."[18] This is one way in which works of art transcend religious doctrine and their own time. What we respond to in such works is the recognition of a shared humanity. This example clearly establishes the relevance of the past and helps us to appreciate why William Arrowsmith, a classical scholar, once remarked that the cultural heritage literally trembles with relevance.

Given such considerations, it is difficult to accept the belief that efforts to acquaint the young with the best that has been created in the cultural heritage are politically oppressive. The very choice of terms tends to prejudice the matter. If instead of speaking of imposition, with its associations of the forcible and illegitimate, we speak of providing access; if instead of fearing the suppression of individual interests, we emphasize liberating young minds from nature for culture; and if instead of denouncing the exercise of dominant power, we talk about enfranchising the young in matters of understanding and appreciation, then the language of political oppression assumes a strained quality. To place within the reach and grasp of the young that which has the capacity not only to intensify experience but also to enlarge the scope of human awareness is neither authoritarian nor maleficently elitist. On the contrary, it is to wish for the large majority what heretofore has been the privilege of the minority.

The belief that persons should be given the kind of culture they want can be countered by pointing out that persons, especially young people, are usually uncertain about their interests and tastes and thus need to know something of the range of what it is possible to enjoy and admire before they can make intelligent cultural decisions for themselves. Certainly it is presumptuous to assume that given the opportunity to cultivate a taste for the best, persons will turn their backs on it. There is too much evidence to the contrary. Certainly it is not evident to Marva Collins, in whose school for minority children in Chicago respect for persons and the best in the tradition are not considered incompatible. It has even been said that to treat people as if they already knew what they like or ought to like is to treat them as less than human.[19]

Were there space, it would be worth summarizing Robert Penn Warren's 1974 Jefferson Lecture, *Democracy and Poetry*. Warren, who was this country's first poet laureate, states that the values of democracy and poetry, and by *poetry* he means art in general, are indeed compatible. He writes that an outstanding work of art is valuable not only as a vital affirmation and image of the organized self, but also as "a permanent possibility of experience" that "provides the freshness and immediacy of experience that returns us to ourselves."[20]

The unique power of excellent art as a permanent possibility of worthwhile experience is an appropriate place to end these remarks. Everything *Excellence* says on the matter of quality underscores the realization that while democracies value the common man they do not ultimately value what Ortega y Gasset called the commonplace mind, a mind that not only knows itself to be commonplace but also proclaims the right to impose its commonplaces whenever possible.[21] Matthew Arnold also realized that with the coming of mass democracy, the freedom and energy of large numbers of people would be dissipated if not employed in the service of an ideal higher than that of the ordinary self, that is to say, unless they were employed in the service of the best possible self.[22] It is the potentiality for transcendence, for becoming uncommon, that is important. We may say that art at its best is one of those things of the world that is a perpetual reminder of the possibility of transcending the ordinary and that excellent art constantly calls us away from a pedestrian existence. Arts education should do no less.

NOTES

1. Perhaps more substantive and creative as well. See, e.g., Allan Bloom's discussion of the 1950s and 1960s in *The Closing of the American Mind* (New York: Simon and Schuster, 1987), 313–35.

2. Ralph A. Smith, *Excellence in Art Education: Ideas and Initiatives*, updated version (Reston, Va.: National Art Education Association, 1987). For the first printing, I was advised and encouraged by an NAEA Committee on Excellence in Art Education, whose members were Randall S. Craig, Margaret DiBlasio, Arthur Efland,

James U. Gray, W. Dwaine Greer, Grace Hampton, Marilyn Johnston, Clyde McGeary, Jean C. Rush, and Nancy MacGregor, ex officio.

3. Moses Hadas, *The Greek Ideal and Its Survival* (New York: Harper Colophon Books, 1966), 13.

4. For a discussion of this literature, see my *Excellence in Art Education*, chap. 5.

5. Ibid, chap. 2.

6. Kenneth Clark, *What Is a Masterpiece?* (New York: Thames and Hudson, 1979).

7. Smith, *Excellence in Art Education*, chap. 3.

8. The notion of a sense of art was suggested by Arthur Danto's *The Transfiguration of the Commonplace* (Cambridge, Mass.: Harvard University Press, 1981).

9. The idea of a service unit is borrowed from Boyer's report *High School: A Report on Secondary Education in America* (New York: Harper and Row, 1983), chap. 12.

10. Clark, *What Is a Masterpiece?*, 10–11.

11. Such objectives have been suggested for humanities education by Albert William Levi in his *The Humanities Today* (Bloomington: Indiana University Press, 1970). Also see his "Literature as a Humanity," *Journal of Aesthetic Education* 10, no. 2–4 (1976).

12. John Goodlad, *A Place Called School* (New York: McGraw-Hill, 1984), 218–20.

13. Kenneth Clark, "Art and Society," in *Moments of Vision* (London: John Murray, 1981).

14. This is the position of Herbert S. Gans in *Popular Culture and High Culture* (New York: Basic Books, 1974).

15. For a description of such festivities, see John Canaday, *Lives of the Painters* (New York: W. W. Norton, 1969), 1:15–16. For a report on the reactions of the residents of Reggio di Calabria to the discovery of the classical figures in question, see the *New York Times*, 12 July 1981.

16. See, e.g., Stuart Hampshire's remarks in "Private Pleasures and the Public Purse," a review of Janet Minahan's *The Nationalization of Culture* (New York: New York University Press, 1977), in the *Times Literary Supplement*, 13 May 1977.

17. Hannah Arendt, *The Human Condition* (Chicago: University of Chicago Press, 1958), 167.

18. Nelson Edmonson, "An Agnostic Response to Christian Art," *Journal of Aesthetic Education* 15, no. 4 (1981): 34.

19. Hampshire, "Private Pleasures and the Public Purse."

20. Robert Penn Warren, *Democracy and Poetry* (Cambridge, Mass.: Harvard University Press, 1975), 72.

21. Ortega y Gasset, *The Revolt of the Masses* (New York: W. W. Norton, 1932), 18.

22. For a discussion of Arnold's notion of the best self, see G. H. Bantock, *Studies in the History of Educational Theory*, vol. 2, *The Minds and the Masses, 1760–1980* (Boston: George Allen & Unwin, 1984), chap. 9.

The Arts and the Humanities

Aesthetic Education: A Critical Necessity

A S THE PROBLEMS of the world magnify and assume proportions that are adversely affecting the quality of life, aesthetic education is becoming more and more a critical necessity. Ever increasing modernization, for all its benefits, is eroding crucial human values and muting the dialogue that is necessary to keep the discussion of such values alive.[1]

This is not the place to dwell on the ills of modern civilizations, but it has been said that civilizations can survive their pathologies if they have the determination, talent, and energy to address them. When civilizations do decline, it is from a lack of confidence and hope, which causes them to crumble from within. At this point the human spirit surrenders to despair and a sense of helplessness and alienation.[2] During times of preoccupation with the discontents of civilization, I think the arts and aesthetic education can perform the important function of reminding persons of human possibility and accomplishment and thus help restore confidence and hope. As the distinguished art historian Kenneth Clark once said, "When we are beginning to despair of the human race we remember Vézelay or Chartres, Raphael's *School of Athens* or Titian's *Sacred and Profane Love*, and once more we are proud of our equivocal humanity. Our confidence has been saved by the existence of masterpieces, and by the extraordinary fact that they can speak to us, as they have spoken to our ancestors for centuries."[3] To examples of memorable works of Western civilization we may certainly add those of all civilizations.

How can we explain this redemptive power of outstanding works of art? For a reply to this question I refer to the words of another distinguished art historian. "Michelangelo and Raphael, Rubens and Rembrandt, Van Gogh and Cézanne," E. H. Gombrich writes, "are not only objects of art-historical study or investments or status symbols for collectors. They are centers of attraction and repulsion to be loved, admired, criticized, or rejected, living forces with which we get involved." And he goes on to say that such works "are culture heroes, Gods of our secular Pantheon, beneficent or baleful, serene or capricious, but like Gods they must be approached with respect

111

and humility for they can light up for us whole areas of the mind which would have been dark without them."[4] To complete a trilogy of tribute to memorable art, I refer to Arnold Hauser, who, though of an accent and philosophical persuasion different from those of either Clark or Gombrich, likewise states, "Great art gives us an interpretation of life which enables us to cope more successfully with the chaotic state of things and to wring from life a better, that is, a more convincing and more relevant meaning."[5] Anyone who has tried to enter into the world of a great work of art knows the truth of such remarks.[6]

I have said that aesthetic education is becoming a critical necessity. There are four reasons for making this assertion: aesthetic education not only cultivates a disposition to appreciate excellence in art, it also generates a capacity for aesthetic vision, an ability to think critically, and a willingness to entertain cultural alternatives.[7] The appreciation of excellence, aesthetic vision, critical thinking, and respect for alternatives are all traditional objectives of the humanities and exemplify the time-honored ideal of humanistic learning. The interpretation of aesthetic education I present, then, is from the point of view of the humanities.

EXCELLENCE IN ART

The first major value of aesthetic education—the appreciation of artistic excellence—presupposes the development of a number of dispositions: a disposition to prize artistic skill and artisanship over shoddy work; a disposition to prefer the complexity and strength of design to ill-conceived composition; a disposition to prefer profundity of expression over shallow understanding; a disposition to tolerate allusions and ambiguity in contrast to an insistence on the literal and the straightforward; and a disposition to prefer the transcendent and spiritual to strictly material experience. All this is to say that works of art at their best include habits that are part of a worthwhile life. In my writings on excellence in art, I have set out in greater detail what some of our most perceptive writers regard as the criteria of artistic excellence, and I will mention just a few of them here.[8]

In his discussion of the criteria of excellence in past and present art, Jacob Rosenberg concludes that both representational and nonrepresentational art reveal such qualities as sensitivity, articulateness, consistency, selectiveness, range of concepts, richness of formal relationships, intensity, expressiveness, a sense of balance, and a feeling for the medium.[9] Sherman E. Lee, a distinguished scholar of Asian art, finds similar qualities in non-Western art.[10] He concedes, moreover, that we have arrived at the point of dismissing as irrelevant any comparisons of the relative excellence of Michelangelo and Cézanne or of Chinese and Greek art. Yet he thinks it is possible to distinguish more or less superior qualities of works within the same kind, even if such works are from different historical periods. For example, he judges the finest examples of Greek vase painting to be superior to similar Neoclassical works of the late eighteenth and early nineteenth centuries; Renaissance painters to be superior to their nineteenth-century imitators, the Nazarenes; and an earlier Ma Yuan painting from the Sung dynasty of the thirteenth century to be superior to one done a century later.

Qualities of formal organization and expressiveness are not, of course, the whole story. Major works of art are compelling centers of attraction because they also express a profound sense of human values. As Clark points out, masterpieces characteristically disclose the ways in which artists have reworked traditional ideas and forms in order to make them expressive both of themselves and of the times in which they lived, all the while retaining a significant link with the past.[11] Employing terms similar to those used by other writers, Clark also finds the excellence of masterworks in their impeccable virtuosity, supreme compositional power, intensity of feeling, masterful design, uncompromising artistic integrity, and originality of vision and, once again, in their understanding of the human condition.

Such qualities of excellence can be found in both traditional and modern art as well as in newer media. The American film critic Stanley Kauffmann, for example, writes that the achievement of good films derives from their inventiveness, imaginative energy, dramatic content, technical competence, and— particularly relevant to the medium of film—dialogue and characterization, capacity to transform literary into cinematic values, psychological complexity, and spiritual power. Of the Italian filmmaker Michelangelo Antonioni, Kauffmann says his *L'avventura* reveals Antonioni's immense talent "to make the film respond formally and morally to our changing times, yet without forsaking what is still viable in the tradition."[12]

It may be thought that such criteria of excellence are primarily typical of the high cultures of Western and Eastern civilizations but less so of the traditional societies of West Africa, Oceania, and pre-Columbian America and Mesoamerica. Yet H. Gene Blocker, in a philosophical study of such art, thinks that it also submits to judgments of artistic excellence.[13] He believes that there is enough similarity between Western notions of aesthetic consciousness and artistic excellence and the art of the societies he studied to warrant claiming that such works also possess a unique sense of artistic excellence. "The best works in this style," he observes, have "a directness, a presence, a monumentality expressive of continuity and stability, a contained spiritual presence or power, whether firmly contained in a cool aloofness or barely contained in a fierce aggressiveness, and resulting in a quality varying from arresting to terrifying."[14] Harold Osborne, moreover, thinks that because they are often redundant to a work's efficacy in a ceremonial function, such qualities would not be present but for the existence of an aesthetic consciousness. He further adds that such societies often prefer more skillfully crafted and expressive works. It is therefore possible to detect degrees of artistic excellence and to discuss innovation and creativity within these societies' artistic traditions.

My brief references to authors whose aim was to describe the excellences of art are meant to suggest that apart from viewing the works of art themselves, there is no better way to renew one's faith in their powers and delights than to read what perceptive writers say about their special qualities. We further learn from this literature that the reasons given in support of judgments of artistic excellence are both aesthetic and nonaesthetic, that is to say, cognitive and moral as well as aesthetic. We may say, then, that we value works of art for three reasons: for the artistic virtuosity evident in the completed product; for its capacity to sustain perception in a distinctive mode of attention called aesthetic experience; and for its stature, where *stature* implies the ways in which works suggest imaginative models for thinking about human nature and the world.[15] In major works we characteristically find a blend of all these aspects and capacities.

AESTHETIC VISION

I have indicated what I think is the important function that works of art can perform in troubled times, reviewed criteria of artistic excellence, and referred to the kinds of reasons that can be given in assessing excellence in art. But what about the character of the *experience* of excellence, its peculiar features? Following Walter Kaufmann, we may call such experience aesthetic vision. If works of art at their best are valuable for their capacity to induce aesthetic vision, aesthetic vision in turn is valuable for its twofold function of shaping the self in positive ways and in providing humanistic insight, that is to say, for their constitutive and revelatory powers. At their best, works of art have the potential not only for integrating and shaping the self in positive ways but also for providing what has been called *aesthetic wisdom.*[16]

The notion that works of art can shape the self in beneficial ways recalls a line of thought in Western thinking that extends from Plato in antiquity to Friedrich von Schiller in the eighteenth century to Herbert Read, John Dewey, and a number of theorists in the twentieth. Schiller's *On the Aesthetic Education of Man in a Series of Letters*, published in 1795, stands out as a work that celebrates the constitutive values of aesthetic vision.[17] A poet and playwright as well as a philosopher, Schiller wrote during a century of great democratic revolutions. He believed that true civil and political freedom could be achieved only through the formation of a good character and that before people can be given a political constitution they must themselves be soundly constituted. And he believed that aesthetic education was the key to political and individual freedom. Occupying a middle state between brute force and the rule of law, aesthetic learning was to be the means by which individuals attained character.

How, then, was aesthetic education itself to be constituted? Schiller placed great faith in the study of masterworks for their capacity to release the living springs of human experience. It was particularly the form of artworks—their structure, balance, symmetry, harmony, and integrity—that constituted the peculiar essence of both art and a realized self. To acknowledge this is to say that aesthetic education did not stand in contrast to moral education; it had itself an important moral function.

Aesthetic education performed a similar function in Herbert Read's writings. For Read moral education consisted essentially of education through aesthetic discipline. Where Schiller spoke of aesthetic education's contribution to an ennobled character, Read designated human grace as its end result. In *The Redemption of the Robot: My Encounters with Education Through Art*, he writes, "We must give priority in our education to all forms of aesthetic activity, for in the course of making beautiful things there will take place a crystallization of the emotions into patterns that are the moulds of virtue."[18]

Dewey likewise recognized the role that organic unity plays not only in the perception of the external world but also in successful works of art and the integration of human consciousness. As he points out in *Art as Experience*, art not only breaks through conventional distinctions and stereotyped thinking—that is, performs a function that is part intellectual as well as aesthetic—it also composes psychological stresses, conflicts, and oppositions into a greater, richer, and more harmonious personality.[19]

If aesthetic vision has potential for shaping the self in positive ways, it is also a means of acquiring humanistic understanding. This is the point of revelatory theories of art characteristic of the modern Romantic era. What is revealed through such experience are not the warranted assertions of scientific inquiry but rather the human truth of things expressed in aesthetic or dramatic form. For example, Albert William Levi points out that in the work of Giotto, Fra Angelico, and Giovanni Bellini we gain insight into the nature of religious commemoration, adoration, and inspiration; in the work of Poussin, Constable, and Van Gogh we are granted access to the transcendent values of landscape; and in the work of Holbein, Rembrandt, and Ingres, all great portrait painters, we come to understand various features of human character.[20]

The influence of Schiller, Read, and Dewey is apparent in contemporary writing about aesthetic education. Contemporary theorizing is also heavily influenced by cognitive studies of the mind. The writings of Nelson Goodman and Howard Gardner and their followers place emphasis on art as a way of understanding that calls into play such mental powers as perception, memory, discrimination, analysis, and judgment.[21] Although theorizing of this kind acknowledges the important role that feeling plays in the apprehension of works of art, it does not sufficiently stress the cluster of identifiable feelings and emotions characteristic of aesthetic vision. In contrast, Beardsley refers to several criteria of the aesthetic that feature its affective character. He speaks of a feeling of response being directed by and to an object of some presence; a feeling of exhilaration that comes from making disparate phenomena cohere; a feeling that things are working themselves out in fitting and appropriate ways; a feeling of momentary escape and freedom from life's problems and frustrations; a feeling of significant discovery; and, not least important, a feeling of wholeness or integration.[22] Such a constellation of feelings is what makes aesthetic vision both compound and disjunctive. It is compound because it cannot be reduced to a single feeling but is rather a combination of several; and it is disjunctive in the sense that it tends to separate itself—though not without some overlap—from other types of experience. From the characterization of aesthetic vision it is but a logical next step to see it as a model for human experience in general and, as some philosophers of education and curriculum theorists are recommending, as a model for teaching, learning, and educational assessment.[23]

CRITICAL THINKING

A third benefit of aesthetic education is the development of critical dispositions. By this I mean nothing more than an inclination to reflect rationally about values. Such inclination does not exhaust the definition of critical thinking, but it is what bears on my remarks. Because works of art are among the most intriguing things in the world that sustain interest, we are constantly trying to interpret their meanings and assess their merit, which, of course, involves thinking about them. D. N. Perkins, among others, has pointed out how works of art can be perplexing and that intelligent people enjoy solving puzzles.[24] Not the least puzzling aspect of works of art is their nonliteral, metaphorical import. Accordingly, making sense of art involves a fair amount of hypothetical thinking that relies on more or less explicit assumptions about the nature, meaning, and value of art. The construal of works of art as puzzles generated interest in a case-study approach to the teaching of aesthetics that is based on the supposition that learning can be made more interesting and productive if instead of teaching a history of aesthetic theories from which principles can then be derived, teachers present a puzzling case and then draw on theory to try to resolve it.[25] This method of teaching aesthetics is also being used in aesthetic education classes and workshops.[26] In brief, interpreting meaning or assessing the merit of a work of art involves critical reasoning. And such reasoning obviously requires a good use of language. "Critical judgment, appreciation, stylistic analysis, disputations about taste, historical comparisons, and efficient instruction itself," writes Jacques Barzun, "depend on the appropriate use of words." He goes on to note "the pleasure that comes of being able to see and hear works of art more sharply and subtly, more consciously, to register that pleasure in words and compare notes with other people similarly inclined."[27] In addition to their puzzling and ambiguous character, works of art can effectively stimulate critical thinking because they have greater immediate impact than more abstract or ephemeral entities and are more accessible for checking, comparison, and contrast. What is more, as the mind scans a work of art of some magnitude, critical reasoning is supplemented by various sensory modalities that are also brought into play.[28]

Finally, works of art are worth studying not only because they make direct contact with a range of human concerns but also because they provide opportunities for effecting transfer of learning. Those who have internalized the concepts of art and aesthetic vision have no difficulty in imagining the human career itself as a carefully crafted performance or in understanding the self as a dramatic text that can be rewritten as the occasion requires.[29] It follows from what I have said that aesthetic education is equally capable of fostering respect for the arts and values of alternative cultures.

CULTURAL ALTERNATIVES

Developing an understanding and respect for cultural alternatives is an abiding concern of the International Society for Education Through Art. But it is one thing to underline the importance of appreciating cultural diversity and another to decide how best to accomplish it

Elsewhere, I have suggested there are right and wrong ways to celebrate cultural diversity.[30] Finding useful for my purposes some distinctions between ways of understanding made by Kaufmann, I have discussed the differences between what I call *exegetical, dogmatic, agnostic,* and *dialectical* multiculturalists.[31] Kaufmann had used these terms to discuss the art of reading a classic text for purposes of experiencing culture shock and self-examination, and he likened the reader of a literary classic to a tourist who visits an alien culture. Tourists who travel to different cultures in search of alternative experiences can also be said to exemplify Kaufmann's types. In my discussion of Kaufmann I dealt only briefly with the first three of his types of visitor—the exegetical, the dogmatic, and the agnostic—because I found them, as Kaufmann did for his purposes, insufficient for mine. Instead, I concentrated on the dialectical visitor. Thanks to the British art educator Rachel Mason and others—and perhaps because of the paucity of conceptualizations of multiculturalism at the time I wrote—these distinctions have become part of the literature of multiculturalism.[32] Another reason may have come from my quoting Harold Osborne, who believed that the only way to shed one's ethnocentrism is by entertaining the values of a radically different society. But perhaps a more important reason for the adoption of the types of multiculturalist I described is that they represent real types and are not mere abstractions. And so I refer to them once again.

Exegetical multiculturalists typically endow a different culture with superior merit and then read their own sentiments and allegiances into it for the purpose of receiving them back, reinforced and substantiated. Their next step is to convert others to their position. The limitation of the exegetical point of view is that its prior emotional commitment to certain ideas and values risks missing the whole picture, thereby inviting deception and old-fashioned chauvinism. Exegesis is thus educationally restrictive because it can subvert one of the principal objectives of humanities education—to help persons think critically and to judge for themselves what is or is not worthwhile.

Dogmatic multiculturalists can be dismissed because they err on the side opposite from that of exegetical types. Multiculturalists of this temper assume that their own culture is superior to the one under scrutiny and that the sooner the latter can be transformed the better. There is no effort to seek culture shock for purposes of self-reflection.

As far as agnostic multiculturalists are concerned, their interest lies either in surface phenomena, a tiny part of the whole, or in the antiquarian aspects of a culture. Such interest resembles that of the amateur stamp collector. Although preferable to dogmatic multiculturalists, agnostic multiculturalists are guilty of taking an easy road; they prefer the comforts of home away from home. Taking in only brief glimpses of things along the way, they give themselves little opportunity for genuine culture shock and thus serious self-examination.

The most illuminating and educationally rewarding way of studying a culture for purposes of experiencing culture shock and self-examination is not the exegetical, dogmatic, or agnostic way but the dialectical way. *Dialectical* implies an extended and significant encounter with the arts of a different culture, and it has three components: Socratic, dialogical, and comparative. The Socratic component presupposes a commitment to self-examination. *Dialogical* refers to an open-mindedness that initially presumes neither the superiority of one's own culture nor the one under scrutiny. *Comparative* suggests the necessity to compare and contrast one's own value system with that of another. What is more, inquiry of this kind is nonauthoritarian and attempts to be as objective as possible. It releases observers from parochialism and cultural conditioning and, as Kaufmann puts it, allows them to experience the freedom that comes from an awareness of alternatives that permits the creation of new ways. The comparative component of dialectical inquiry requires an individual's ability to compare and contrast and implies a solid understanding of his or her own cultural value system.

Kaufmann envisions three concentric circles as an aid to seeing what is going on in a different culture. As far as aesthetic education is concerned, the innermost circle would consist of the art of a culture to which we typically respond with our own premises and values. Yet because we are self-consciously attempting to perceive art in what we know to be a different culture, we must place such art within the second concentric circle, wherein we try to understand its relation to a culture's other aspects. In what ways does its art express the distinctive voice of a culture, its cast of mind and mode of feeling, its style, its sense of personhood, its relation to tradition and innovation, and so forth? A third circle compares and contrasts what we have thus far discovered with our own cultural assumptions and ways of knowing and feeling.[33] Not only should these circles be understood as having overlapping content, but it is also assumed that one travels back and forth among them.

To illustrate the dialectical encounter and its various components, I have referred to Clifford Geertz's study of theatrical performances in Balinese culture.[34] Although it might initially seem that there is much in Balinese life that is consistent with Western assumptions about the importance of aesthetic values, and indeed exemplifies these values more vividly than is the case in Western societies (for example, the ways in which aesthetic etiquette pervades Balinese life), closer examination reveals some dramatic differences. In Balinese theatrical performances, for example, there is no sense of the Aristotelian unities—of beginnings, middles, and ends—which, says Geertz, leaves the visitor perplexed about what is happening or what has gone on before. Consequently, the observer is prevented from having Dewey's conception of an experience that is marked by dramatic organization and unity. According to Geertz, Balinese life mutes such experience or any experience that is too personal and subjective. It subdues a strong sense of self in favor of the absorption of the person into the fabric of social life. Dialectical encounters that reveal such differences can, of course, be carried out in other cultures. My point is that a proper stance toward another culture is becoming more and more important with the ease of travel.

CONCLUSION

In summary, I reiterate that our times necessitate a return to the appreciation of artistic accomplishment wherever we find it if we are to help restore faith in human capability and effectively address new challenges. Part of this task entails the cultivation of aesthetic vision, which I have called the capacity for aesthetic perceptiveness and experience, and such capacity is complemented by thoughtful reflection. Both vision and reflection are brought into play in any discussion of cultural alternatives.

The four major benefits of an aesthetic education K–12 curriculum understood from a humanities point of view—appreciation of excellence, aesthetic vision, critical thinking, and respect for alternatives—are interrelated and overlapping. How these benefits can be realized through aesthetic learning will vary from culture to culture and within cultures. One image of a curriculum I have suggested entails a number of phases. In the early years there would be familiarization with a wide range of artworks, introduction to the principles of art making and aesthetic perception, and initiation into the cultural institution known as the artworld. The middle years would concentrate on a more formal introduction to the history of world art, leaving to the later years the study in depth of selected exemplars, with perhaps seminars coming at the end of schooling in which older adolescents could begin to fashion their own ideas about art and its significance.[35] All these phases of aesthetic learning would contribute to the building of a comprehensive sense of art, the possession of which enables persons to realize the inherent values of art.

It should be clear that I place great importance on the historical dimension of art. The history of art is an undeniable record of artistic accomplishment. It not only provides criteria of artistic excellence and informs aesthetic vision and critical thinking; it also engenders appreciation of difference and contributes to cultural literacy. Most significantly, we study the achievements of the past to admire some of the most precious creative moments in the history of humankind, moments that, to recall some earlier remarks, "light up for us whole areas of the mind," make us "proud of our equivocal humanity," and help us wring from life "a more convincing and relevant meaning."

NOTES

1. My sentiments are similar to Monroe C. Beardsley's in his "Aesthetic Experience Regained," in *The Aesthetic Point of View: Selected Essays*, ed. Michael J. Wreen and Donald M. Callen (Ithaca: Cornell University Press, 1982), 77.

2. Max Lerner has some perceptive remarks along these lines in his *America as a Civilization*, 2nd ed. (New York: Henry Holt, 1987), 1008.

3. Kenneth Clark, *What Is a Masterpiece?* (New York: Thames and Hudson, 1979), 5.

4. E. H. Gombrich, *Ideals and Idols* (New York: E. P. Dutton, 1979), 15–16.

5. Arnold Hauser, *Philosophy of Art History* (New York: Alfred A. Knopf, 1959), 5.

6. I am also reminded of a remark made by Rudolf Arnheim in *Parables of Sun Light* (Berkeley and Los Angeles: University of California Press, 1989), 218. He said that when in the presence of a great work of art, he often feels as if he had been admitted by mistake inasmuch as the full significance of such a work eluded his grasp. It was, he said, as if a careless priest had let him have a peek at the Athena in the cella of the Parthenon.

7. These objectives of the humanities are conventional ones, but they are well discussed in Walter Kaufmann's *The Future of the Humanities* (New York: Thomas Y. Crowell, 1977).

8. First in *Excellence in Art Education: Ideas and Initiatives* (Reston, Va.: National Art Education Association, 1986; slightly updated version 1987), chap. 2; and later in *Excellence II: The Continuing Quest in Art Education* (Reston, Va.: National Art Education Association, 1995), chap. 5.

9. Jacob Rosenberg, "Conclusions," in *On Quality in Art: Criteria of Excellence, Past and Present* (Princeton, N.J.: Princeton University Press, 1967).

10. Sherman E. Lee, "Painting," in *Quality: Its Image in the Arts*, ed. Louis Kronenberger (New York: Atheneum, 1969). Reprinted in Lee's *Past, Present, East and West* (New York: George Braziller, 1983), 187–204.

11. Clark, *What Is a Masterpiece?*, 10–11.

12. Stanley Kauffmann, "Film," in Kronenberger, *On Quality*, 374–78.

13. H. Gene Blocker, *The Aesthetics of Primitive Art* (New York: University Press of America, 1994).

14. Ibid., 314.

15. Harold Osborne, "Assessment and Stature," in *Aesthetics and Arts Education*, ed. R. A. Smith and Alan Simpson (Urbana: University of Illinois Press, 1991), 95–107.

16. For a discussion of the constitutive and revelatory theories of art, see Albert William Levi and R. A. Smith, *Art Education: A Critical Necessity* (Urbana: University of Illinois Press, 1991), chap. 2.

17. Friedrich von Schiller, *On the Aesthetic Education of Man in a Series of Letters*, trans. Elizabeth M. Wilkinson and L. A. Willoughby (New York: Oxford University Press, 1976).

18. Herbert Read, *The Redemption of the Robot: My Encounters with Education Through Art* (New York: Simon and Schuster, 1969), 43.

19. John Dewey, *Art as Experience* (Carbondale: Southern Illinois University Press, 1987), 252–53.

20. Levi and Smith, *Art Education*, chap. 2.

21. Nelson Goodman, *Languages of Art: A Theory of Symbol Systems* (Indianapolis: Hackett, 1976); Howard Gardner, *Frames of Mind: The Theory of Multiple Intelligences* (New York: Basic Books, 1983).

22. Monroe C. Beardsley, "Aesthetic Experience," *The Aesthetic Point of View: Selected Essays,* 288–89.

23. See Vernon Howard, *Learning by All Means: Lessons from the Arts* (New York: Peter Lang, 1992); Elliot W. Eisner, *The Educational Imagination: On the Design and Evaluation of School Programs,* 3rd ed. (New York: Macmillan, 1994); and Donald Arnstine, *Democracy and the Arts of Schooling* (Albany: State University of New York Press, 1995).

24. David N. Perkins, *The Intelligent Eye: Learning to Think by Looking at Art* (Los Angeles: Getty Center for Education in the Arts, 1994).

25. Margaret P. Battin, John Fisher, Ronald Moore, and Anita Silvers, *Puzzles About Art: An Aesthetics Casebook* (New York: St. Martin's Press, 1989).

26. See, e.g., Marilyn Galvin Stewart, "Aesthetics and the Art Curriculum," in *Aesthetics for Young People,* ed. Ronald Moore (Reston, Va.: National Art Education Association, 1995), 77–88.

27. Jacques Barzun, "Art and Educational Inflation," *Journal of Aesthetic Education* 12, no. 4 (1978).

28. For an example of how various sense modalities are activated during aesthetic experience, see Harry S. Broudy, "The Structure of Knowledge in the Arts," in *Aesthetics and Criticism in Art Education: Problems in Defining, Explaining, and Evaluating Art,* ed. R. A. Smith (Chicago: Rand McNally, 1966), 34–35. The passage is also quoted in the appendix on aesthetic experience in R. A. Smith, *Excellence II,* 203–4. Cf. Broudy, *Enlightened Cherishing: An Essay on Aesthetic Education* (Urbana: University of Illinois Press, 1994). Broudy is often regarded as the principle theorist of aesthetic education in the United States.

29. For some discussion of the self as text, see Iredell Jenkins, "Performance," in *Aesthetic Concepts and Education,* ed. Ralph A. Smith (Urbana: University of Illinois Press, 1970), 204–26.

30. Ralph A. Smith, "Celebrating the Arts in Their Cultural Diversity: Some Wrong and Right Ways to Do It," in *Arts in Cultural Diversity,* ed. Jack Condous, Janterie Howlett, and John Skull (New York: Holt, Rinehart and Winston, 1980), 82–88. Cf. my "Forms of Multi-cultural Education in the Arts," *Journal of Multicultural and Cross-cultural Research in Art Education* 1, no. 1 (Fall 1983): 23–32; "The Question of Multiculturalism," in both *Arts Education Policy Review,* 94, no. 4 (1993): 2–18 and *General Knowledge and Arts Education* (Urbana: University of Illinois Press, 1994), chap. 5; "The Uses of Cultural Diversity," *Journal of Aesthetic Education* 12, no. 2 (1978): 5–10; "On Observing a Different Society," *Journal of Aesthetic Education* 23, no. 1 (1989): 5–7, a special issue devoted to arts education in China; and "Multiculturalism and Cultural Particularism," *Excellence II,* chap. 7.

31. Walter Kaufmann, *The Future of the Humanities* (New York: Thomas Y. Crowell, 1977), chap. 2.

32. For example, in *Art Education and Multiculturalism* (New York: Croom Helm, 1988), Mason adopts a dialectical approach to inquiry for her study of multiracial inner-city schools.

33. My description of a third concentric circle is a modification of Kaufmann's. Since he was talking about literature, he took it to involve the relation of the two inner circles to the body of work of an author.

34. Clifford Geertz, "Person, Time, and Conduct in Bali," in *The Interpretation of Cultures* (New York: Basic Books, 1973).

35. I have sketched such a K–12 curriculum in *The Sense of Art: A Study in Aesthetic Education* (New York: Routledge, 1989), chap. 6; "Toward Percipience: A Humanities Curriculum for Arts Education," in *The Arts, Education, and Aesthetic Knowing*, Part 2, ed. Bennett Reimer and R. A. Smith, Ninty-first Yearbook of the National Society for the Study of Education (Chicago: National Society for the Study of Education, 1992), chap. 3; *Excellence II*, chap. 9; and *General Knowledge and Arts Education*, chap. 6.

Toward Percipience: A Humanities Curriculum for Arts Education

THE EMPHASIS on cognition in art education is predicated on the increasingly accepted belief that art is a basic form of human knowing. Although it may share features with other forms of knowing, artistic expression is considered to be distinctive enough to be appreciated for its own characteristic values. This view of art achieved prominence in the modern era with the writings of the German philosopher Ernst Cassirer (1874–1945). In *An Essay on Man* he popularized a conception of knowledge that features six symbolic forms of human culture: myth, language, religion, history, science, and art. These forms of human culture constitute the characteristic work of man and defined what Cassirer called the circle of humanity. "A 'philosophy of man' would therefore," he writes, "be a philosophy which would give us insight into the fundamental structure of each of these human activities, and which at the same time would enable us to understand them as an organic whole."[1] The proposition that it is possible to understand varieties of knowing as forming an organic whole is perhaps more controversial than the supposition that there are different kinds of knowing. The theoretical assumptions and terminology of writers may vary, but the root idea remains the same: there are realms of meaning, ways of knowing, types of intelligence.[2] Since it is one of the principal functions of schooling to introduce students to this variety, it seems only reasonable to suggest that instruction in aesthetic knowing should be made available. Knowledge about the structure of art would provide the basic content or subject matter for such instruction, while the psychology of human development would yield suggestions for scheduling appropriate learning activities. In the following, I concentrate on the substantive dimensions of aesthetic knowing.

First, however, it will be helpful to indicate the basic situation around which to organize teaching and learning in the arts. This situation is one in which persons confront works of art for the sake of realizing the worthwhile benefits that such works are capable of providing. Because we typically find works of art in the cultural institutions of the artworld, we may understand arts education as preparation for traversing the world of art with intelligence and sensitivity. Intelligent and sensitive encounters in art in turn presuppose certain capacities and inclinations that are enfolded in the term *percipience*. It follows that the general goal of arts education is the cultivation of percipience in matters of art and culture.[3] The learner, then, is appropriately viewed as a potentially reflective observer and artworld sojourner. A perceptive stance is an appropriate educational objective because it is the attitude persons characteristically assume toward works of art. To be sure, a number of theorists and practitioners continue to stress competence in creative and performing activities as the cornerstone of arts education. I, too, believe that such activities are important, but I view them as but one set among several competencies that contribute to the development of what I hereafter call *aesthetic percipience*.

One might think it a relatively straightforward matter to organize the components of aesthetic learning, yet pluralism reigns, and a multiplicity of aims and purposes must be accepted as professional facts of life. How, then, does one develop a context for responding to art under these circumstances? We may speak of two types of objectives: the more general objectives of the humanities and the more specific objectives of arts education. The former are framed as a response to the cultural conditions that require a restatement of the role of the humanities in the human career. The latter concern the more practical matters of teaching, curriculum design, and assessment.

THE HUMANITIES TODAY

Albert W. Levi has argued that the humanities are eternally relevant because they are the liberal arts of communication, continuity, and criticism. He associates communication with languages and literatures, continuity with history, and criticism with philosophy in its sense of critical reasoning. How did he arrive at such an interpretation, and why did he feel the need for it?

Levi felt that his writings on the topic were a response to many of the problems besetting contemporary society: the need to restore historical memory and recall the ideal of human excellence; the need of a democratic, egalitarian society to come to terms with an essentially aristocratic tradition of learning; the need to articulate a plausible relation between the taught and the lived humanities; and the need to defend the humanities against their newest rival, the social sciences. In responding to these challenges, Levi, a strong believer in historical continuity, recalls two ways of interpreting the humanities and suggests a third option that combines both.[4]

From the tradition of the Renaissance, Levi recalls a substantive definition of *the humanities* as "subject matters." This definition is consistent with the tendency of Renaissance thinkers to recover and transmit the literary texts of antiquity. From the earlier tradition of the Middle Ages, he recalls a procedural definition that construed the humanities as skills or ways of organizing and understanding human experience. These skills ultimately became known as the liberal arts. Levi's third option consists of a synthesis of the Renaissance and the medieval traditions in which he defines the humanities procedurally as the liberal arts of communication, continuity and criticism, and substantively as languages and literatures, history, and philosophy. Thus Levi foresaw, and attempted to avoid, the trap of educational formalism into which E. D. Hirsch Jr. thinks American schooling has fallen—the tendency to separate the teaching of skills from specific content or background knowledge.[5]

If we subsume the creative and fine arts under languages and literatures, which is surely permissible inasmuch as we commonly speak of artistic expression as aesthetic communication, then we will have assimilated another *c*—the arts of creation—to Levi's interpretation. This emendation enables us to say that the humanities are indispensable and eternally relevant because they are the arts of creation, communication, continuity, and criticism. Teaching the arts as humanities would then mean bringing to bear at appropriate times and junctures the ideas and procedures of these arts. Works of art would be understood as artistic statements created in the stream of time whose meanings and significance are disclosed through historical and art criticism. The basic problem for a humanities interpretation of arts education would be the orchestration of these arts of thought and action for purposes of curriculum design and learning.

Pedagogical considerations would center on what is involved in coming to understand and appreciate works of art. To help bring about such understanding, the following questions may be asked of any work of art: (1) Who made it? (2) How was it made? (3) When was it made? (4) For whom was it made? (5) What is its message or meaning, if any? (6) What is its style? (7) What is the quality of experience it affords? (8) What was its place in the culture in which it was made? (9) What is its place in the culture or society of today? and (10) What peculiar problems does it present to understanding and appreciation?[6] A degree of competency in answering these questions constitutes evidence of a well-developed sense of art and is prerequisite for engaging works of art. Such competence makes the young less dependent on the judgments and value preferences of others and enables them to venture into the artworld with a measure of autonomy. What kind of a curriculum would conduce to the cultivation of such percipience?

A HUMANITIES CURRICULUM FOR ARTS EDUCATION

In the following, *percipience curriculum* and *humanities curriculum* are used interchangeably, as are *percipience* and *aesthetic percipience*. A percipience curriculum extends from kindergarten through twelfth grade and is part of a program of required general studies for all students. If, with Cassirer, we believe that art is a basic symbolic form of human culture, then all members of a democratic society deserve the opportunity to reap its benefits, for such opportunity gives meaning to the idea of becoming more fully human through art.[7] I further assume that efforts to cultivate aesthetic percipience will have different accents at various points along the instructional path. The curriculum should also be cumulative in the sense that early learning should be foundational for what comes later. I am not recommending a lockstep series of highly specific behavioral objectives, but I am saying that it pays to know the lay of the land before exploring it in greater detail. Assessment of aesthetic learning would estimate the extent to which a learner's framework for understanding and experiencing art is expanding and developing in appropriate ways.

I have said that arts education is concerned with whatever is necessary to get persons to confront works of visual, auditory, or verbal art with a well-developed sense of art for the sake of realizing the benefits that works of art are capable of providing. I further supplement this image of a reflective percipient with a view of the curriculum as an itinerary and of the aesthetic learner as potential artworld sojourner. Artworld sojourners know not only where to seek aesthetic value but also how to realize it. True, when in the privacy of one's home we examine a painting, listen to music, or read a poem, we do not ordinarily imagine ourselves as participating in the artworld, which has a public, institutional connotation. Yet many of the same conditions and problems obtain whether we attend to a work in a private or a more social setting. But before we can prepare artworld sojourners, we must ask ourselves, What characteristic role do works of art play in the human career? Without coherent ideas about how to answer this question, arts education will suffer from a lack of purpose, and the problem of justification will go unresolved.

THE VALUES OF ART

It has been persuasively argued that works of art are valuable for their capacity to induce a high degree of aesthetic experience in a well-prepared percipient. Aesthetic experience in turn is important because it serves a two-fold function: it shapes experience in desirable ways and provides humanistic insight. Another way of characterizing the positive effect of works of art is to say that they have both constitutive and revelatory powers; that is, they have potential for integrating the self and for conveying what may be called *aesthetic wisdom.*[8]

Constitutive Values of Art

Regarding the constitutive values of works of art—their capacity to shape experience in beneficial ways—we can trace a line of thought from Plato in antiquity to Friedrich von Schiller in the eighteenth century to Herbert Read and John Dewey and other theorists in the twentieth. In this literature, Schiller's *On the Aesthetic Education of Man in a Series of Letters* (1795) stands out as a work that celebrates art's constitutive powers.[9] Writing during the politically charged century of great democratic revolutions, Schiller, a poet and playwright as well as a philosopher, argued that true civil and political freedom could be achieved only through the formation of an ennobled character and that before citizens could be given a constitutional government they themselves need to have become soundly constituted. Schiller believed that the latter result could be achieved through aesthetic education, which, in his idea of it, placed great importance on the study of the immortal works of the masters. In other words, aesthetic education was the key to the problem of political and individual freedom. It occupies a middle state between the realm of brute force and the rule of law, a sphere where character building develops. What was it about masterworks that released what Schiller called the living springs of human experience? Schiller thought it was their form, by which he meant not merely a work's shape but also its structure, balance, symmetry, harmony, and integrity. These qualities were at once the essence of the work of art and of the properly constituted self. In short, aesthetic education, for Schiller, did not exist in contrast or as an addition to moral education; it had itself an important moral function.[10]

Aesthetic education plays a similar role in the thinking of Herbert Read, who makes aesthetic discipline central to moral education generally. Where Schiller spoke of aesthetic education's contribution to an ennobled character, Read, in *The Redemption of the Robot*, designates grace as the end result. "We must," says Read, "give priority in our education to all forms of aesthetic activity, for in the course of making beautiful things there will take place a crystallization of the emotions into patterns that are the molds of virtue."[11]

John Dewey likewise recognized that it was a purpose of art to bring about organic unification in both the perception of the external world and in the integration of human consciousness. In *Art as Experience* he writes that art not only breaks through conventional distinctions and stereotyped thinking, which is a moral as well as an aesthetic function; it also composes psychological strains, conflicts, and oppositions into a greater, richer, and more harmonious personality structure.[12]

Revelatory Powers of Art

In addition to exercising and shaping constitutive powers, art is a source of revelation, of humanistic insight. Revelatory theories, which were prominent in the modern Romantic period, underline the exaltation of self, animation of spirit, and discovery of self that are typically experienced in encounters with major works of art. What is revealed through such experience is not verifiable fact couched in warranted assertions but rather the human truth of things expressed in aesthetic or dramatic form, a truth more like aesthetic wisdom. We avail ourselves of such wisdom whenever we contemplate artists' visions of relations to the external world, to others, and to themselves. As Levi has noted, we have Giotto, Fra Angelico, Giovanni Bellini, and Raphael on religious commemoration, adoration, and inspiration; van Ruisdael, Poussin, Constable, and Van Gogh on the transcendental values of landscape; Holbein, Rembrandt, Velázquez, and Ingres on human character in portraiture—all testifying to the revelatory powers of artistic expression.

Constitutive and revelatory theories of art are inherently cognitive in the sense that they presuppose the exercise of a range of mental functions such as perception, memory, discrimination, analysis, and judgment in the making of and responding to works of art. Revelatory theories, however, contain a cognitive bonus inasmuch as they concentrate on a work's meaning as well as its potential shaping power. This does not imply that feelings or emotions play no strategic role in either group of theories. Simply being told what a work means or being informed that it has potential for shaping the self does little for persons unless they feel or realize for themselves in a personal sense an artwork's form and content. The point that knowing is suffused with feeling, that we know with our emotions, is well made in the cognitive theory of Nelson Goodman.[13] Although a narrow, overintellectualized conception of the nature and role of cognition in aesthetic experience ought to be avoided, the important role that intelligence and knowledge do play in such experience should nonetheless be acknowledged.

A Synthesis

A third option combines the insights of both constitutive and revelatory theories. For an example, I turn to the later writings on aesthetic experience by Monroe C. Beardsley. In these writings Beardsley specifically takes into account the cognitive character of aesthetic response, largely, he says, as the result of the influence on his thinking of E. H. Gombrich, Rudolf Arnheim, and Nelson Goodman.[14]

Aesthetic experience, Beardsley believes, is both compound and disjunctive. By *compound* he means that aesthetic experience cannot be reduced to a single emotion or attitude; rather, it consists of a number of characteristics that tend to cluster. By *disjunctive* he means that experiences with aesthetic character separate themselves quite readily from ordinary experiences, even though the latter may also have some aesthetic features. Accordingly, Beardsley suggests five criteria of the aesthetic, although he is prepared to admit the possibility of there being more or fewer features. These criteria are object directedness, felt freedom, detached affect, active discovery, and personal integration or wholeness. The following is a condensed account of his analysis.

The feeling of object directedness involves a realization that things in one's phenomenally objective field of awareness—for example, works of visual, auditory, and verbal art—are working or have worked themselves out in fitting and appropriate ways. Presupposed is some presence or object to which attention is directed and that in turn guides perception. We regard intensely and seriously what is happening in a painting, a musical composition, a work of sculpture, a poem, or a film, and if we feel the rightness of what is unfolding, then the first criterion of the aesthetic is satisfied. Felt freedom is a feeling of having suddenly put aside or pushed into the back of one's mind troubling or obtrusive thoughts in favor of freely giving oneself to phenomena of perception. It is a sense, says Beardsley, "of being on top of things, of having one's real way, even though not actually having chosen it or won it" (290). One willingly accedes to a change of attitude because of the pleasure or gratification derived from doing so.

The feeling of detached affect implies the act of experiencing a work at a certain emotional distance in order to avoid two undesirable outcomes. The first is losing ourselves in the object, in which case we would give up contact with its intricate and demanding form and content and thus with its peculiar richness. The second is deceiving ourselves into thinking that we are perceiving real rather than imaginary or fictional objects. Implicit in the notion of detached affect is the tendency of works "to lend some degree of detachment to the effects they produce." They give "an air of artifice, of fictionality, of autonomy and reflexiveness, of separation from other things, and so on" (291). This feeling may not always be experienced, but it is experienced often enough to suggest that detached affect is an important feature of many aesthetic experiences.

It should be clear that aesthetic experience is fueled by knowledge and that perception is a cognitive act. True, we freely give our attention to an object because we discern or feel something special that invites further scrutiny. This scrutiny would remain unrewarded, however, unless it were animated by perceptual skills and background knowledge. But it is in the feeling of active discovery, Beardsley's fourth feature of aesthetic experience, that its cognitive character becomes most evident. Beardsley came to realize that one of the central components in our experience of art "must be the experience of discovery, of insight into connections and organization, the elation that comes from the apparent opening up of intelligibility." This opening up draws attention "to the excitement of meeting a cognitive challenge, of flexing one's powers to make *intelligible*—where this combines *making sense of something with making something make sense*" (292). Sense making is, of course, what aesthetic experiences have in common with other kinds of experiences. A feeling of discovery is certainly not alien to the scholar and the scientist who experience the same exhilaration of discovery. When there is little to discover there can, of course, be little sense making, and aesthetic experience will be thin. This obvious fact is why masterworks rank high on the list of things that have the capacity to stimulate aesthetic experience.

If Beardsley's notion of active discovery underscores the cognitive character of aesthetic awareness, his fifth feature, wholeness, draws attention to art's constitutive powers. In discussing the ways in which the experience of an artwork can generate a feeling of wholeness, Beardsley concentrates on the coherence of aesthetic experience, by which he means both "the coherence of the elements of the experience itself, of the diverse mental acts and events going on in one's mind over a stretch of time" and "the coherence of the self, the mind's healing sense . . . of being all together and able to encompass its perceptions, feelings, emotions, ideas, in a single integrated personhood" (293).

I have used Beardsley's theory of aesthetic experience to suggest an alternative to theories that stress either the constitutive or revelatory power of art. Just as Levi in his redefinition of the humanities combined the medieval and Renaissance traditions of the humanities into a third option that features the liberal arts of communication, continuity, and criticism, to which I have added the arts of creation, so I have combined elements of Classic and Romantic theories of art in describing art's peculiar values. Having offered an answer to the question why the art world is worth traversing, I return to the more concrete question of curriculum design.

PHASES OF AESTHETIC LEARNING (K–12)

At their best, works of art require years of study and half a lifetime of experience and growing familiarity may be necessary for their full appreciation. So opined Harold Osborne in *The Art of Appreciation*.[15] Aesthetic learning in the schools is a similarly long journey. It begins early and gradually extends into the middle and secondary years. Its overall purpose is the cultivation of percipience, which involves acquiring a well-developed sense of art.

This goal can be reached through a number of learning phases that build toward the learner's having a rich apperceptive mass. Learning, moreover, occurs most efficaciously when new information is related to a person's conceptual framework. Concepts, organized in a hierarchy, undergo change as new information is assimilated. This view of learning means that teachers must have a good grasp of the conceptual character of art and an understanding of how to relate new information to the learner's existing schemes of knowledge.[16]

Learning in the arts proceeds from simple exposure and familiarization as well as practice in art making and perception in the elementary grades to more demanding historical, appreciative, and critical studies during the secondary years. As particular objectives change, so will teaching and learning methods. Assessment will center on the progress that learners make in expanding their conceptual frameworks. The entire scheme is built on the assumption that phases of aesthetic learning are instrumental to the goal of attaining greater percipience (see accompanying illustration).[17]

Phase 1: Perceiving Aesthetic Qualities (K–3)

Although very young children are hardly prepared to engage works of art in all their formal complexity and dramatic intensity, to say nothing of their thematic and symbolic import, they are sensitive to the simple sensory and expressive qualities of things. Hence the years from kindergarten through third grade are the time to exploit and expand this capacity. This can be done through exposure to the aesthetic qualities found in all sorts of things, in nature, in ordinary objects, or in works of the children's own making. During this phase it might be said that the general goal is an appreciation of the qualitative immediacy of life. The young learn to enjoy things for their freshness and vividness. They are encouraged to delight in the looks, sounds, tastes, and smells of things. But since visual, auditory, and verbal works of art are the principal loci of such qualities, it is important that young students' attention also be directed toward artworks. Learners in the early grades should be led to notice their aesthetic qualities and to understand that artworks are special objects found in special places that society maintains at considerable effort. Thus do young learners begin to develop an elementary understanding of art and the art world. At the same time they intuitively acquire a sense of object directedness, which is a fundamental feature of aesthetic experience.

In short, formal aesthetic learning begins during phase 1. The understanding the young bring to school undergoes modification and expansion. The job of building dispositions gets under way. An initiation occurs into

A Percipience Curriculum (K–12)

General Goal: Cultivating Percipience in Matters of Art by Teaching the Concepts and Skills of Art Conceived as a Humanity

The Concepts and the Skills

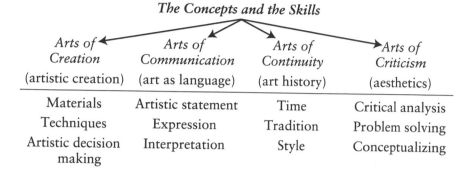

Arts of Creation	*Arts of Communication*	*Arts of Continuity*	*Arts of Criticism*
(artistic creation)	(art as language)	(art history)	(aesthetics)
Materials	Artistic statement	Time	Critical analysis
Techniques	Expression	Tradition	Problem solving
Artistic decision making	Interpretation	Style	Conceptualizing

The Learning Continuum

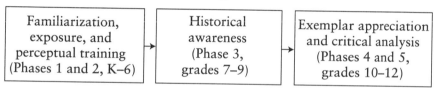

Familiarization, exposure, and perceptual training (Phases 1 and 2, K–6)	Historical awareness (Phase 3, grades 7–9)	Exemplar appreciation and critical analysis (Phases 4 and 5, grades 10–12)

Teaching and learning proceed along a continuum from exposure, familiarization, and perceptual training to historical awareness, exemplar appreciation, and critical analysis, stressing discovery and reception learning, didactic coaching, and dialogic teaching methods. Evaluation of aesthetic learning centers on the development of aesthetic conceptual maps and the conditions conducive for doing so.

the mysteries of art and into a cultural institution known as an artworld. In making their own works of art, young learners also gain insight into the nature of the artistic creative process. They come to realize that a work of art is a product of an artist's having combined the special qualities of materials in an aesthetic object that features medium, form, and content. They learn, in other words, the way of aesthetic communication. In terms of a humanities interpretation of aesthetic education, this is, in effect, to bring the arts of creation and communication to bear on the study of art. During phase 1, instruction should not be overly formal and it should keep children's natural propensities constantly in mind. And although all phases of aesthetic learning are instrumental to the achievement of a certain level of percipience, aesthetic learning will, once more, afford students numerous moments of intrinsic satisfaction when ulterior objectives recede or are ignored.

Much of what now goes on in the early years of school could suffice for achieving the objectives of phase 1. But if teachers plan these activities and lessons with the long-term goal of aesthetic percipience in mind, they might go about their teaching in slightly different ways. The important consideration is that all learning should have a point and lead in a definite direction, most immediately toward the greater perceptual finesse that is the goal of phase 2 of aesthetic learning.

Phase 2: Developing Perceptual Finesse (Grades 4–6)

A precise dividing line between learning phases cannot, of course, be drawn, but by the upper elementary years the young are capable of concentrating their energies and powers. They can perceive greater complexity in their own works of art as well as those of mature artists. Gradually, however, attention shifts to the latter, for it is only through the perception of works of some complexity that perceptual skills can be honed and developed.

In addition to the immediate qualities of artworks, their complex webs of relations and meanings are now brought more fully and clearly into view. It is time for looking at artworks more closely while simultaneously learning about the artworld, in which works of art find a home and caretakers. Still not inordinately formal, learning in phase 2 is more structured than it was in phase 1. In addition to making, seeing, and listening, students begin to acquire during this period a vocabulary or language for talking about art and its various components.

Although it is possible to teach even the very young a methodical way of doing something, it is during phase 2 especially that some system can be introduced. Harry S. Broudy recommends a scheme of paying close attention to a work's sensory, formal, expressive, and technical aspects.[18] The scanning of such aspects can be a useful method for making initial contact with artworks, provided it does not become oversimplified, rigid, or burdened with excessive claims for its effectiveness. It might therefore be helpful to see scanning within a larger pattern of response.

The art historian Kenneth Clark once described his own perceptual habits this way.[19] First, there is the initial impact that a work of art makes, which can be quite idiosyncratic, and then a period of close scrutiny and examination during which one attempts to find what is actually in a work to be perceived and enjoyed. The phase of scrutiny is followed by one of recollection. Relevant information, biographical and historical, for example, is summoned in order to render a work intelligible. After that, additional periods of scrutiny and recollection renew and revitalize initial responses. The point is that aesthetic experience is difficult to sustain for very long, and the senses need time to regroup. What is more, although one's initial impressions of a work are fresh and spontaneous, they are often not a reliable key to a work's character or import. At the end of phase 2, far more than at the end of phase 1, students should be able not only to convey to others the character of their first impressions (impact), but also to engage in formal analysis (scrutiny) and apply what knowledge they have acquired (recollection) in sustaining their interest in a work (renewal). When they practice the skills of aesthetic perception during what may be called the complete act of informed aesthetic response, learners become acquainted with, though not necessarily self-consciously, those additional features of aesthetic experience that Beardsley termed *felt freedom, detached affect,* and *active discovery*, that is, feelings of freely taking up a special point of view toward something for the sake of what can be discovered while doing so. During phases 1 and 2 it is, of course, appropriate to show and discuss works created by members of different groups and from other cultures and civilizations. A humanities curriculum, in other words, should have a multicultural dimension. However, I understand multiculturalism not as an ideological attack on the values of Western civilization but simply as a recognition that the study of alternatives is a revered humanistic objective, a way of avoiding a narrow ethnocentrism.[20] Indeed, a well-developed sense of art implies an awareness of a broad range of artworks.

Phase 3: Developing a Sense of Art History (Grades 7–9)

Having learned how to appreciate the qualitative immediacy, relational properties, and meanings of works of art, students are now ready to examine works under the aspects of time, tradition, and style. In what could be a well-designed survey course, students could discover, among other things, how works of art have both celebrated and criticized a society's beliefs and values. Learning still serves the same general goal of a percipience curriculum, but now the development of historical awareness deepens the learners' cognitive stock and helps them to solidify their sense of art.

Phase 3 also contributes to an understanding of how works of art reflect the evolution of civilization. They do this is two ways. One is by providing a record of extraordinarily successful efforts to impose form and style on raw, unshaped material.[21] But beyond that, artworks are preeminent symbols of the human striving to liberate existence from the domination of necessity in favor of greater freedom and leisure, in which human powers can be cultivated for their own sakes. The study of such works further serves to emphasize that just as works of art have survived their severance from religion, magic, and myth,[22] so they often transcend gender, class, and race. Finally, and not least important, the study of art history contributes to an appreciation of tradition.

In contrast to the pedagogy of the first two phases of aesthetic learning, that of phase 3 is necessarily more formal and involves systematic instruction. Although there will not be time in a survey course to linger long over any particular work, students will develop important insights into the processes of historical continuity and change and will come to realize that continuity is by far the greater part of the story. An appreciation of continuity and change can be attained through the study of practically any culture or civilization. But for American youth, priority should be given to the cultural heritage of their own society. Even Richard Rorty, the controversial philosophical revisionist, acknowledges this as common wisdom.[23] The war against Eurocentrism waged by advocates of multiculturalism is thus ill-advised and counterproductive. It promotes cultural particularism rather than the nobler goal of cultural pluralism.[24]

Phase 4: Exemplar Appreciation (Grades 10–11)

The purpose of phase 4 is neither skill training nor historical study so much as appreciation in the best sense of the term. The time has arrived for studying selected works of art in some depth. During this phase students pause to admire some of the finest achievements of humankind—great works of art uniquely resplendent in their beauty, form, significance, and mystery. Moreover, the ethnic origin or gender of the artist is less relevant than a work's excellence.

Such exemplar study also provides an opportunity to understand the role of contextual factors in experiencing art. One can appreciate a work of art on its own terms without much regard for the historical factors that helped to shape it. But as Levi remarked, we fail to give the arts their full due unless we pause to examine the ways in which they exemplify or integrate the different cultural elements of a society or epoch. We may call this the figure-ground relationship of exemplar appreciation, with the artworks being the figure. This relationship should not be reversed; contextual information is primarily an aid to appreciation and should not be allowed to dissolve the artwork into its context.[25]

Given the aim of cultivating an appreciation of artistic excellence during the fourth phase of aesthetic learning, it follows that examples of artistic excellence from different cultures can be candidates for appreciation. Once more, one would expect masterworks from the Western cultural heritage to be featured, but efforts should also be made to present selected exemplars of artistic quality from non-Western cultures.

Phase 5: Critical Analysis (Grade 12)

Beyond exemplar appreciation, the percipience curriculum offers opportunities for critical reflection on the role of art in human life and society and on the innumerable conundrums such relations generate.[26] The principal purpose of the last phase of aesthetic learning is to encourage adolescents to fashion something of their own philosophies of art. This would include formulating beliefs and staking out positions, at least tentative ones, on such questions as the relations of art and morality, art and the mass media, art and the environment, art and politics, and so forth. Certainly prominent among the questions to be probed are ones about artistic value and worth. When students address these problems, they put to good use the apperceptive mass that they had built up throughout the preceding phases of learning. Given the contentious public reactions that often attend artistic events, there should be no difficulty finding material to stimulate the interest of twelfth graders. In truth, older students are curious about artistic controversies and want to know how to respond to them. In senior seminars, a start can be made by asking the right questions and sorting out the relevant issues.

TOWARD NEEDED REFORM

A humanities justification of arts education is grounded in a redefinition of the traditional humanities in procedural and substantive terms. Under this redefinition the teaching of the arts involves bringing to bear in appropriate ways and at relevant times the arts of creation, communication, continuity, and criticism. The mastery of these arts at levels suitable for the ages of learners eventually yields percipience in matters of art and culture, the ultimate goal of arts education. Being aesthetically percipient, the well-educated nonspecialist can be expected to traverse the artworld with knowledge and sensitivity, not to mention with a degree of autonomy. A student achieves this level of percipience through a series of learning phases: exposure and familiarization, perceptual training, historical study, exemplar appreciation, and critical analysis.

Before a percipience curriculum can be implemented in the schools, major progress would obviously have to be made in reforming teacher education.[27] Prospective teachers of art, for example, would need considerably more work in the humanities. And there would have to be more widespread acknowledgment on the part of society of the importance of the constitutive and revelatory powers of art for affecting the human personality in beneficial ways.

The potential in art thus has not only individual but also social benefits. A society is more likely to enjoy cultural health when constituted by persons with aesthetic intelligence. In this sense arts education is a critical necessity.

NOTES

1. Ernst Cassirer, *An Essay on Man* (New Haven: Yale University Press, 1944), 68.

2. For representative works, see Philip H. Phenix, *Realms of Meaning* (New York: McGraw-Hill, 1964); P. H. Hirst, *Knowledge and the Curriculum* (Boston: Routledge and Kegan Paul, 1974); L. A. Reid, *Ways of Understanding and Education* (London: Heinemann, 1986); and Howard Gardner, *Frames of Mind* (New York: Basic Books, 1983).

3. I borrow the notion of *percipience* from Harold Osborne's *The Art of Appreciation* (New York: Oxford University Press, 1970), chap. 2, "Appreciation as Percipience." The term *artworld* is intended in the sense that Arthur Danto uses it in his *The Transfiguration of the Commonplace* (Cambridge: Harvard University Press, 1981). That is, "to see something as art at all demands nothing less than this, an atmosphere of artistic theory, a knowledge of the history of art" (135). My notion of percipience presupposes such theory and knowledge.

4. See Albert William Levi, *The Humanities Today* (Bloomington: Indiana University Press, 1970), chap. 1; "Literature as a Humanity," *Journal of Aesthetic Education* 10, no. 3–4 (1976): 45–60; "Teaching Literature as a Humanity," *Journal of General Education* 28, no. 4 (1977): 283–89.

5. E. D. Hirsch Jr., "Cultural Literacy and the Schools," in *Cultural Literacy* (New York: Vintage Books, 1988). Cf. Ian Westbury and Alan C. Purves, eds., *Cultural Literacy and General Education*, Eighty-seventh Yearbook of the National Society for the Study of Education, Part 2 (Chicago: National Society for the Study of Education, 1988); and Ralph A. Smith, ed., *Cultural Literacy and Arts Education* (Urbana: University of Illinois Press, 1991).

6. Levi, "Literature as a Humanity," 60. Levi's questions are slightly amended for purposes of this discussion.

7. I refer here to Edmund B. Feldman's *Becoming Human Through Art* (Englewood Cliffs, N.J.: Prentice-Hall, 1970), one of the more substantive art education textbooks of the 1970s.

8. The following discussion is condensed from Albert William Levi and Ralph A. Smith, "The Arts and the Human Person," in *Art Education: A Critical Necessity* (Urbana: University of Illinois Press, 1991).

9. Friedrich von Schiller, *On the Aesthetic Education of Man in a Series of Letters*, trans. Elizabeth W. Wilkinson and L. A. Willoughby (New York: Oxford University Press, 1976).

10. Ibid., esp. 7, 9, 55, 215.

11. Herbert Read, *The Redemption of the Robot: My Encounters with Education Through Art* (New York: Simon and Schuster, 1969), 143.

12. John Dewey, *Art as Experience* (Carbondale: Southern Illinois University Press, 1987), 252–53.

13. Nelson Goodman, *Languages of Art*, 2nd ed. (Indianapolis: Hackett, 1976), 245–52.

14. Monroe C. Beardsley, "Aesthetic Experience," in *The Aesthetic Point of View: Selected Essays*, ed. Michael J. Wreen and Donald M. Callen (Ithaca: Cornell University Press, 1982), 285–97. All quotations are from this essay.

15. Harold Osborne, *The Art of Appreciation*, 36.

16. For a discussion of such principles, I have found the writings of Joseph D. Novak quite helpful. See his *A Theory of Education* (Ithaca: Cornell University Press, 1986) and David P. Ausubel, Joseph D. Novak, and Helen Hanesian, *Educational Psychology: A Cognitive View*, 2nd ed. (New York: Holt, Rinehart and Winston, 1978).

17. The following discussion is a condensed version of the accounts given in Ralph A. Smith, *The Sense of Art: A Study in Aesthetic Education* (New York: Routledge, 1989), chap. 6, and in Levi and Smith, *Art Education: A Critical Necessity*, chap. 8.

18. Harry S. Broudy, *The Role of Imagery in Learning* (Los Angeles: Getty Center for Education in the Arts, 1987), 52–53.

19. Kenneth Clark, *Looking at Pictures* (New York: Holt, Rinehart and Winston, 1960), 16–17.

20. For example, in *The Future of the Humanities* (New York: Thomas Y. Crowell, 1977), Walter Kaufmann writes that the objectives of the humanities arc four: the conservation and cultivation of the greatest works of humanity, the teaching of vision, the fostering of a critical spirit, and thoughtful reflection on alternatives (xvii–xxi).

21. This is the theme of Kenneth Clark's *Civilization* (New York: Harper and Row, 1969) and *Towards Civilization: A Report on Arts Education* (Washington, D.C.: National Endowment for the Arts, 1988).

22. Hannah Arendt, *The Human Condition* (Chicago: University of Chicago Press, 1958), 167.

23. Richard Rorty, "The Dangers of Over-philosophication: Reply to Arcilla and Nicholson," *Educational Theory* 40, no. 1 (1990): 41–44.

24. See Diane Ravitch, "Multiculturalism: E Pluribus Plures," *American Scholar* 59, no. 3 (1990): 337–54 and "Multiculturalism: An Exchange," *American Scholar* 60, no. 2 (1991): 272–76 for Ravitch's response to a critique of "Multiculturalism" by Molefi Keti Asante, which appears in the same issue. See also my "Forms of Multicultural Education in the Arts," *Journal of Multi-cultural and Cross-Cultural Research in Art Education* 1, no. 1 (1983): 23–32; and Rachel Mason, *Art Education and Multiculturalism* (London: Croom Helm, 1988), esp. 1–2, "Four Types of Multiculturalism."

25. What one must avoid is what Hilton Kramer in *The New Criterion* 9, no. 4 (December 1990) calls the postmodernist mode of analysis termed deconstruction, whose aim is "to deconstruct every 'text'—which is to say, every art object—into an inventory of its context and thus remove the object from the realm of aesthetic experience and make it instead a coefficient of its sources and social environment" (7).

26. For a number of such conundrums, see Margaret P. Battin, John Fisher, Ronald Moore, and Anita Silvers, *Puzzles About Art: An Aesthetics Casebook* (New York: St. Martin's, 1989).

27. I have discussed some initiatives for such reform in my *Excellence in Art Education: Ideas and Initiatives*, updated version (Reston, Va., National Art Education Association, 1987), chap. 5.

Teaching Music as One of the Humanities

CAN MUSIC, notable for what Aaron Copland calls its sensuous, expressive, and sheerly musical planes, be understood as one of the humanities, especially music of the highest quality known as masterworks?[1] To be sure, masterworks are only a part of the world of music, but they pose some of the more interesting problems of musical understanding and appreciation.

LEONARD MEYER: THE SCIENCES, ARTS, AND HUMANITIES

Any response to the question asked at the beginning must proceed from a definition of the humanities, and I honor custom by distinguishing the humanities from the sciences. In doing so I draw on a far-ranging and insightful essay by Leonard Meyer in which he discusses creation, criticism, invention, and application in terms of their procedures and goals.[2] Published in the 1970s, Meyer's essay reflects a time when devising taxonomies and classifications of knowledge were in fashion. But I am less interested in Meyer's comprehensive categories of disciplines than in the ways in which he characterizes the sciences and the arts and understands the role of the humanities.

Meyer begins by locating the important differences between the behavior of scientists and artists in two areas. One is the nature of their respective accomplishments and the relations of their achievements to their own traditions and to contemporary efforts. The other is the manner in which the structures and properties of the sciences and those of the arts affect audiences for science and art. I will put these differences in the following form: Whereas X (science) is or does so and so, Y (art) is or does otherwise. That is, whereas scientists discover relationships already present in nature, artists create works that have never before existed; whereas scientific theories are propositional in form, works of art are presentational in character; whereas scientific theories tend to supersede, displace, or invalidate previous scientific hypotheses, great works of art remain continuous sources of vital experience; whereas science studies phenomena for purposes of framing theoretical generalizations, artists produce works the principal significance of which is their status as objects for aesthetic response and appreciation; whereas science strives to build an abstract edifice of scientific knowledge characterized by systematic relations among its hypotheses, works of art are valued for their concrete individuality and particularities, for their nonrecurring as well as their recurring features; and finally, whereas the reputations of scientists are based on their creation of new paradigms for studying the phenomena discovered, usually early in their careers, artists' reputations have typically been based on their creative contributions to already existing styles, contributions that, moreover, generally became more meaningful and profound in their mature years. Meyer provides numerous examples of these differences, as well as some points of similarity. However, I pass over these and move to his discussion of the humanities.

In his account of the humanities Meyer distinguishes *understanding* from *explanation* and describes three interrelated areas of humanistic inquiry: theory, style analysis, and criticism. He furthermore contrasts the role of the critic to those of the creative artist and the scientist. Meyer believes that it is the humanist-theorist or critic and not the artist who is most comparable to the scientist. Just as the scientist formulates hypotheses to explain relationships among phenomena, so the humanist-theorist formulates explanations of the relationships in works of art as they are experienced by beholders. I cannot dwell on Meyer's interesting discussion of these points but would like to mention two: first, his description of the role of tacit knowing in scientific research and artistic creation and, second, his reasons for holding not only that understanding must precede explanation but also that it is possible to understand something without being able to explain it—notions implied in Michael Polanyi's assertion that we often know more than we can tell.

But when we do explain something, we must have recourse to general principles. Meyer thinks three kinds of hypothesis are brought to bear in attempts to explain an artwork's structure and internal relationships and the ways in which they stimulate aesthetic experience. There are "(a) general laws, which are presumed to be constant over time and place; (b) restricted principles, derived from and applicable to the norms and procedures of a specific style; and (c) ad hoc reasons, which . . . are necessary adjuncts to the first two types when particular works of art are being explained" ("Concerning the Sciences," 191–92). General principles may be formulated by humanist-theorists themselves or be taken from other disciplines and applied deductively, as Meyer illustrates in his borrowings from information theory.

The humanist-theorist, however, cannot rely solely on general principles when explaining works of art. There must also be reliance on ad hoc or commonsense reasons that command assent because of their congruence with a culture's beliefs and way of living. We can decide, for example, to convey an ordinary understanding of the impression of indomitable force and irresistible authority that issues from Michelangelo's *Moses* by associating these qualities with the statue's colossal size rather than by recourse to Freudian theory. Similarly, we can explain the extension of a phrase in music not as the result of some quirk in the composer's personality but by saying that had the cadence come precisely at the point at which it was expected, it would have sounded too obvious and uninteresting. In short, we are obliged to engage in ad hoc or commonsense reasoning because general principles and style taxonomies do little to explain the nonrecurring features of a work of music and because no satisfactory account of music's capacity to move and affect us is as yet available.

I wish to draw attention to the part played by the restrictive principles of style analysis and ad hoc reasoning in music criticism as well as in the teaching of music. By the term *criticism*, Meyer understands that activity that "seeks to describe and explain as precisely and explicitly as possible how the structures and processes peculiar to a specific work of art are related to one another and to the aesthetic experience of a competent audience" (197). It is worth noting the twofold nature of the task: it attempts to describe and explain not only the musical character of a work but also the work's effect on the aesthetic responses of a competent listener, a point to which I return later.

To repeat, the humanist-critic is akin to the scientist in the effort to explain relationships; the vital difference between the two lies in the fact that the scientist strives to develop hypotheses that account for relationships discovered among phenomena in the natural world. This involves isolating, limiting, and controlling the relevant variables, while the humanist is more concerned with the unique character of a work of art and its capacity to generate aesthetic experience. Given its focus on the idiosyncratic features of works of art, criticism transcends general theory and style taxonomies and asks what makes a particular work of art different from all the others, even different from other works in the same form, style, and genre.

Understanding the role of the humanist-critic is important in a program of general music education that pursues the goal of developing percipience in matters of music and culture, that is, a capacity recognized by an informed appreciation of music and the atmosphere in which it exists. Similar to the humanist-critic, a music teacher working in such a program would also use general principles and ad hoc reasons not only when drawing attention to the processes, qualities, and structures of musical works, but also when pointing out what is valuable and significant and explaining how musical values impinge on aesthetic awareness. The difference is that teachers typically do not formulate the general principles they use; that is the humanist-theorist's job. As Meyer puts it:

> Theorists and style analysts use particular works of art as exemplars—as data—for the discovery and formulation of general principles and for the description of the characteristics typical of some style; the critic [and, I would add, the teacher of music], working the other way around, uses the general principles and taxonomies thus developed to explain and illuminate particular works of art. (199)

As if to confirm his conviction of the limited usefulness of general principles when it comes to explicating the idiosyncratic or nonrecurring features of artworks, Meyer adds that "there are many examples of antecedent-consequent structures, in common time, the minor mode, and with homophonic texture, whose melodies begin with an upbeat skip to the fifth of the scale and then descend to the tonic. But there is only one such combination of relationships, which is Chopin's *Prelude no. 4 in E Minor*" (199–200). It is not only the critic's but also the teacher's task to explain why this is so.

The humanist-critic and the teacher of music appreciation thus occupy a middle ground—between the composer and the performance of a work on one side, and the audience for the work on the other—but they do their work somewhat differently. Certainly the critic can also be said to perform an educative service for the public; but the critic's educational responsibility is less direct and stringent than that of the teacher. The music teacher's principal aim is the cultivation of musical percipience in young people to the point where they will be able not only to enjoy and participate in music at a respectable level of comprehension but also to engage in intelligent conversation about it. Or we may say that the teacher of music is distinguished from the music critic by virtue of the teacher's self-image as an educator committed first of all to bringing about learning. A teacher of music, then, is not a specialist in philosophy or theory or history but a professional educator who draws on all these disciplines and activities in order to develop appropriate degrees of musical awareness in students. This is what makes the teacher's task unique. The central pedagogical question centers on models that should guide the development of musical percipience. Here the music critic would provide what is perhaps the most important paradigm. The critic's connoisseurship is compounded of natural talent and disposition; performance skills, or at least an advanced ability to assess them; and a vast knowledge of music's history and theory, not to mention love of and devotion to music. How far can education go in developing such critical finesse? Some distance, I think, but no further than would be commensurate with the overall objective of general education, namely, to produce intelligent and sensitive nonspecialists. An effective interpretive capacity is what I think we are after.[3]

But to suggest that the teaching of music should take music criticism as its model is in effect to say that music should be taught as one of the humanities. This raises the question of whether a broadly humanistic interpretation of music education can in fact define the aims of the field in a new and clearer light. It is one thing, and perhaps adequate for some purposes, to suggest that music education should pursue the objective of developing musical percipience in the young so that they may realize the benefits of music. But it is another matter altogether to work out in detail what ought to go into building a sense of music that would be adequate to attaining this goal. I believe we should start by looking for a definition of the humanities that would be especially suitable for music education, and indeed for arts education in general. Luckily, such a definition can be extracted from the writings of Albert William Levi.

THE HUMANITIES AS THE LIBERAL ARTS

In *The Humanities Today* and other writings, Levi takes stock of the humanities in the contemporary world and asks how we can preserve their traditional aims and purposes while adapting them to changed conditions.[4] How, for example, do we deal with the humanities' having become practically unmanageable as a result of their trying to encompass the works of all civilizations, non-Western as well as Western? How can a democratic society grounded in egalitarian ideals defend a tradition of learning whose origins are rooted in an essentially aristocratic culture? How can we make good on the promise of music's civilizing influence? And how can we maintain the claims of the humanities against their new rivals, the social sciences? For Levi these were not merely matters for idle philosophical speculation. As a charter member of the National Council for the Humanities, he was sensitive to policy questions bearing on research and teaching, and he had a strong interest in the social role of the humanities. What is more, in his three years as rector of Black Mountain College, an experiment in the liberal education of artists, he was required to cope with the day-to-day practical problems of teaching and administration. Levi was, then, a philosopher of the humanities with a keen interest in their uses, and he believed that the taught humanities were meaningless unless they ultimately became the *lived* humanities.

Levi's persuasive redefinition of the humanities begins by recalling two traditions, one going back to the Middle Ages and the other to the Renaissance. The tradition dating from the Renaissance is most prominently characterized by a penchant for the rediscovery and recovery of ancient texts, which helps to explain why the humanities have become understood *substantively*, that is, in terms of literary artifacts or subject matter to be studied and mastered. This tradition lives on in the curriculums of higher education today where the humanities are taught as texts or works. The tradition dating from the Middle Ages defines the humanities *procedurally*, that is, in terms of methods, approaches, skills, or ways of interpreting human experience; it consequently favors a conception of the humanities as liberal arts rather than as subject matters.

Levi's synthesis combines these two traditions, the substantive and the procedural, into a conception of the humanities as the liberal arts of communication, continuity, and criticism. These arts, in turn, are associated with subject matters distinctive of each: the arts of communication are identified with languages and literatures, the arts of continuity with history, and the arts of criticism with philosophy in its ordinary sense of critical reasoning. Levi thus reconnects what critics think have become unduly separated in American schooling: skills and specific content.[5] For Levi, then, the aims of the humanities are three: to enable students to communicate successfully, to encourage them to walk proudly with their cultural heritage, and to help them to think critically. He writes:

> In the case of the arts of communication this has meant the presentation of languages as forms of enlarging a limited imagination and producing that mutual sympathy which Kant took to be the defining property of social man. In the case of the arts of continuity, comprehending both history proper and the use of the classics of literature and philosophy, presented as elements in a continuous human tradition, this has meant the presentation of a common past in the service of social cohesiveness and enlarged social sensitivity. And finally, in the case of the arts of criticism, this has meant the enlargement of the faculty of criticism, philosophically conceived as intelligent inquiry into the nature and maximization of values. A humane imagination, the forging of a universal social bond based upon sympathy, and the inculcation of a technique for the realization of values then become the ultimate goals of the liberal arts. (*The Humanities Today* 85–86)

Where do the arts of creation and performance fit into this picture? I think it is possible to subsume them under the arts of communication and criticism, if, that is, we are willing to tolerate some lingustic license. We would thus stretch the meaning of language and communication to include artistic expression and performance and construe criticism as the disclosure of whatever it is that art communicates. Yet this may not be a satisfactory solution for those who attach great importance to creative and performing activities and who would consider them slighted by such subsumption. For this reason Levi and I in *Art Education: A Critical Necessity* agreed to add to the arts of communication, continuity, and criticism the arts of creation.[6] I now propose that for educational purposes, arts education may be usefully conceived as the study of a distinctive mode of communication that has a history of outstanding accomplishments (that is, exhibits continuity), challenges our appreciation of it with puzzling issues and situations demanding judgment (that is, calls for critical reasoning), and cannot be well appreciated in the absence of training in artistic creation and performance. In this manner the standard definition of a music education aimed at the development of musical ideas, concepts, and skills has been augmented by a number of larger humanistic objectives, the attainment of which should be part of any liberal or general education.

It might be claimed that cultivating historical and critical capacities in music education takes time away from performing and listening activities, or even that acquiring historical and critical knowledge serves extra-aesthetic outcomes and contributes nothing significant to musical percipience. But such objections would be misguided. We need only recall that the music critic has been suggested as an important model for the music teacher. There are probably few good music critics who are not also performers, and certainly none who does not bring to the task a strong sense of music's history (and often the history of the other arts) and an intimate familiarity with the conundrums that beset discussions about music. Indeed, ideas, concepts, and skills from relevant disciplines and practical activities are what the critic thinks with; and I cannot see why, to an appropriate extent, that should not be true of the teacher of music as well.[7]

Although the teacher need not command the full panoply of the critic's expertise, in certain respects the teacher's work is even more demanding than that of the critic. In a discussion of teaching and learning in the arts, Henry Aiken points out that the teacher's task is stricter and more austere than that of the critic because of the teacher's daily concern to help the young apprehend the forms unique to works of art. This involves cultivating in students a fuller awareness of the idea that artworks are the product of the creative life that constitutes one primary level of everyone's subjective nature. Aiken goes on to say that teachers who perform this task through their talk, gestures, and attitudes provide a model of the ability to discern possibilities in a work of art, what it is, for example, to discover a significant artistic form and to develop an authentic taste.[8]

UNDERSTANDING MUSIC

It should be clear by now that teachers of music must draw on a number of disciplines and activities if they are to do a good job of developing musical percipience in young people. And although I suggest that music is a language that communicates something significant, I am fully aware of views that assert the contrary. What then, someone may ask, does music say? Does it really communicate anything at all? Consider Beethoven's Third Symphony (the *Eroica*). Peter Kivy, a philosopher of music, holds that it is difficult to see not only how this symphony could be about anything profound, but how it could be about anything at all. Indeed, he believes that it is nothing but "a magnificent abstract structure of sound: one big beautiful noise, signifying nothing."[9] He acknowledges that it is a deeply satisfying entertainment but thinks that it totally lacks subject matter, content, and meaning. And if there is no message to be decoded, how can such a work teach or educate us about anything important? Let us, therefore, says Kivy, enjoy music of this kind for what it is, a pure, contentless, abstract form, and stop burbling about its profundity. Let us find other grounds for justifying the study of music in a required program of liberal education.

Kivy is one of the more interesting writers about the aesthetics of music, and his works figure strategically in my teaching. For example, I have shown students the photograph of the sad-looking St. Bernard that serves as the frontispiece of Kivy's *Sound Sentiment*.[10] Why, I would ask, would a serious thinker begin a philosophical discussion about music with such an image? The St. Bernard, of course, introduces an analysis of expression in music in which Kivy argues the case for what he calls emotive criticism. As an example of such criticism, Kivy quotes Donald Francis Tovey, who remarked that the second movement of Beethoven's *Eroica* "concludes with a final utterance of the main theme, its rhythms and accents utterly broken with grief" (5–6). Kivy's aim is to resolve what he calls the paradox of music description: the fact that the kind of music criticism that is the most objective and scientific is also the least humanistic and thus unable to say much about music's power to move us (p. 9). The value of emotive criticism for descriptions of the emotional qualities of great music notwithstanding, Kivy believes that music's lack of content and profundity disqualifies it from being taught as one of the humanities. A different case can, of course, be made for literature, the theater, and the visual arts.

Mindful of contrary theoretical positions on this topic, I nonetheless suggest that music can after all provide us with deep understanding—an apprehension of an aspect of reality, no less—and that music can therefore be taken to teach and educate in its own way. My progress toward this view represents a shift in my thinking of a magnitude of perhaps a few more inches than the small distance that Bennett Reimer admits to having moved in his position on this question. For although I have always derived something I consider profound from listening to musical masterworks, I was persuaded, as Kivy apparently still is, that theories of musical meaning are undermined by both the facts of music and the requirements for something to count as a language.

Monroe Beardsley was another writer who had started out being skeptical about semiotic theories of musical meaning. Instead, he regarded music simply as a process, as perhaps the closest thing to pure process that we have. In his major work on aesthetics, Beardsley wrote that "to understand a piece of music is simply to hear it, in the fullest sense of this word . . . to organize its sounds into wholes, to grasp its sequences of notes as melodic and rhythmic patterns, to perceive its kinetic qualities and, finally, the subtle and pervasive human qualities that depend on all the rest."[11] Beardsley consequently thought it was a mistake to cast about for something outside music with which to connect or compare music. Although I was uncomfortable with the implications of this view—that since music cannot signify anything and therefore has no meaning, all interpretive statements about musical meaning are false and have no place in music teaching—I felt compelled to accept it. But a strong doubt about something is no substitute for an argument.

It was characteristic of Beardsley that whenever possible he tried to accommodate new and challenging ideas. Hence in an essay titled "Understanding Music," published more than twenty years after his original views about musical meaning, he covers much of the same ground while reviewing the theories of musical meaning of Deryck Cooke, Donald N. Ferguson, Gordon Epperson, and Wilson Coker. He finds all their efforts to explain musical meaning in semantic terms unsatisfactory.[12] During that same period, however, aesthetic theory was reflecting the influence of Nelson Goodman's ideas about the nature and function of the arts as symbol systems. According to Goodman's theory, music has the ability to refer by virtue of a symbolic function technically called *exemplification*. It is not enough for Goodman, as it was for Beardsley, simply to say that music possesses aesthetic qualities and to leave it at that. For it seems to be Goodman's position that aesthetic qualities can have elements of overt display, of active featuring, of drawing attention that are more fittingly captured by the term *exemplification*. In short, exemplification is claimed to be a form of reference and hence to perform a cognitive function. Goodman, then, is the fifth theorist Beardsley discusses in "Understanding Music." He judged Goodman's *Languages of Art* to be an enormously valuable book, gave it a sympathetic reading, and then asked to what extent his own thinking might be adjusted to a semantic explanation of art, that is, one in terms of art's cognitive function and ability to provide understanding.[13]

Beardsley makes a number of illuminating observations about the way exemplification works; how, that is, certain properties and qualities can be referred to by a musical performance. His emendation of Goodman's theory, however, would require that someone must actually put something on display or feature it before exemplification can occur. Thus a tree in the forest may possess qualities of majestic height and spread, but as long as no one is putting the tree on display the tree cannot exemplify these properties. However, a fashion model who walks down a runway is putting something on display, is featuring, say, a trimly severe or a loose and billowy look. Such expressive qualities, Beardsley would say, are being exemplified. As he explains it: "Property-displaying is, or involves, reference when, and only when the property-displaying object is itself object-displayed."[14]

Now, the performance of a piano sonata in a concert hall satisfies the condition of something's being put on display. The question is what, if anything, the sonata exemplifies, for a particular performance of a sonata need not exemplify all the properties of that sonata, only those that are noteworthy in the context of concert giving and concertgoing. These are the properties whose presence has a direct bearing on the sonata's capacity to interest us aesthetically. We may, of course, recalling Meyer's discussion of the critic's role, need the intercession of a music critic to realize which structures and relations of a musical work bear on our aesthetic response to it.

In order to help us understand how we might give a semantic explanation of a musical work in Goodman's terms, Beardsley asks us to consider a performance of Beethoven's Piano Sonata in A Major, op. 101. Which of the sonata's properties are exemplified for our aesthetic interest? The first movement's being in the key of A, with few restricted modulations, does not amount to its having a property that particularly enhances or inhibits the aesthetic effectiveness of the sonata. However, the first movement's uncommonly hesitant, diffident, and indecisive character does figure prominently in our aesthetic response. This quality plays a crucial part in the sonata as a whole, especially in the finale that we must await in order to experience the liberating resolution of the unusual musical business in the first movement. But what, to be more specific, is being referred to by the music? Beardsley emphasizes that reference is not being made to objects, events, processes, or emotional states as they occur in or belong to the external world. Rather, the reference is to qualities within the music itself. So far, I think, Beardsley and Kivy are in accord; the description of such qualities Kivy would call *emotive criticism* and Beardsley *aesthetic criticism*. Nor is Beardsley talking about the devices composers often use to establish some kind of connection with external reality—devices such as sound imitation, conventional associations, and kinetic parallelisms—for he does not construe these connections as instances of reference or meaning. What Beardsley has in mind is something more complicated, more profound, and it suggests a response to Kivy's claim that music—at least abstract instrumental music—has no meaning.

To illustrate his point, Beardsley follows an interpretation of a Beethoven sonata by Kay Dreyfus, an Australian musicologist who had made a study of Beethoven's last five piano sonatas. Dreyfus claims that the finale of this opus provides the clue to Beethoven's musical statement. The statement, Dreyfus claims, is not one concerned with a conflict or confrontation of op-

posing ideas. Rather, it has to do with the nature of the musical ideas introduced in the opening movement, which consist of the unleashing of a capacity
for sustained growth and development. As Beardsley puts it, the music moves
from unexpected constriction and constraint in the first movement to great
breadth of activity and assertiveness in the finale. From Dreyfus's description
of the first movement we learn that the movement employs a technique of
delayed resolution as a substitute for development that is marked by tonal
inconclusiveness, and that it is extremely brief in duration. All these things are
important, says Beardsley, but "so much happens so vividly, in a mere nine-
teen and one-half minutes, between the first notes and the last, in the way of
musical growth, that the sonata can be said to show its 'concern' with growth
in general, to exemplify that property" ("Understanding Music," 69).

But why should the exemplification of growth be so important? Beardsley
thinks it is significant because growth is a basic kind of alteration found in
human experience at its most rewarding, especially when it is successful in
overcoming obstacles; and music, being itself a form of change, can mirror
or match this process. He goes on to say that "music exemplifies—indeed,
exploits and glories in—aspects of change that are among the most fundamental and pervasive characteristics of living." As a mode of continuation,
music in its movement toward completion is "marked by the sense that possibilities are opening or closing, that there is development or retrogression,
that there is continuity or abruptness, doubt or decisiveness, hesitancy or
determination, building or disintegration" (70).

Such modes of continuation are features of all experience, and Beardsley
thinks that if music has them, then it exemplifies them, and therefore it refers
to aspects of reality in one of its humanly important dimensions. It is sometimes said—for example, by Meyer in the essay I discussed earlier—that no
satisfactory theory exists to explain music's power to move and delight. But
perhaps part of the explanation lies in music's ability to exemplify modes of
continuation that are firmly woven into our personal and social destinies. An
echo of some of Meyer's remarks may be detected in Beardsley's statement that

> suspense is disturbing in whatever form it assumes, and the release from it cor-
> respondingly heartening and gladdening. So, too, disintegration is threatening,
> reversal astonishing, loss of power and drive unsettling, delayed fulfillment
> anxiety-producing, missed opportunity poignant; but growth is encouraging, re-
> vival inspiriting, arrival satisfying. Triumph over obstacles arouses confidence,
> and endurance, respect. (71)

Although we do not really undergo any of these situations and their corresponding emotions as we listen to music, Beardsley says that their distinctive forms of continuation as they occur in music nonetheless have great power
to affect us.

Does music, then, provide knowledge after all? Can its profundity help us to attain a better understanding of ourselves and our relations to others and to the world? Does music afford us a kind of insight? To the extent that Beardsley came to believe in such possibilities, he also accepted Goodman's argument for the cognitive character of music. Music, Beardsley concluded,

> can make extremely delicate discriminations between kinds of continuation, between two slightly different forms of ambiguity or of headlong rushing or of growth. It thereby can sharpen our appreciation of such differences, and give us concepts of continuation that we might miss in ordinary experience, under the press of affairs, but yet that we can bring to experience (as "models," perhaps) with fresh perceptiveness and clearer cognitive grasp. (72)

I think such an interpretation offers us what we need for a humanities interpretation of music; it gives meaning to the notion of teaching music as one of the humanities.

I have dwelled on the question of the cognitive status of music because it is an issue that is difficult to avoid in the context of a humanities interpretation of music education. Indeed, if the problem of the cognitive status of art is the only one that keeps aesthetics alive, then I think Beardsley contributes to that discipline's health and longevity. Music, we may now claim, not only has the capacity to provide magnificent enjoyment, it can also yield insight into human reality. It would be helpful at this point to sketch a curriculum designed around a humanities approach to music education, but all I can do here is to indicate that such a curriculum would encompass roughly five stages of musical learning, that is, the phases of exposure to music's qualitative aspects and increasing familiarization with them, perceptual training, historical inquiry, the study of masterworks in some depth, and perhaps a seminar in which adolescents would have an opportunity to fashion an elementary philosophy of music. Performing activities would find a place at most levels, but their role and centrality would vary according to the learning phase in question. I have variously called this kind of curriculum an *excellence* curriculum, an *artworld* curriculum, and a *percipience* curriculum; here I refer to it as a *humanities* curriculum.[15]

NOTES

1. Aaron Copland, *What to Listen for in Music*, rev. ed. (New York: Mentor Books, 1957), 18–23.
2. Leonard Meyer, "Concerning the Sciences, the Arts–AND the Humanities," *Critical Inquiry* 1, no. 1 (1974).
3. In this connection, see Harry S. Broudy, B. Othanel Smith, and Joe R.

Burnett, *Democracy and Excellence in American Secondary Education* (1958; New York: Robert E. Krieger, 1978).

4. See Albert William Levi, *The Humanities Today* (Bloomington: Indiana University Press, 1970); "Literature as a Humanity," *Journal of Aesthetic Education* 10, no. 3–4 (1976); and "Teaching Literature as a Humanity," *Journal of General Education* 28, no. 4 (1977). Cf. Ralph A. Smith, *The Sense of Art: A Study in Aesthetic Education* (New York: Routledge, 1989), 127–32.

5. See, e.g., E. D. Hirsch Jr., *Cultural Literacy: What Every American Needs to Know* (New York: Random House Vintage Books, 1988).

6. Albert W. Levi and Ralph A. Smith, *Art Education: A Critical Necessity*, Vol. 1 of *Disciplines in Art Education: Contexts of Understanding*, 5 vols. (Urbana: University of Illinois Press, 1991).

7. The notion of *thinking with* has been advanced by Harry S. Broudy in his extrapolations from Michael Polanyi's writings about tacit knowing. See Broudy's "On Knowing With," in *Philosophy of Education*, ed. Harold B. Dunkel, Proceedings of the Twenty-sixth Annual Meeting of the Philosophy of Education Society (Edwardsville, Ill.: Philosophy of Education Society, 1970).

8. Henry D. Aiken, "Teaching and Learning in the Arts," *Journal of Aesthetic Education* 5, no. 4 (1971): 107.

9. Peter Kivy, "Music and the Liberal Education," *Journal of Aesthetic Education* 25, no. 3 (1991): 85.

10. Peter Kivy, *Sound Sentiment: An Essay on Musical Emotions* (Philadelphia: Temple University Press, 1989). First published as *The Corded Shell: Reflections on Musical Expression* (Princeton: Princeton University Press, 1980). The 1989 version contains additional chapters.

11. Monroe C. Beardsley, *Aesthetics: Problems in the Philosophy of Criticism*, 2nd ed. (1958; Indianapolis: Hackett, 1981), 337.

12. Monroe C. Beardsley, "Understanding Music," in *On Criticizing Music: Five Philosophical Perspectives*, ed. Kingsley Price (Baltimore: Johns Hopkins University Press, 1981).

13. Nelson Goodman, *Languages of Art*, 2nd ed. (Indianapolis: Hackett, 1976). Goodman has continued his analysis in a number of subsequent books, e.g., *Ways of Worldmaking* (Indianapolis: Hackett, 1978); *Of Mind and Other Matters* (Cambridge: Harvard University Press, 1984); and, with Catherine Z. Elgin, *Reconceptions in Philosophy and Other Arts and Sciences* (Indianapolis: Hackett, 1988). Cf. *Journal of Aesthetic Education* 25, no. 1 (1991), a special issue titled "More Ways of Worldmaking."

14. Beardsley, "Understanding Music," 66.

15. See, e.g., *Excellence in Art Education*, updated version (Reston, Va.: National Art Education Association, 1987), *The Sense of Art: A Study in Aesthetic Education* (New York: Routledge 1989), and Albert William Levi and Ralph A. Smith, *Art Education: A Critical Necessity* (Urbana: University of Illinois Press, 1991).

Remoralization and Aesthetic Education

THERE ARE SEVERAL ways to understand Harry Broudy's aims and accomplishment in *Truth and Credibility: The Citizen's Dilemma.*[1] One might say he is concerned to assess the deteriorated conditions of commitment in a society that has been demoralized by a breakdown in conventional morality and an erosion of the legitimacy of its major institutions. On a more positive note, Broudy could be said to hold out the hope that such conditions of commitment might be rediscovered in the democratic values of the American Creed, in the cognitive and evaluative maps developed by general education, and in the enduring capacity of individuals to remoralize themselves and their society. Alternatively, the book may be viewed as having justified warranted commitment (fashioned largely from the resources of the humanities) and warranted assertion (the truth of scientific inquiry).[2] For Broudy, as if in a Deweyan moment, integrates science and the humanities, fact and value, objectivity and subjectivity, the explicit and the tacit, and other ostensible dichotomies. One might go even further and credit Broudy with having forged a synthesis of classical humanism, Deweyan instrumentalism, and Kierkegaardian existentialism (although to what extent he carries this off is for his fellow philosophers to decide). In brief, Broudy answers affirmatively the question Robert Penn Warren asked in his Jefferson Lecture: whether making our world more humanly habitable involves acceptance not only of the knowledge that comes from science but also of the insights that come from the feelingful acts of the imagination characteristically found in literature and the humanities.[3] Indeed, the cultivation of the imagination figures importantly in Broudy's educational philosophy.

Yet another approach might place Broudy's social analysis within the framework of the Galbraithian economic perspective that explains how—as Dewey never tired of claiming in the 1930s—a reduction of all values to economic considerations adversely affects the development of other values, including aesthetic values.[4] All the above, and more, can be said to characterize aspects of Broudy's volume. Its special feature lies in its being addressed not to his professional colleagues in the fields of philosophy and education, but to ordinary citizens and the predicaments of living during the last quarter of the twentieth century.

The plight of citizens is most acute when they try to act rationally in a complex society in which their dilemma arises from problems of credibility. Everywhere citizens turn they encounter attacks on conventional norms, corruption and hypocrisy in public life, disagreement between experts, superficiality and distortion in the news media, and an ever expanding specialism and fragmentation that inhibits understanding and communication. In *The Public and Its Problems* Dewey wrote that for the Great Society to become a Great Community, society will have to depend heavily on socially responsible artists of mass communications.[5] Such persons would accept the obligation to interpret the results of inquiry for average citizens in order to enable them to act intelligently on matters pertaining to the common good. Dewey thought such humanization of knowledge was possible as long as the transmission of information availed itself of the potentialities of art, as long, that is, as events and their meanings were rendered vivid and memorable.

Dewey's thinking rested on three foundations: his belief in the use of knowledge to improve the quality of life and to guide social change; his realization that the human import of abstract knowledge must be elucidated for citizens; and his faith in the propensity of the members of a democratic society to act in behalf of the general welfare. For this, Dewey usually meant acting in behalf of the lasting values of freedom, individualism, and intelligence. Broudy, too, believes that a free and morally responsible press is a citizen's best ally, as are editors, critics, the clergy, and intellectuals. Dewey's dream of a Great Community, however, is far from being realized, and those who ought to be concerned about bringing it to pass have instead become part of the problem by contributing to the twin tendencies of devaluation and demoralization.[6]

An example from imaginative literature may serve to demonstrate the astuteness of Broudy's analysis. In *The Dean's December*, Saul Bellow has a columnist say of Professor Corde, the novel's principal character, that he is "very hard on journalism, on the mass media. His charge is that they fail to deal with the moral, emotional, imaginative life, in short, the true life of human beings, and that their great power prevents people from having access to this true life." The columnist goes on to describe Corde's belief that the communications industry merely breeds misunderstanding and hysteria, not to mention academics who, supposedly different from corporate functionaries, are in fact little better than philistines ruled by consensus and public opinion. The fictional Corde is convinced that academics, instead of discharging their responsibility as humanists by producing new models, "have been incapable of clarifying our principal problems and of depicting democracy to itself in this time of agonized struggle."[7] The point here is not to claim that Bellow's views coincide with those attributed to the characters in his novel. Rather, it is that a respected contemporary novelist considered the credibility of the academic calling and the performance of journalists to be fitting thematic material.

Broudy's *Truth and Credibility*, then, can now be seen as an attempt to answer charges of the kind brought by the protagonist of Bellow's novel, for Broudy's aim is precisely one of "clarifying our principal problems and of depicting democracy to itself in this time of agonized struggle." For Broudy, the struggle of the ordinary citizen, what he calls the citizen's dilemma, is to find a way to act rationally in a society in which the credibility of persons and institutions is increasingly called into question and in which knowing *whom* to believe is as difficult as knowing *what* to believe. What is Broudy's remedy, and what place does aesthetic education have in it?

Truth and Credibility is an elaboration of the 1980 John Dewey Lecture presented to the John Dewey Society. Broudy is neither a student of Dewey nor a Dewey scholar, but on this occasion he paid respect to Dewey's career and writings. He accepted in its essentials Dewey's formulation of the complete act of thought (CAT) as one legitimate source of knowledge available to citizens for their deliberations. (In another context, Broudy might well quibble with aspects of Dewey's epistemology.) Broudy agrees with Dewey's notion of warranted assertion as the best truth we can expect from scientific inquiry. But warranted assertions, which we associate with the truth of propositions, are not enough for rational action today. Something else must be brought into view, what Broudy calls credibility or warranted commitment, which is associated not so much with the truth of propositions but with the character of the persons uttering them. It is when experts differ that credibility becomes an issue.

Broudy recalls for his readers the radical nature of the democratic idea, especially Dewey's belief that scientific method could be domesticated for purposes of learning and guiding social change.[8] It was Dewey's brand of liberalism, Broudy reminds us, that extended the relevance of the CAT beyond the classroom. To complement Dewey's conviction of the ordinary citizen's ability to think scientifically, Broudy offers a radical proposition of his own. He writes that "warranted assertion may not be sufficient grounds for warranted commitment" and that "an enlightened citizenry willing to use information in making rational decisions may not be able to do so" (*Truth and Credibility*, 12). For "we cannot act on information alone; the information must first be understood, then interpreted for relevance, and finally command belief and commitment" (13). This is to say that the criteria for warranted acceptance of the import of matters of fact are not the same as those for warranted assertion about matters of fact. And if the citizen increasingly finds it difficult to frame a situation in order to define and examine it, it is because a rupture has occurred between the grounds of warranted belief and the grounds of warranted commitment. Before this rupture can be healed, the nature of warranted commitment must be understood.

Briefly stated, considerations of warranted commitment or credibility take us into the moral realm where motives can be questioned and truth is validated existentially by a willingness to accept the consequences of one's acts. Claims to credibility are thus not couched in the language of warranted assertion but are made by reference to such terms as *authenticity*, *sincerity*, and *purity of heart*. Broudy next discusses those groups (journalists, editors, critics, the clergy, intellectuals) whose credibility is crucial to a democracy but whose reliability has been considerably diminished by a number of twentieth-century developments. Understanding is hampered by technological and information overload; specialism and its byproduct, proceduralism; and the pitfalls inherent in planning. All contribute to the devaluation of substantive inquiry and the demoralization of human behavior. Accordingly, says Broudy, the remoralization of society is "tantamount to reintroducing the moral dimensions into cognition, for morality [in contrast to science] has to do with intentions, principles, and motives" (53–54). In the middle chapters of Broudy's volume, he cites examples of obstacles to rational activity and strains on credibility. Professors, economists, and journalists are tried before the court of credibility and found wanting. Broudy discerns strains on credibility in the often glaring disparity between statements of principles and actual sentiments, in instances where principles are violated with impunity, in the biases of journalists, and in the refuge sought in numbers for purposes of justification and accountability.

In developing the themes of credibility and rational action, Broudy is perhaps harshest with those, principally legislators, who approve policies the consequences of which they know will not affect them personally. He also questions the credibility of affirmative action programs that emphasize quotas and punish (as in the *Bakke* case) those who could not possibly have been responsible for society's past injustices. Further targets of his criticism are students who vehemently protested the Vietnam War from the safety of their campuses and certain organizations, such as the American Civil Liberties Union (ACLU), that while professing to protect the principles of free speech and assembly often find themselves unwittingly defending those who would deny such rights to others. Then there is the communications industry, which is always ready to question everyone's credibility but its own. Universities and professors fare little better. Although the credibility of scholarship is still intact, it is also true that professors are increasingly esteemed not for their teaching, scholarship, and promotion of the good life, but for the amount of time they spend away from campus serving as consultants and lecturing in exotic capitals and mountain retreats. Relativists get called to account for their unwillingness to examine the relativity of their own basic premises.[9] What clearly emerges in this recital of instances of strained credibility is Broudy's condemnation of persons unwilling to bear the consequences of their beliefs; theirs is the ultimate breach of authenticity.

Broudy finds reductionism in the realm of values equally distasteful because the good life requires a just and artful balancing of the various kinds of value—personal, social, economic, civic, and aesthetic. Thus remoralization also calls for the reintegration of values. To make this point, Broudy quotes the art critic Robert Hughes as supplying an illustration of value reductionism:

> What do the soaring prices being paid for art mean? On the most obvious level, it means what everyone knows: that money is losing value. . . . The culture is now getting to the point where everything that can be regarded, however distantly, as a work of art is primarily esteemed not for its ability to communicate meaning, or its use as historical evidence, or its capacity to generate aesthetic pleasure, but for its convertibility into cash. (103)

This, adds Broudy, is true not only of art, inasmuch as the monetary value of many other things has now achieved a hallowed status. Even affectional experience, religious devotion, and humanitarian service are increasingly certified by a dollar amount. Reductionism, however, exacts a human cost:

> Measuring all values on an economic scale desensitizes us to the intrinsic differences in the qualities of experience and to their subtle relations. Each value domain has its distinctive quality as experienced and satisfies distinctive needs of the human personality. Each domain can enhance and inhibit the others; the art of life is to maximize and harmonize their totality." (105)

In short, without such value reintegration, the good life suffers.

To repeat, the remedy for devaluation and demoralization is remoralization. Remoralization does not imply throwing out the CAT, but it does involve reinvigorating the arts and humanities, which are the loci of credibility and existential truth, and it is in this sense that Broudy's volume assumes special relevance to aesthetic education. Lionel Trilling often remarked that the truth that literature yields is the truth of the self and of the self's right relation to others and to culture. Broudy is in complete accord, for imaginative literature is the preeminent source of existential truth; it provides the staging areas and the battlegrounds for the triumphs and defeats of selves in their striving for sincerity and authenticity. Central to such struggles are the active imagination and the crucial mechanism of sublimation through which persons humanize themselves by transforming lust into love, feeding into dining, and death into heroism. In a section that brings Kierkegaard into the picture and stresses the importance of imagination and the arts, Broudy writes:

> Because feelings of the self about itself and about the natural world can be objectified in images, the arts present us with images of human import that, as Wordsworth put it, can be recollected in tranquility. And so recollected, they convert the inner subjective reality into an object of contemplation. In this sense we can speak of art yielding feelingful knowledge and knowledgeful feeling, the synthesis of fact and value. (115–16)

The arts, it might be said, supply the aesthetic component of remoralization. The ethical component derives forthrightly from Kant's categorical imperative never to treat persons merely as means. And the rational component is vouchsafed by the tendency of humans to strive for consistency and reasonableness in their thinking.

A curriculum for remoralization—a credibility curriculum—takes form along lines recognizable to those familiar with Broudy's writings. It is a curriculum of genuinely liberal studies that are dedicated primarily to the cultivation of the self in contrast to their serving special interests or subservience to social expediency. Intellectually, a credibility curriculum is charged with fashioning the cognitive and evaluative maps that prospective citizens need in order to act rationally in behalf of the public good. Morally, the curriculum is justified by its commitment to democratic values, especially those tenets of the American Creed articulated by Gunnar Myrdal in his study of race relations in the United States. The particular rationale for liberal studies rests in a conception of the uses of knowledge—replicative, applicative, interpretive, and associative—of which the last two are central to building a sense of warranted commitment (though readers will have to follow the details of the argument for the uses of knowledge in Broudy's writings).[10] All that can be said here is that Broudy, drawing on Michael Polanyi's work on tacit knowing, believes that school learnings acquired explicitly during the school years function tacitly later when individuals interpret a broad range of situations:

> The disciplines studied explicitly in school become resources used tacitly in life; their details are forgotten, leaving frames or lenses or stencils of interpretation, both of fact and value. Perspective and context are the functional residues of general education. We understand *with* them, even though we are not attending to them. I believe that a convincing case can be made for the functionality of formal course work in the associative and interpretive uses of knowledge, even though the content of the formal courses cannot be recalled on cue. (137)

The arts and humanities are especially helpful in developing the interpretive and associative uses of learning. Associative learning is the means by which one acquires concepts and images that build the layers of meaning by which life is felt, understood, and evaluated. All kinds of experience contribute to what Broudy calls an imagic-conceptual store, but the arts are preeminently suited to achieve this purpose. This is where aesthetic education comes in. The arts, instead of being a luxury or refinement, are necessary to make the truth existentially significant. And finally:

> The arts help the imagination invent and contemplate new forms of bravery, honesty, temperance, wisdom, and so forth, as well as the corresponding vices. ... The humanities, including literature, history, and philosophy, represent the learned tradition in the systematic examination, critique, and redefinition of the virtues and the diverse formulae for the good life. This tradition, although not free from silly solemnity, pedantry, and pretense, still has high credibility in the realm of truth about value-existential truth. Regardless of time and circumstance, the schools at all levels can induct the young into this consensus with the confidence that it is about as near as we can get to an abiding, if not absolute, truth about the good life. (142)

Here, then, is classical humanism adapted to the modern world. It consists of recommendations for teaching virtue in new forms, a kind of value or character education grounded in a democratic ethic and the common good, in the uses of knowledge, and in an optimistic faith in human nature. Given sufficient investments of energy and a wholehearted commitment, a curriculum promoting these values could, Broudy thinks, help bring about a society that provides maximum achievement potential (or opportunities for value possibility), justice, and compassion, which are Broudy's criteria for the good society. Aesthetic education plays its role in remoralization by means of the value possibilities inherent in the aesthetic realm and its ability to strengthen the imagination through the study and appreciation of aesthetic exemplars. Overall, the formula is the CAT + the humanities + the American Creed.

Any commentator on a book, no matter how persuaded of its merits, feels obliged to raise a critical point or two. How good are the prospects for a reintegration of values? I will simply present some questions. Is it perhaps asking too much of ordinary citizens, imposing too great a burden, to expect them to fashion their selves from the resources of the disciplines? Can every citizen be a Socrates? Will not anxiety be raised to intolerable levels? What, moreover, are parents to think of a rationale for liberal studies that claims that much of school learning will be forgotten but can nonetheless function interpretively later in life? In this respect, Broudy argues at length for context building as against context deprivation, but in appealing to the mysterious workings of tacit knowing he may be calling for a leap of faith (perhaps the credibility of tacit knowing is at stake). Again, *I* am a believer, but those coming upon the thesis for the first time may not be easily converted. Meanwhile, we can be grateful to Broudy for having illuminated our common predicament.

NOTES

1. Harry S. Broudy, *Truth and Credibility: The Citizen's Dilemma* (New York: Longman, 1981).

2. Broudy's discussion of warranted commitment might be compared to the notion of commitment advanced by Solon Kimball and James E. McClellan in *Education and the New America* (New York: Random House, 1962).

3. Robert Penn Warren, *Democracy and Poetry* (Cambridge: Harvard University Press, 1975), 47–48.

4. See John Kenneth Galbraith, *The New Industrial State*, rev. ed. (Boston: Houghton Mifflin, 1972), 401–02.

5. John Dewey, *The Public and Its Problems* (New York: Henry Holt and Co., 1977), 179–84.

6. Regarding the meanings of devaluation and remoralization, Broudy writes: "De-valuation refers to diminishing or denying the relevance of all but one type of value to an issue; de-moralization denies the relevance of moral questions. The reduction of all values—intellectual, civic, health, among others—to a money value would be an example of de-valuation; the slogan 'business is business' is an example of de-moralization" (99).

7. Saul Bellow, *The Dean's December* (New York: Harper and Row, 1982), 334.

8. Although, Broudy remarks, whether science twice domesticated, namely, first in Dewey's CAT and then in Kilpatrick's project method, retains the true spirit of science is another question.

9. On relativism, Broudy writes: "As a general principle, relativism is self-defeating, both logically and strategically. Logically, it is self-contradictory, for if nothing is absolutely true, then this principle is no exception. Strategically, the force of the principle is to free action from the constrictions of absolutes. However, relativizing all claims to truth frees all claims from criticism or question; that is, it absolutizes them. The price of relativism is the multiplication of absolutes" (91–92).

10. For further discussion of the uses of knowledge, see Harry S. Broudy, B. Othanel Smith, and Joe R. Burnett, *Democracy and Excellence in American Secondary Education* (Chicago: Rand McNally, 1964; reprint, Huntington, N.Y.: R. E. Krieger, 1978). Also, Broudy's "The Humanities and Their Uses: Proper Claims and Expectations," *Journal of Aesthetic Education* 17, no. 4 (1983): 125–38.

Art and Diversity

The Uses of Cultural Diversity

ONE OF THE LAST writings by Lionel Trilling was an incomplete essay titled "Why We Read Jane Austen."[1] Although the essay has, to be sure, much to say about Jane Austen, it also introduces a fair number of other topics. Among them are the assumptions underlying traditional human-istic education, literary figures and style-phases in culture, the concept of self or personhood, the uses and functions of art, the motives of youth for read-ing literature, and the ways in which individuals and cultures confront them-selves and their destinies.

Of particular relevance here is the portion of the essay discussing liter-ary criticism and the kind of anthropological explanation exemplified in Clifford Geertz's studies of Indonesian village life, and the uses of both to-ward an improved understanding of culturally different societies. It is at this point that, implausible though it might at first appear, a link can be estab-lished between a contemporary American literary critic writing on a nine-teenth-century English novelist and the agenda for a world congress of the International Society for Education Through Art.

What, we may ask, was the genesis of Trilling's mental itinerary that extends from the world of *Mansfield Park* to that of village life in Indonesia, separated by both hemisphere and historical time? Its origin can be traced to Trilling's decision in 1973 to teach a course on the novels of Austen. As Trilling notes, the response to this course offering was marked by an uncom-mon, and sometimes almost hysterical, moral intensity in those wanting to register.

Such enthusiasm puzzled Trilling, for it was only five years earlier, at the peak of the counterculture, that the literary interests of Columbia Uni-versity students centered on William Blake. This instance of rapid shift in literary taste prompted Trilling to query students about their reasons for wishing to take the course. He concluded that students wanted to read the novels of Austen for the use they might make of them in building their own distinctive sense of self. By reading Austen's novels, students appeared to sense the possibility of neutralizing the general state of maleficence into which they thought their culture had fallen—a state brought about by the principal dehumanizers of the modern human condition: industrialization, urbanization, and the multiversity. These young men and women seemed to think, writes Trilling, that "they could in some way transcend our sad contemporary existence, that from the world of our present weariness and desiccation, they might reach back to a world which, as it appears to the mind's eye, is so much more abundantly provided with trees than with people, a world in whose green shade life for a moment might be a green thought."[2]

In other words, students construed reading Austen as an act that could not only strengthen their adversarial relation to society but also simultaneously satisfy their craving for spiritual nourishment. Although in the course of his career Trilling had grown increasingly skeptical about such uses of literature by young people, he acknowledged that in expressing this attitude, students were manifesting adherence to what has long been one of the principal assumptions of humanistic education, this assumption being that apart from whatever pleasure literature might afford, it may also be consulted for its personal and moral relevance. What is more, despite the diversity of circumstance that everywhere affects human nature, it has been supposed that humankind is essentially the same under the skin, and that the contemplation of this unity within diversity is crucial to the task of building a sense of self. Humanistic education also presumed to know the method by which the universals of human nature could be discerned. It was the method of empathic experience, which is to say, the effort made by the imagination to identify with the characters of a literary work of art.

While teaching the course, however, and somewhat to his surprise, Trilling began to question these assumptions about universality and method. As the ways in which the characters of Austen's novels confronted themselves and their destinies were examined, Trilling discovered the inability of his students to understand, and thus to sympathize with, many of the attitudes expressed in the novels, for example, the attitudes toward close family relations, toward being and doing, and toward duty. Was it therefore possible, queried Trilling, that traditional humanistic education had things all wrong, that it failed to appreciate just how complicated a matter it is to understand literature? I stress the term *complicated*, for as Trilling's lifelong friend and colleague Jacques Barzun, pointed out in a memoir, Trilling's avowed intellectual purpose was to develop in his readers an awareness of complexity and difficulty.[3] Complicators, of course, can be expected to appreciate others of a similar cast of mind, and in the writings of the anthropologist Clifford Geertz, Trilling found ostensible reinforcement for his own developing skepticism regarding the devices of literary appreciation.[4] What Trilling finds interesting in Geertz is the minimal role the latter assigns to empathy in anthropological description. Rather, Geertz writes, "I have tried to arrive at this most intimate of notions [namely, how people define themselves as persons] not by imagining myself as someone else . . . but by searching out and analyzing the symbolic forms—words, images, institutions, behaviors—in terms of which, in each place, people actually represent themselves to themselves and to one another."[5] Thus according to Geertz, "finding one's feet" with the culture of a people, or learning its informal logic so as to be able to carry on a conversation with its members, is extraordinarily difficult. The implication for literary criticism of Geertz's semiotic theory of anthropology is perhaps obvious. If anthropological inquiry and literary criticism are analogous in the sense that both try to uncover the realities and meanings of seemingly alien worlds, the assertion that anthropology possesses a possibly more potent method of understanding will have repercussions for literary study: the methods of literary criticism stand in danger of appearing superficial. Trilling, however, while admitting the complexity of the questions and problems, thought that the barriers to understanding may not be insurmountable. Neither did he think that the professed values of Indonesian culture, specifically those of Java and Bali, are so alien or irrelevant to Western temperaments as Geertz suggested.

Trilling's drawing attention to this possibility would seem to indicate that he thought the time was right to move beyond the concept of self as it has been the understood in the West and, in the interest of the self, to subject this concept to sympathetic criticism. What is that sense of personhood to which Trilling directs us?

Javanese culture, he writes, "has as one of its definitive functions to induce its members to become as much as possible like works of art: the human individual is to have the shapedness, the coherence, the changelessness of an object, if not actually of high art, then at least of *vertu*." The appeal of this ideal of the individual consists in its propensity to find value in what is "fixed, moveless, and silent."[6] The purpose of Balinese culture as a whole is the same. Trilling quotes Geertz as saying that

> there is in Bali a persistent and systematic attempt to stylize all aspects of personal expression to the point where anything idiosyncratic, anything characteristic of the individual mainly because he is who he is physically, psychologically, or biographically, is muted in favor of his assigned place in the continued, and so it is thought, never changing pageant that is Balinese life. It is dramatis personae, not actors, that in the proper sense really exist. (223)

Those who have read Trilling's *Sincerity and Authenticity* know how far removed this sense of self is from Western concepts.[7] And irrelevant to it as well? It depends. Trilling is obviously not asking that we superficially imitate Javanese and Balinese cultural forms, that we assume, for example, an

Indonesian look in matters of appearance. The question is a more basic, structural one. It involves the possibilities of life approximating art. This possibility, of course, is one held out by one prominent strand of modern aesthetic thought; and it is worth remarking that it is to this tradition of aesthetic thought that Trilling gives the last word. What starts out as an apparent rejection of the aesthetic model is followed by an affirmation of the part it can play as one term of a continuing dialectic:

> We of the West are never finally comfortable with the thought of life's susceptibility to being made into aesthetic experience, not even when the idea is dealt with as one of the received speculations of our intellectual culture—sooner or later, for example, we find ourselves becoming uneasy with Schiller's having advanced, on the basis of Kant's aesthetic theory, the idea that life will be the better for transforming itself into art, and we are uneasy again with Huizinga's having advanced the proposition, on the basis of Schiller's views, that life actually does transform itself into art: we feel that both authors deny the earnestness and literalness—the necessity—of which, as we of the West ultimately feel, the essence of life consists. (224)

But in the same passage he concludes, "It is, I think, open to us to believe that our alternations of view on this matter of life seeking to approximate art are not a mere display of cultural indecisiveness but, rather, that they constitute a dialectic, with all the dignity that inheres in that word" (224).

NOTES

1. In Lionel Trilling, *The Last Decade: Essays and Reviews, 1965–75*, ed. Diana Trilling (New York: Harcourt Brace Jovanovich, 1970), 204–25. All references are to the volume in the Uniform Edition.

2. Ibid, 209.

3. Jacques Barzun, "Remembering Lionel Trilling," *Encounter* 47, no. 3 (1976). Also see the preface to Lionel Trilling's *The Liberal Imagination* (New York: Harcourt Brace Jovanovich, 1979) for his discussion of the values and uses of literature.

4. Trilling refers to Clifford Geertz, "From the Native's Point of View: On the Nature of Anthropological Understanding," *Bulletin of the American Academy of Arts and Sciences* 28, no. 1 (1974). Relevant reading in conjunction with this essay is Geertz's "Thick Description: Toward an Interpretive Theory of Culture" in *The Interpretation of Cultures* (New York: Basic Books, 1973).

5. Geertz quoted in Trilling, "Why We Read Jane Austen," 216.

6. Trilling, "Why We Read Jane Austen," 222.

7. Lionel Trilling, *Sincerity and Authenticity* (New York: Harcourt Brace Jovanovich, 1980).

Index

About the Author

R ALPH A. SMITH is Professor Emeritus of Cultural and Educational Policy Studies at the University of Illinois at Urbana-Champaign. He received his Bachelor of Arts degree from Columbia College and his graduate degrees in Fine Arts Education from Columbia Teachers College. After teaching at state universities in Ohio, Wisconsin, and New York, he received an appointment at the University of Illinois, where he designed courses in aesthetic education and initiated the interdisciplinary *Journal of Aesthetic Education*, which he edited continuously for thirty-four years. His major publications include *The Sense of Art: A Study in Aesthetic Education*, *Art Education: A Critical Necessity* (with Albert William Levi), *General Knowledge and Arts Education*, *Excellence II: The Continuing Quest in Art Education*, and the edited volumes *Aesthetics and Criticism in Art Education*, *Public Policy and the Aesthetic Interest* (coedited with Ronald Berman), *Aesthetics and Arts Education* (coedited with Alan Simpson), *The Arts, Education, and Aesthetic Knowing* (an NSSE Yearbook, coedited with Bennett Reimer), and *Discipline-Based Art Education*. He is a Distinguished Fellow of the National Art Education Association, a Senior Scholar in the University of Illinois College of Education, and a Distinguished Member of the Illinois Art Education Association, and his contributions to aesthetics and aesthetic education have been recognized by the American Society for Aesthetics.